PAT METHENY
THE ECM YEARS, 1975–1984

OXFORD STUDIES IN RECORDED JAZZ
Series Editor JEREMY BARHAM

PAT METHENY
THE ECM YEARS, 1975–1984

MERVYN COOKE

OXFORD
UNIVERSITY PRESS

Oxford University Press is a department of the University of Oxford. It furthers
the University's objective of excellence in research, scholarship, and education
by publishing worldwide. Oxford is a registered trade mark of Oxford University
Press in the UK and certain other countries.

Published in the United States of America by Oxford University Press
198 Madison Avenue, New York, NY 10016, United States of America.

Library of Congress Cataloging-in-Publication Data
Names: Cooke, Mervyn, author.
Title: Pat Metheny : the ECM years, 1975–1984 / Mervyn Cooke.
Description: New York : Oxford University Press, 2017. | Series: Oxford
studies in recorded jazz | Includes bibliographical references and index.
Identifiers: LCCN 2016028859| ISBN 9780199897674 (hardcover : alk. paper) |
ISBN 9780199897667 (pbk. : alk. paper)
Subjects: LCSH: Metheny, Pat—Criticism and interpretation. |
Jazz—1971–1980—History and criticism. | Jazz—1981–1990—History and criticism.
Classification: LCC ML419.M477 C66 2017 | DDC 787.87/165092—dc23
LC record available at https://lccn.loc.gov/2016028859

9 8 7 6

Paperback printed by Marquis, Canada
Hardback printed by Bridgeport National Bindery, Inc., United States of America

FOR SALLY—AND OSLO 2005

SERIES PREFACE

THE OXFORD STUDIES in Recorded Jazz series offers detailed historical, cultural, and technical analysis of jazz recordings across a broad spectrum of styles, periods, performing media, and nationalities. Each volume, authored by a leading scholar in the field, addresses either a single jazz album or a set of related recordings by one artist/group, placing the recordings fully in their historical and musical context, and thereby enriching our understanding of their cultural and creative significance.

With access to the latest scholarship and with an innovative and balanced approach to its subject matter, the series offers fresh perspectives on both well-known and neglected jazz repertoire. It sets out to renew musical debate in jazz scholarship, and to develop the subtle critical languages and vocabularies necessary to do full justice to the complex expressive, structural, and cultural dimensions of recorded jazz performance.

Jeremy Barham
University of Surrey
Series Editor

ACKNOWLEDGEMENTS

THANKS ARE DUE first and foremost to the series editor of the Oxford Studies in Recorded Jazz, Jeremy Barham, not only for the initial invitation to contribute a volume to the series, but for his constant support and encouragement along the way, and to the stalwart staff of Oxford University Press in New York—principally Suzanne Ryan, Adam Cohen, Andrew Maillet, and Jamie Kim—for their constant enthusiasm and undiminished patience during a number of those inevitable and unavoidable delays in meeting deadlines which must be the bane of a publisher's existence. During the production process, the text has benefited enormously from the expertise of both copy-editor Patterson Lamb and project manager Damian Penfold. I should also like to acknowledge the valuable input of the anonymous readers who commented in detail on the work as it took shape.

Researching and writing about the work of a living musician can uncover all sorts of unexpected twists and turns, and in the present instance it has been a particular delight to discover the still undimmed sense of sheer excitement in the creative process—and in life on the road as a crucial part of the jazz musician's formative experiences—shared by those who worked closely with Pat Metheny during the period with which this book is concerned. Band members Mark Egan, Danny Gottlieb, and Paul Wertico have all been exceptionally generous with their time and shared many fascinating reminiscences about those years with me, and I am also grateful to others closely connected with the ECM recordings under consideration here for taking the time to answer my many queries: these include William Clift, Deborah Feingold,

Klaus Frahm, Rainer Kiedrowski, Richard Niles, Rob Van Petten, and Gerd Winner. Most importantly, however, I am hugely indebted to Pat Metheny himself for his interest in the project, for the many insights into his music and career he has been willing to share along the way, and for his considerable patience in addressing my many queries and tolerating my (I hope not too frequent) ineptitudes.

The following libraries have offered invaluable support in tracking down essential but often elusive source materials: Baylor University Libraries, British Library, Cleveland State University Libraries, Five Towns College Library, Hallward Library (University of Nottingham), University of Houston Libraries, McIntyre Library (University of Wisconsin), and New York Public Library. I am particularly indebted to Jonathan J. Quick for his kindness in supplying a copy of a hard-to-obtain Metheny article from his personal collection, and to Ed Hazell for his generous assistance in locating a transcript from a Metheny workshop held at Berklee College.

Copyright in the music reproduced here is acknowledged in the captions to individual examples, which comprise transcriptions from audio recordings by the present author prepared for this volume and appearing here for the first time (AT), brief extracts from the *Pat Metheny Song Book* (SB), and hybrid examples in which *Song Book* material is combined with additional transcribed passages (ASB). Guitar parts in the examples are notated one octave higher than sounding pitch in accordance with conventional practice.

For their help with sundry matters, I am grateful to the following: Mike Brannon, Peter Elsdon, Martina Fischer and Anna Schneider (Haus der Kunst, Munich), Dan Forte, Christopher Harting, John Hilderbrand, John Howland, Andrew Justice and John Murphy (University of North Texas), Sandro Kancheli (ECM), Ted Kurland Associates, Simon Paterson, Ken Prouty, Kenneth Robinson, John Shore, Alison Stevens, Joseph Vella, Gary Walker, Philip Weller, Justin Williams, Katherine Williams, and wattsjazz (Ann Arbor, MI). I should particularly like to thank ECM for their generosity in allowing me to use their sleeve artwork by way of illustration, Rob Van Petten for permission to reproduce his original (uncropped) *American Garage* photograph, Deborah Feingold for permission to reproduce her *Offramp* session photograph, and Stuart Greenbaum for allowing me to quote from his unpublished full-score transcription and detailed analysis of 'First Circle'. I am indebted to Alexander Gagatsis for having constantly refreshed my perceptions of jazz and jazz scholarship through many endlessly fascinating and stimulating discussions on the subject, and special (and woefully overdue) thanks are also due to Kim Roper for having first introduced me to the music of Pat Metheny and Lyle Mays very many years ago.

Last, but most important of all, my love and gratitude are as always extended to my cherished wife Sally, who has shared many special Metheny moments with me over the years, both at home and abroad, and who has been a truly amazing source of sustained moral support during the writing of this book.

CONTENTS

FIGURES AND TABLES

FIGURES

5.2   *Offramp* sleeve art. Design by Dieter Rehm; photograph by
       Gerd Winner. © ECM Records, 1982. Used by permission.   198

TABLES

MUSIC EXAMPLES

LIST OF MUSIC EXAMPLES

PAT METHENY
THE ECM YEARS, 1975–1984

CHAPTER 1

INTRODUCTION
A NEW PARADIGM

[W]e all have to rise to this challenge, and it's a big one:
the challenge to recreate and reinvent [jazz] to a new paradigm
resonant to *this* era, a new time. It's simply not gonna cut it
to just keep looking back, emulating what has already been done
with just a slightly different spin on it ... we have to get our
collective imagination working hard on a vision that is more concerned
with what this music can *become* than what it has already *been*.[1]

PAT METHENY'S CEASELESS desire to create music of contemporary
relevance within a broad jazz aesthetic inevitably conjures up an image
of constant travelling, often boldly, towards new and exciting artistic
frontiers. In a very real sense, his entire career (spanning more than
four decades at the time of writing) has been a never-ending journey
of exploration, and metaphors of journeying and narrative are never far
below the surface when his music is discussed. Although in academic
circles it has long been unfashionable to chart the trajectory of an artist's
creative achievements in a linear fashion, in Metheny's case a strong
sense of ongoing continuity and inter-connections across his oeuvre is

---

1 Pat Metheny, keynote address for conference of the International Association of Jazz
Educators, New York City, January 2001, in Lloyd Peterson, *Music and the Creative
Spirit: Innovators in Jazz, Improvisation, and the Avant-Garde* (Lanham, MD: Scarecrow,
2006), 322.

inescapable. Indeed, he has himself described his whole recorded output to date as one continuous album, or 'one long set'.[2] The present study examines the substantial body of eleven albums he recorded for the label ECM at the start of his recording career and shows how this single-minded sense of purpose—manifested in practice by formidably strong band-leadership—has in no way prevented his music from achieving an astonishing technical and expressive diversity along the way.

On a basic level, these albums appear to fall into two broad categories, although the division is by no means always clear-cut. On the one hand, Metheny's 'straight-ahead' jazz playing is reflected in vibrant recordings with trios (*Bright Size Life*, 1976; *Rejoicing*, 1984) and a quintet (*80/81*, 1980), mainly featuring his own compositions but also celebrating the music of Ornette Coleman, Charlie Haden, and others. On the other hand, no fewer than seven of the albums document the concurrent evolution of the Pat Metheny Group, in which—alongside an undiminished commitment to improvisation—Metheny furthered his compositional aspirations occasionally in conjunction with keyboardist and sometimes co-composer Lyle Mays, with several resourceful rhythm sections. The core quartet that laid the foundations for this music appeared first under Metheny's name (*Watercolors*, 1977), and then as the Pat Metheny Group (*Pat Metheny Group*, 1978; *American Garage*, 1979; *Offramp*, 1982; *Travels*, 1983; and *First Circle*, 1984), with one vitally important Metheny–Mays album issued under their joint names during a break in the full group's activities (*As Falls Wichita, So Falls Wichita Falls*, 1981). The remaining album in the collection, *New Chautauqua* (1979), is a unique solo project notable for an innovative musical language involving fresh soundscapes and multiple guitars, and one that had a significant impact on his other work.

Metheny's high international profile and huge fan base are arguably matched by no other jazz performer in the world today: as Ian Carr put it, he has long been the kind of 'jazz superstar' whose like has not been seen since the career of Miles Davis was at its peak.[3] Across the world, Metheny and his various bands routinely fill theatres and open-air stadia with cheering crowds while at the same time creating music endowed with an intellectual and emotional sophistication that offers considerable technical and interpretative interest to the professional analyst and

2 Richard Niles, *The Pat Metheny Interviews*, ed. Ronny S. Schiff (Milwaukee, WI: Hal Leonard, 2009), 103. For more on Metheny's strong personal sense of goal-directed journeying from the outset of his career, see also Niles, *Pat Metheny Interviews*, 91–2.

3 Ian Carr, 'Bright Size Life', BBC Radio 3, June 27 to July 25, 1998; introduction to episode 1.

critic. Carr's comparison with Davis is not fanciful, nor based merely on phenomenal audience pulling-power: as John Scofield memorably said of the trumpeter, in terms equally applicable to Metheny, 'Nobody else could do big long tours every summer and fall and sell out stadiums all over Europe. And these people were not jazz snobs, they just dug Miles. He could make a believer out of a non-jazz person with the beauty of his sound and the rhythm of his notes.'[4] The comparison is relevant not only because of the contemporaneity of both musicians' work, which enabled it to appeal well beyond a mainstream and potentially limited jazz demographic, but because their success was only possible as a result of punishingly hard touring schedules, embracing literally hundreds of live gigs each year, and a deep commitment to maintaining exceptionally high performance standards no matter the size of their audiences or venues. Since the present series of books is concerned primarily with recorded artefacts, it is necessary constantly to remind ourselves that the recordings examined here are inextricably associated with the innumerable live appearances in the course of which the music had for the most part already been shaped. These recordings are the residue of the enormous amount of hard work that went into perfecting Metheny's music time and time again on the road during the period with which this book is concerned, a tremendously exciting and rewarding (if utterly gruelling) activity which carried with it transient and elusive musical qualities that were to some extent impossible to recapture in the recording studio.

The albums chart a clear trajectory from an early emphasis on original composition—rather than the interpretation of standards—into creative territory that involved the exploration of increasingly complex (and sometimes electronically generated) timbres and extended musical structures. The music represented here deftly balances, to varying degrees in different contexts, spontaneous improvisation, avant-garde experimentation, straightforward melodic appeal, and firm structural control. The Metheny Group's early output in particular initiated a move towards increasingly large-scale formal conceptions which was ultimately to culminate in *The Way Up*, a complex and uninterrupted *c.*76-minute piece toured across the globe and recorded in 2005. Metheny has himself commented that *The Way Up* was

> a pretty ambitious undertaking on a number of levels, certainly, compositionally. That level of detail is something that we probably

---

4 John Scofield, interview for *Wire* (September 1991), quoted in Stuart Nicholson, *Is Jazz Dead? (Or Has It Moved to a New Address)* (New York: Routledge, 2005), 2.

have been heading towards from the very beginning. Right from the start, one of the major tenets of the group was that we wanted to go beyond song form type material whenever we could.[5]

Central to the present project are considerations of the various musical influences on Metheny and how these affected the course of his stylistic development; the improvisational methods of the extraordinarily fluent guitarist, especially where these arise directly from chord patterns he himself devised (which tend to fall into two distinct types: harmonic changes that readily enable the fertile exploitation of musical ideas that come naturally to him, and those which contrastingly require a more considered creative response to self-imposed challenges and restrictions); the relationship between improvised material and pre-composed structures; the music's harmonic language and its implications for long-term structural articulation; the exploration of different guitar sonorities and tunings, and synthesizers driven by both guitar and keyboard controllers, and how these timbral potentialities gradually impacted upon the musical language; the relationship between studio recordings and live performances; and the roles of the record producer—at first ECM's founder Manfred Eicher but later Metheny himself—and recording engineers in defining unique sonic environments.

Implicit in the list of diverse musical parameters in the preceding paragraph is the concept-driven mentality that has always been at the core of Metheny's creativity. In all of his projects, an initial concept is first explored (privately) in the shape of written musical ideas which grow naturally from it; the most fruitful of those ideas are then communicated to players chosen specifically for the conceptual purpose at hand. The impressive roster of stellar performers whom Metheny has hired throughout his career has inevitably enabled much beneficial collaboration to take place as part of the ongoing process of fully realizing his creative ideas; but—in the case of the Metheny Group in particular—a potentially misleading mythology of some kind of creative 'co-operative' driving his work has grown up over the years. In part, this misconception may unwittingly have been triggered by the public credit he always gave his collaborators for their input, but the 'co-op' mentality is also an attractive ideal in academic studies of jazz

5 Anon., 'A Fireside Chat with Pat Metheny' (February 24, 2005). http://www.allaboutjazz. com/php/article.php?id=16664&page=1 (August 11, 2013).

in which the concept of musical democracy in various (more plausible) historical instances is highly and rightly prized. The most accurate description of how Metheny's potent leadership skills work in practice is perhaps the notion of a benevolent dictatorship, and it has always been his own strong belief that being a bandleader and a conceptualist are symbiotic manifestations of the same creative impulse. The singular artistic vision at the helm of all his projects remains, however, deeply rooted in practical considerations: much initial material is rejected in the search for music that will remain both rewarding to play and to hear during the eventual recording process, and which when played live on extended tours can withstand performance after performance for nights on end. As he put it in an interview published in 2014, the basic musical materials need to be of a kind that the players 'can pound on ... rhythmically, harmonically or melodically and they bounce back to retain their original shape no matter what'.[6] In the case of compositions from his early period which, at the time of writing, are in some cases now around forty years old, this quality of robustness has meant that music which was originally conceived with a highly specific bandleading vision in mind has subsequently been able to develop an entirely unforeseen creative life of its own.[7]

As well as offering the first substantial historical account of Metheny's professional activities during his early years, and providing (also for the first time) a detailed analysis of how the style of his music evolved through these groundbreaking albums, this book also illustrates the wider significance of the ECM label in establishing a variety of internationally appreciated musical idioms which in some cases departed radically from blues-based, bebop, and fusion styles. Many notable US jazz musicians recorded with ECM at some stage in their careers, as shown in the following chapter. In Metheny's case, the present study provides a timely opportunity to investigate how one of the most gifted musicians of his time was enabled to find a distinctive personal voice through the creative opportunities offered by an enterprise—described by Thomas Steinfeld as 'probably the finest garage company ever to exist'[8]—which today continues to maintain its strong presence in the jazz and modern classical markets.

---

6 Metheny, interviewed in Gil Goldstein, *Jazz Composer's Companion*, 3rd edn. (Mainz: Advance Music GmbH, 2014), 102.

7 *Ibid.*

8 Steve Lake and Paul Griffiths (eds.), *Horizons Touched: The Music of ECM* (London: Granta, 2007), 386.

As shown by the quotation at the head of this chapter, Metheny's artistic credo from the very outset was firmly anchored in the strong belief that jazz musicians must reflect in their work the specific times in which they live, and not remain rooted in the comfortable but sometimes remote haven of past styles. He expounded this view persuasively in his 2001 address to the International Association of Jazz Educators:

> It is jazz's very nature to change, to develop and adapt to the circumstances of its environment. The evidence of this lies in the incredible diversity of music and musicians that have evolved, and lived and flourished, under the wide umbrella of the word 'jazz' itself from the very beginning . . .
>
> There is an important and consistent element in the jazz tradition of young people coming along and molding—reinventing—the nature of the form itself to fit their times and their circumstances, as only they could possibly know how to do . . .
>
> I always encourage musicians (who are of course citizens of the world first, and jazz musicians second) to address *all* of the music that they love and that they are attracted to as people, regardless of its style, regardless of its content, as a unified set of materials when they consider their full options—and potentials—as modern-day jazz musicians.[9]

In short, it was not enough to be a technically fluent improviser and/ or capable composer if the music produced by either method was not 'embodied in a conception'[10] relevant to the musician's own times. A healthy eclecticism of the kind Metheny outlines above is reflected in his own music by its absorption and reworking of influences as diverse as bebop, free jazz, rock, pop, country & western, Brazilian music, classical music, minimalism, and the avant-garde. Narrow definitions of the label 'jazz', which have historically caused unwarranted consternation amongst commentators inclined towards purism and an often elusive quest for the white whale of authenticity, are rendered entirely pointless by a holistic approach to stylistic diversity in music of the kind Metheny both advocates and practises. As Eric Porter has observed, problems of this kind tend to arise in jazz criticism when certain 'value

9 Peterson, *Music and the Creative Spirit*, 318-20.
10 Metheny, quoted in Nicholson, *Is Jazz Dead?*, 18.

components' such as 'experimentation, black vernacular practices, composition, populism, etc.' are 'used in excess, that is, to the extent that they are seen as pushing a particular musical project into territory more properly encompassed by a different genre'.[11] Metheny's music, in all its shapes and forms, has nevertheless always remained deeply rooted in jazz stylistically, with a commitment to improvisation the key factor:

> I've always felt very lucky that somehow, early on, no one ever told me, 'Well, this is jazz and this is that.' It was never an issue for me. And yet everything I've been involved with as a musician has had to do with improvising which, from my point of view, has made everything that I play jazz, with no fear of style.[12]

His distinctive blend of improvisation and pre-composition in a stylistically diverse environment, and (crucially) the ability to place an immediately recognizable personal stamp on a multitude of musical possibilities and thereby avoid incoherence, are two of his most notable achievements. The ECM recordings demonstrate an increasingly bold exploration of this phenomenon.

Metheny once described the attempt to bring together improvisation and composition as 'one of the most treacherous areas in jazz',[13] but he noted that in essence such initiatives—which are as old as jazz itself—simply unite 'similar tasks that happen at wildly different temperatures'.[14] In 1998, he told Carr that the principal creative challenge in his work with his own band had been one of 'constructing environments for improvisation that are malleable yet at the same time in many cases ... were obviously searching for a certain kind of drama in the music that is dangerous territory'.[15] Creative aspirations are in this context far more important than commercial success, as evinced by the sheer length of the more elaborate pieces in his repertoire, which is not conducive to

---

11 Eric Porter, 'Incorporation and Distinction in Jazz History and Jazz Historiography', in David Ake, Charles Hiroshi Garrett, and Daniel Goldmark (eds.), *Jazz / Not Jazz: The Music and Its Boundaries* (Berkeley: University of California Press, 2012), 17–18.

12 Quoted in Pawel Brodowski and Janusz Szprot, 'Pat Metheny', *Jazz Forum* 97/6 (June 1985): 35.

13 Niles, *Pat Metheny Interviews*, 47.

14 Peterson, *Music and the Creative Spirit*, 194. Compare Bruno Nettl's view of composition and improvisation as 'part of the same idea', in 'Thoughts on Improvisation: A Comparative Approach', *Musical Quarterly* 61/1 (1974): 6.

15 Carr, 'Bright Size Life', episode 3.

airplay. Although (as suggested above) some of Metheny's followers have been tempted to keep his regular group's output and the 'straight-ahead' recordings made with predominantly improvising musicians apart on structural and idiomatic grounds, he felt creative arranging techniques were just as feasible in (for example) a trio environment, and a challenging project such as *Rejoicing* at times strikingly defies a listener's expectations of what three instrumentalists can achieve in textural and structural terms.

As part of the search for 'a certain kind of drama in the music', electronics became increasingly important during the ECM years as a means of expanding timbral potential, at first with the Oberheim polyphonic synthesizer and later with the far more capable Synclavier and Roland GR-300 guitar synthesizer. Metheny commented that his group work had always been concerned with a 'broader sense of orchestration in a small group setting . . . The group has never been more than seven people and yet at the same time we're really writing on an orchestral scale.'[16] Drawing parallels with Weather Report, which similarly expanded the potential of a standard jazz combo by exploiting electronics during the same period as his recordings for ECM (see Chapter 4), he bemoaned the tendency of critics to want to categorize timbral experimentation as 'less serious or more commercial or less experimental . . . To me it's actually the contrary: to me that's more experimental, *more* difficult.'[17] Metheny once described his group as 'the place where I can play more of the music I like the most,' but also as 'the place to experiment'.[18]

Although some of the music considered here reflected a conscious reassessment of American vernacular idioms, the connection with ECM—the European label famous (at times even notorious) for its promotion of innovative jazz and improvised musics which do not necessarily spring directly from blues-oriented performance traditions, and often created by performers not born in, or native to, the United States—encourages a fresh perspective on another much-debated issue in the history of jazz: its enduring national significance in its country of origin. In his 2001 speech, Metheny commented:

I have always had some misgivings about the whole idea of emphasizing the Americanness of jazz to the point of exclusivity. While, as Americans, we should be proud of its heritage as a key

16 Niles, *Pat Metheny Interviews*, 47–8.
17 *Ibid.*
18 Carr, 'Bright Size Life', episode 3.

component of American culture, the nationalistic celebration of it being something that *must* represent its American roots can also limit the incredible implications of what the form offers, and therefore in fact somewhat diminish its glory. To me, the form demands a kind of deep representation of each individual's personal reality. One of the many things that makes jazz unique is how well suited it is to absorb material and styles and infinite shades of human achievement as well.[19]

The importance of ECM in drawing European jazz thinking to the attention of American players and audiences in the 1970s was highlighted by Metheny's mentor Gary Burton, who also recorded on the label and introduced him to its roster (see Chapter 2).

FUSION

Metheny is routinely described in journalism as a 'fusion' artist, presumably on account of his innovative attempts to combine elements borrowed from an unusually wide range of idioms. This description has been sharply refuted by Metheny on numerous occasions, however, and it may be helpful to explore the reasons for this. In an interview given for an ECM promotional disc released for radio airplay in 1979, he explained that he felt the term 'fusion' only made stylistic sense around 1968–9 when Gary Burton, Larry Coryell, and Keith Jarrett 'grafted their own style' onto popular musical idioms which were not previously familiar to them. As far as his own regular group was concerned, Metheny highlighted their pluralistic approach: being surrounded by a multitude of contemporary styles and influences, they play 'whatever we want to play' without an element of deliberate fusion.[20] In general, it may be argued that juxtapositions of contrasting styles do not necessarily require the constituent elements to be 'fused' for the resulting music to have both intellectual coherence and successfully cross over perceived boundaries of generic classification. The whole notion of fusion can therefore be a red herring. The composer Mike Gibbs, a close associate of Burton's, commented:

I hear this word 'fusion' a lot, and although *fusion* between musics and cultures is going on, I think to label a particular music 'fusion

19 Peterson, *Music and the Creative Spirit*, 192.
20 *An Hour with Pat Metheny: A Radio Special* (PRO-A-810), 1979.

music' is to limit the music. There's a lot of jazz-rock fusion at the moment [i.e., in 1978], and as long as that music is labeled that way, it always remains two musics and the fusions don't have room to take place. I know that the influences I am most aware of are jazz, a lot of contemporary non-jazz music, some classical music, some rock music; but what I put out I don't see as a mixture of all of these . . . There is a fusion going on every time somebody writes music, all the things that have influenced that writing.[21]

The nub of the matter lies in Gibbs's remark that labelling music as 'fusion music' is to limit it, as has been the case more broadly with the similarly vexed label 'jazz'. This problem has been compounded by the use of the term 'jazz-rock fusion', which again ostensibly seems to fit some of Metheny's work, especially when (as in *American Garage*, for example) the rock influences are explicitly audible and self-confessed. But jazz-rock, and the associated term fusion, quickly became specifically associated with the output of the Columbia label in the late 1960s and early 1970s, most famously the music of the electrified ensembles led at first by Miles Davis and later by various of his sidemen. Both Metheny and Michael Brecker have argued that the most interesting music which melded elements from jazz and rock was produced, not surprisingly, before it was categorized and labelled, and one of the most significant examples was the work of Burton in the late 1960s (discussed in Chapter 2). Brecker declared:

My favourite time in the period known as fusion was before the music was *known* as fusion. In the early seventies, when we had no real name for it and when the barriers between rock and jazz were becoming blurry, I found myself, along with my brother [trumpeter Randy] and our contemporaries, interested in finding ways to apply jazz harmony and sensibility to funk grooves . . .
There was an enormous sense of freedom to pursue paths that seemingly hadn't been traversed . . . It certainly was a time of great arrangements as well, and it was a portal through which an endless array of new sonorities and fascinating and visceral harmony and rhythms came . . .
For me, the music was born of a genuine desire and need to do something new and exciting, while coming out of past musical

21 Quoted in Julie Coryell and Laura Friedman, *Jazz-Rock Fusion: The People, the Music*, rev. edn. (Milwaukee, WI: Hal Leonard, 2000), 84.

traditions. It was so exhilarating to play this music for a large audience and really feel that it was being heard, understood and felt.[22]

Metheny commented of his debut album, *Bright Size Life* (1976):

Ironically, I now [in 2003] am classified by people who should know better as a 'fusion' guy, but at that time, first of all, that word didn't exist. In fact, I was a violent reactionary to the fusion of that time. I really didn't want to hear backbeats and rock beats and distorted guitar sounds. I really wanted to deal with harmony. I didn't want to play on one chord or two chords.[23]

These comments refer to a specific style of fusion in which simple, repeated harmonic ideas serve as a basis for virtuosic instrumental showmanship, an approach to performing that Metheny elsewhere described as 'anti-music' that at the time 'made my stomach turn'.[24] He explained his contrasting priorities in his group work, commenting that he did not regard any of his music

as being even remotely close to what [John McLaughlin's] Mahavishnu Orchestra, or [Chick Corea's] Return to Forever, or what Miles was doing at that time. In fact, we were outright reactionaries to that. We wanted to play through complex forms and wrote music that really demanded specific kinds of improvising. I did not want for us to do vamps or solo over a repeated chord, I wanted to play through changes. I wanted to be more driven by the cymbal, not by back beats and the bass drum ... We were committed to playing with dynamics, playing longer song forms, really utilizing the quartet, and I wouldn't use [electric-guitar] distortion. We had this rebellious, reactionary crusade mindset that was a fuel to us to go this different direction.[25]

Metheny told his drummer Danny Gottlieb that he wanted his band's music to bring together jazz and rock without sounding like either

---

22 Quoted in Coryell and Friedman, *Jazz-Rock Fusion*, 290-1.
23 Anon., 'A Fireside Chat with Pat Metheny' (October 29, 2003). http://www.allaboutjazz. com/php/article.php?id=727 (August 11, 2013).
24 Carr, 'Bright Size Life', episode 2.
25 Joe Barth, *Voices in Jazz Guitar: Great Performers Talk about Their Approach to Playing* (Pacific, MO: Mel Bay, 2006), 323-4.

one,[26] and the distinctively fresh timbres that resulted from this aim were spearheaded by Metheny's own trademark guitar sonority in which the combination of his Gibson 175 and Lexicon digital delays sounded neither purely acoustic nor purely electric—only like Metheny (and, since his worldwide fame, countless imitators).

Clearly Metheny, like Gibbs, was also reacting against the implied limitations of the fusion label, and he noted that both Burton's pioneering group and Weather Report were initially labelled as fusion bands but with hindsight were more accurately viewed as essentially jazz outfits.[27] (Conversely, Burton feels that the music he was making in the late 1960s 'eventually became known as "fusion jazz"'.)[28] Metheny reiterated his viewpoint in a *Down Beat* interview published in 1979, in which the authors proposed 'jazz-based' and 'neo-fusion' as less contentious labels for his style and explicitly asked him whether he were 'consciously trying to synthesize jazz and pop, not to mention the obvious country elements in your music?' The reply:

> It might *seem* synthetic now, but 15 years from now it will be seen in an entirely different light. People now are very classification conscious, but when you look back now at the groups that were slightly in the cracks ten years ago, like Gary Burton's group or the early fusion groups, they clearly seem jazz groups today. I think in retrospect we'll seem that way in terms of our emphasis on improvising. So will Weather Report.[29]

On another occasion, Metheny pointed out:

> Hardly any musicians use that term ['fusion']—it's mainly press and record companies which do. I don't think I've ever run across a musician who would say, 'Well, what kind of music do I play?—I play fusion.' I mean nobody says that. I've never felt as uncomfortable with that hyphenated thing, you know—jazz-rock, such and such thing. But even that's clumsy.[30]

26 Rick Mattingly, 'A Different View: Pat Metheny', *Modern Drummer* (December 1991): 80.
27 Brodowski and Szprot, 'Pat Metheny', 39.
28 Gary Burton, *Learning to Listen: The Jazz Journey of Gary Burton* (Boston, MA: Berklee Press, 2013), 208.
29 Neil Tesser and Fred Bourque, 'Pat Metheny: Musings on Neo-Fusion', *Down Beat* 46/6 (March 22, 1979): 43.
30 Brodowski and Szprot, 'Pat Metheny', 38.

As with other groundbreaking movements in music history, however, it may also be the case that the pejorative associations of the term, in addition to its perceived limitations, were partly responsible for the antipathy towards it shown by those who became involuntarily saddled with the label after its first flush of uncritical exposure. (Compare, for example, Debussy's distrust of 'impressionism', Stravinsky's of 'neoclassicism', and Schoenberg's of 'atonality', all of which terms were coined pejoratively.) An interviewer once proposed to Metheny that to call his music fusion—not to mention the far more offensive derivative, 'fuzak'—was in essence to criticize it for being 'too smooth, too bland'.[31] More specifically, bassist and composer Steve Swallow used the term 'fuzak' to mean music that was spoiled by 'overworked formulas',[32] a criticism which would be impossible to apply to Metheny's extraordinarily eclectic output.

In their book on early fusion, Julie Coryell and Laura Friedman—while noting that the label might best remain associated with a specific historical period—nevertheless advance a useful definition: 'a kind of music that, for lack of a better definition, we will call jazz-inspired improvisatory music'.[33] Their book illustrates, through numerous interviews with performers active in the late 1970s, the diversity of musicians who were then working under the umbrella term of 'jazz-rock'. Many of them, as Metheny was later to do, place a strong emphasis on striving to create music that reflects contemporary culture and therefore communicates with modern audiences. Contemporary relevance and jazz improvisation were during Metheny's ECM years increasingly absorbed into innovative and sometimes complex compositions, but this never belied the spontaneity of performance so essential to the jazz tradition. As Metheny once said of Miles Davis, one of his strongest and earliest influences: 'Those records of the great Miles quintet in the Sixties—it sounds like they're playing *free* but the structure is there.'[34]

31 The comment was made in John Shore's article 'Traveling Man: Jazz Guitarist Pat Metheny Discusses His New Album and Life on the Road' in a 1998 issue of SLAMM magazine. I am grateful to Mr Shore for trying to trace a copy of this source, which has so far proved elusive.

32 Joshua Rosenbaum, 'Steve Swallow: Renegade Jazz Bassist', *Guitar Player* (December 1981): 67.

33 Coryell and Friedman, *Jazz-Rock Fusion*, 8.

34 John Fordham, 'Rejoicing', *Wire* 15 (May 1985): 32. For further on fusion-related debates during the 1970s, with special reference to Keith Jarrett's work, see Peter Elsdon, *Keith Jarrett's The Köln Concert* (New York: Oxford University Press, 2013), 29-35.

The notion that Davis's music is '*free* but the structure is there' may be linked to Metheny's strong belief in a narrative model for both composition and improvisation, his playing always clearly aiming 'to try to tell a story rather than just play licks up and down the instrument'.[35] He commented in 2009:

> The idea for me all the way along has been to come up with a narrative, storytelling quality of music that hopefully adds up; once an idea starts, it gets taken to its natural conclusion. Whether that happens on a macro level or micro level, whether it's one phrase or a whole record, that's the quality I'm most attracted to. It can happen in any style or genre.[36]

Narrative models applied directly to music are of course fraught with theoretical dangers; but, as Sven Bjerstedt has argued, empirical evidence based on interviews with musicians generally 'provides a very convincing response to such difficulties' and the understanding of linear musical processes demonstrated by jazz practitioners 'emerges as an important way of dealing with issues of meaning in music'.[37] More specifically, Paul Berliner has described how early jazz performers such as Louis Armstrong, Sidney Bechet, and Lester Young evolved solo structures based on multiple choruses, of which the first would be closely based on the melody, the second would vary it, and the last would either return to the opening formulation or proceed 'to other events such as single-note riffing patterns'.[38] (Metheny's improvising on *Watercolors* was directly compared to Young's playing in an early review, which cited by way of specific comparison not only the story-telling qualities of the two musicians, but also their 'light swing and cool, focused tone'.)[39] Interviewed for

---

35 Tesser and Bourque, 'Pat Metheny: Musings on Neo-Fusion', 43. See also Peterson, *Music and the Creative Spirit*, 194. For further on the narrative model of improvisation, see Ingrid Monson, *Saying Something: Jazz Improvisation and Interaction* (Chicago: University of Chicago Press, 1996), 86.

36 Niles, *Pat Metheny Interviews*, 50.

37 Sven Bjerstedt, 'The Jazz Storyteller: Improvisers' Perspectives on Music and Narrative', *Jazz Research Journal* 9/1 (2015): 37-61; 43.

38 Paul F. Berliner, *Thinking in Jazz: The Infinite Art of Improvisation* (Chicago: University of Chicago Press, 1994), 210.

39 Neil Tesser, review of *Watercolors*, in *Down Beat* 45/1 (January 12, 1978): 24.

Berliner's monumental project on improvisational practices, both Buster Williams and Kenny Barron advocated starting simply, so the solo has somewhere into which it can build: Barron, learning from the example of Dizzy Gillespie, talked of 'hills and valleys' and suggested that the appropriate moment for an improvisation to 'build' was the point at which the tune becomes more interesting harmonically. Drummer Paul Wertico, who joined Metheny's band in 1983, went even further down the narrative road by encouraging his students to develop 'characters and a plot', and to introduce ideas at the start of the solo that can be recapitulated and developed to make 'a little story'; in explaining this, he used the analogy of sentences and paragraphs as the essential building blocks of a novel.[40] This last idea suggests a more abstract approach to structure based on written models, and resonates with comments often made by Metheny that being asked what modes, scales, or chords he liked playing was akin to being asked what verbs he liked using in speech.[41] Interestingly, in Berliner's ten-page discussion of narrative strategies in jazz improvising, there are remarkably few verbal analogies, and the focus is rather on musical developments in the abstract. Yet his index lists a whole host of colourful metaphors for improvisation, including clothing styles, cuisine, dance, foundation building, educational institutions, chess, travel, landing an airplane, love, marriage, preparation for acting, painting, singing, sports, toys, and tape recordings; the most numerous references, however, are to improvisation as speech and types of conversation.[42] Wayne E. Goins, taking a cognitive approach, has examined Metheny's 1992 album *Secret Story* as an emotional journey rooted in models of literary and musical rhetoric (including familiar Baroque affects suggesting a close affinity with classical music), in which the crucial factors are a speech-like manner of articulating improvisations and the overriding ideal of achieving *cantando* instrumental playing.[43]

40 Berliner, *Thinking in Jazz*, 201–2. Wertico explains his narrative conception further in his instructional video *Paul Wertico: Drum Philosophy* (2009 [1997]).

41 See, for example, Dan Forte, 'Pat Metheny: Jazz Voice of the 80's', *Guitar Player* (December 1981): 100. The sentiment is similar to Burton's concept of musical sentence-formation: see *Learning to Listen*, 334.

42 Berliner, *Thinking in Jazz*, 869.

43 Wayne E. Goins, *Emotional Response to Music: Pat Metheny's Secret Story* (Lewiston, NY: Edwin Mellen Press, 2001).

Metheny sometimes likened his goal of musical storytelling to cinema, a medium in which he became increasingly involved during the ECM period (see Chapter 6). 'When I improvise or solo', he once said,

> it's a matter of telling a story, and when you go to see a good movie, or see a painting you like, or hear somebody talk to you, there are certain qualities that make it interesting. You don't wanna hear the guy say the same thing over and over and over again as he's telling you a story. You want him to say it once in the most vivid possible way and then you get the message and you can imagine what it is he's talking about.[44]

Even when his music was at its most complex or experimental, he did not lose sight of this fundamental analogy, and explained in 2002 that 'the details and even the bulk content of the pieces have to primarily succeed as envelopes for emotion and storytelling', noting that the 'fundamental importance' of the music lay in 'the vibe of it . . . and the emotional impact that we are able to achieve through all the work that we put into making all of the elements come together to tell a story as best we can'.[45] At around this time, Metheny gave a question-and-answer session at Berklee College of Music at which he discussed his interest in 'narrative improvisation' and commented that an important consideration was

> what sounds good over the course of an hour or two hour performance. Keeping things moving along a narrative line, usually means shifting and changing and trading off and trying to explore all the little things you can do together and trying not to just do the same thing over and over again. That's a real challenging environment . . .
> [F]or me, thinking in longer ideas is much easier than thinking in shorter ideas. On a structural level, having to come up with little things [one] right after another is one of the hardest things to do . . . Again to use the vocabulary/speaking analogy, it would be very difficult to talk about a different subject one sentence at a time 40 subjects in a row. It's much easier to keep talking about one thing until you've exhausted what you have to say about it, and will take

44 M. Kay, 'Pat Metheny', *Music U.K.* 25 (January 1984): 57.
45 Mike Brannon, 'Pat Metheny: Speaks of Now' (March 2002), formerly available at http://www.allaboutjazz.com. I am grateful to Mr Brannon for his help in connection with this source.

you to the next thing ... [I]f you let one idea lead to the next on the zone you're talking about, you almost start answering your own question as you go along. You make subdivisions and proposals that you elaborate on. To me the linear narrative way of improvising is exactly the same. It's just easier to keep one idea going ... In my case it was really hammered home to me by two people, in particular Gary Burton, who is just an unbelievably evolved improviser in this area—it's mindboggling to me the number of ways he has of getting from point A to point B and make it all connect. And in a very different way, I would say Ornette Coleman, who has the capacity to play one thing that inevitably leads to the next. It's like he's incapable of playing something that doesn't have some reference to something that he played before in that zone on that tune.[46]

Burton's resourcefulness in 'getting from point A to point B and make it all connect' was partly inspired by the occasionally negative example of tenor saxophonist Stan Getz, with whom he played in the early 1960s, who (according to Burton) tended to repeat himself from one solo to the next. Burton, on the other hand, quickly became determined never to lapse into repetition or cliché, though from Getz he did learn the fine art of using dynamics and expression to shape and project a melody convincingly for an audience.[47] In his account of the art of improvisation, Burton went further by commenting that good solos would not only appeal both to the musically trained on a technical level but also offer 'an assortment of well-told stories for non-musicians to follow in their imagination'. This last remark was not remotely intended to be condescending: on the contrary, Burton (like many sensitive musicians) found a 'true magic' in successfully communicating with non-trained listeners through his music-making.[48]

Arguably a yet more treacherous area of jazz than the balancing of composition and improvisation in performance is the minefield of theoretical debate surrounding the alleged inappropriateness of using analytical methods and criteria evolved specifically for the consideration of Western art music for the investigation of jazz improvisation, in

---

46 I am grateful to Ed Hazell for kindly supplying me with a full transcript of this event, an edited version of which was formerly available as 'Improvisational Theater: Making up melodies with guitar great Pat Metheny' (January 23, 2003) on Berklee's website (http://www.berklee.edu).

47 Burton, *Learning to Listen*, 113-14.

48 *Ibid.*, 340.

which even the basic notion of transcription into standard notation (as an analytical tool) has been challenged. Gunther Schuller's pioneering analysis of Sonny Rollins's 'Blue 7' (from the album *Saxophone Colossus*, recorded in 1956) has come to be widely discredited, in a backlash caused at least in part by Schuller's apparent deprecation of jazz which did not meet his own personal criteria for excellence—but also (and more important for the present context) because he self-evidently approached improvised music from the perspective of a classically trained composer and analyst.[49] Only as recently as 2014 has Benjamin Givan thoroughly unravelled the various debates surrounding Schuller's controversial article and its aftermath, arguing that the analysis of any jazz improvisation is only meaningful when the music is placed in the context of the performer's work as a whole: as a result of applying this holistic approach, what may appear in one isolated solo to be what Schuller considered as a consciously and quasi-compositionally manipulated thematic 'motive' (for which Givan prefers the more neutral term 'cell') might equally well come to be viewed as no more than a formulaic lick when the performance is set alongside others by the same artist. After analysing Rollins's music in this more contextualized way, Givan concludes: 'Ironically, the saxophone improvisation that Schuller lauded for its exceptional intellectuality and formal unity may well be Rollins's most casually executed, haphazardly organized performance ever approved for release on a commercial album.'[50]

It should not be overlooked, however, that jazz musicians—especially in the present age—often have a formidable knowledge of classical music, and their approach to creative music-making, whether expressed in improvisation or composition, is inevitably coloured accordingly. In the case of Metheny, an impulse towards intricate composition sits comfortably alongside his passion for improvising, and it would be naïve to assume that these two processes are kept entirely separate. (As noted earlier in this chapter, he regards them as fundamentally similar creative activities taking place at different temperatures.)

49 Gunther Schuller, 'Sonny Rollins and the Challenge of Thematic Improvisation,' *Jazz Review* 1 (November 1958): 6-11, 21; reprinted in *Musings: The Musical Worlds of Gunther Schuller* (New York: Da Capo Press, 1999), 86-97. On the backlash, see Ingrid Monson, *Saying Something*, 135-6.

50 Benjamin Givan, 'Gunther Schuller and the Challenge of Sonny Rollins: Stylistic Context, Intentionality, and Jazz Analysis', *Journal of the American Musicological Society* 67/1 (Spring 2014): 167-237; quotation from 226. I am grateful to Alexander Gagatsis for his thoughts on this article and for many stimulating discussions on related issues.

Musicians of this kind will not surprisingly—even if at an instinctive rather than necessarily conscious level—approach improvisation with a compositional mentality founded on principles that are not in fact dissimilar to the Schuller model. Similarly, in his own seminal contribution to the mechanics of jazz analysis, Lewis Porter concluded that in John Coltrane's improvisations 'we hear a composer at work, shaping, developing, and connecting musical ideas while attempting, often successfully, to keep the musical whole in perspective'.[51] Sentiments of this kind were also expressed by Duke Ellington, the musician who has oftentimes caused a degree of consternation amongst critics perplexed at—rather than impressed by—his ability seamlessly to fuse compositional sophistication with the spontaneity and timbral expressiveness of 'authentic' jazz.

Certainly, some of Schuller's rather rigid tenets do not fit well with Metheny's music-making, even though the guitarist singled out Rollins as a prime example of an improviser 'who seems incapable of playing a phrase without coming up with two or three of the most logical and stimulating responses to his own melodic postulations every time out'.[52] In the same statement, Metheny commented:

> The whole idea of melodic development in a linear way has been fascinating to me ever since I really started listening to music . . .
>
> I really try to stay on the subject at hand as much as possible—in other words, if I have started an idea that involves, say, a large interval leap, I try to continue to use that as an idea for as long as seems natural, trying to let each idea come to its natural conclusion.
>
> At its best, the duration of this way of thinking can be an entire solo, but often it is just for a few phrases. But the thing is, even if it is just for a few phrases, by concentrating on the idea of development, you invariably wind up having a narrative shape to the 'story' aspect of your improvisation that if you were just 'running the changes', you probably wouldn't.

While the guitarist's improvisations (representative examples of which are examined in detail in subsequent chapters) generally conform to Schuller's desideratum of motivic coherence, as suggested by these

---

51 Lewis Porter, 'John Coltrane's *A Love Supreme*: Jazz Improvisation as Composition', *Journal of the American Musicological Society* 38 (1985): 621.
52 http://www.patmetheny.com/qa/questionView.cfm?queID=2451 (September 5, 2014).

remarks, Schuller's complaint against performers whose solos bear no relation to the pre-composed sections of the same piece might at times be felt to be borne out by Metheny's fondness—even in the middle of a structurally intricate composition—for improvising over 'blowing changes' which can be both disarmingly simple and apparently of little direct relevance to the rest of the composition. (As shown by specific examples considered later in this book, however, such blowing changes are in fact always strategically important in harmonic terms, even when at their most economical.) But here, of course, the improviser's innate skills take over, enticing the listener into a compelling musical journey with its own logic and a sense of pacing which, in overview, makes a vital contribution to the trajectory of the structure of the piece as a whole. The narrative metaphor remains crucial. As noted above, this concept in jazz stretches back at least as far as Armstrong, and Porter observed that 'musicians themselves rarely speak of form except to say that a good solo should tell a story, should have a beginning, middle, and end'.[53] Roy Eldridge's description of Armstrong's ability to link improvised phrases in a cumulatively developmental fashion, which he likened to 'a plot that finished with a climax',[54] could be applied to Metheny's approach without incongruity, and the analyses advanced in subsequent chapters explore this concept of linear musical narrative more fully.

BRAVE NEW WORLD

Metheny's brand of what Leonard Feather once termed a 'brave new world of . . . music to which young, rock-reared audiences can relate' (see p. 33) began life in the small Missouri town of Lee's Summit, where he grew up. Born in nearby Kansas City in 1954, Metheny developed compositional and playing styles that were strongly influenced by his Midwestern roots (see Chapter 3), being reflected from the late 1970s onwards in his reworking of country-music idioms in a jazz context; but his early years also exposed him to a wide range of other musics, and his eclectic tastes were typical of emerging musicians of his generation. As a teenager playing in Kansas City, he learnt much from the example of trumpeter Gary Sivils, whose soulful playing he regarded as a continuation of a venerable KC tradition stretching back to Lester

---

53 Porter, 'John Coltrane's *A Love Supreme*', 594.
54 Brian Harker, *Louis Armstrong's Hot Five and Hot Seven Recordings* (New York: Oxford University Press, 2011), 41.

Young, and from bebop drummer Tommy Ruskin.[55] Both musicians strengthened Metheny's awareness of two essential concepts that were to underpin all his mature music, and which he repeatedly stressed in many interviews throughout his career: the need for improvisations to be melodically memorable rather than formulaic, and the narrative model for musical structure discussed above.

During his formative years in KC, Metheny was thoroughly schooled in a bebop manner of jazz playing, much of it in the context of small groups with organ, and he would continue to regard this as something all aspiring jazz musicians needed to master—though he quickly distanced himself from a manner of improvising based largely on pre-learnt formulae. Apart from Young, the region was also inextricably identified with the legendary Charlie Parker, with whom some of the young guitarist's collaborators had played. By the age of 15, Metheny had immersed himself in the music of Ornette Coleman, John Coltrane, Miles Davis, Bill Evans, Herbie Hancock, and McCoy Tyner, and he was especially influenced by trumpeters such as Freddie Hubbard and Clifford Brown. This was not merely because Metheny's first instrument before taking up the guitar had been the trumpet: more fundamentally, melodic trumpet playing remained his primary inspiration when striving to achieve a sustained lyricism in his guitar solos. Many years later he commented of his fundamental 'horn playing aesthetic': 'I still think in terms of trumpet most of the time. I think in terms of how one would tongue a phrase in the back of my mind . . . I have worked very hard trying to simulate that kind of articulation that, to me, rings true as a horn player.'[56] On a promotional disc made for ECM, he recalled that both his father and brother were trumpet players; he followed the family tradition at the age of nine but switched to guitar at 13 and was playing with organ trios from 15.[57]

Asked in later life to identify three recordings by jazz guitarists which had a seminal influence on his own playing, Metheny chose two albums by Wes Montgomery and one by Kenny Burrell.[58] In April 1968, at the age of 13, Metheny had met Montgomery and secured his autograph at the KC Jazz Festival, at a time when (on his own admission) his playing was virtually a clone of his idol's. Heading the list of three albums was the famous *Smokin' at the Half Note*, documenting performances which

55   Tesser and Bourque, 'Pat Metheny: Musings on Neo-Fusion', 13.
56   Barth, *Voices in Jazz Guitar*, 314.
57   *An Hour with Pat Metheny: A Radio Special* (1979).
58   Barth, *Voices in Jazz Guitar*, 318.

took place in New York in June and September 1965 with the Wynton Kelly Trio. Metheny commented that the album 'just defined so many things for me. Rhythm section playing, melodic playing, Wes's solo on "If You Could See Now" is the greatest guitar solo I have ever heard'.[59] Fellow guitarist Anthony Wilson identified the characteristics which made this solo typical of Montgomery's playing,

> with its sinuous single lines for most of the chorus, with a foreshadowing of the octaves to be used in the second chorus. The logic of the melodies, the insatiable swing and flawless execution, the voluptuous tone, the cohesion of themes and motifs and a joy beyond comprehension make this, for me, one of the greatest solos ever played on the guitar.[60]

Wilson's words might easily be adapted as a description of a Metheny solo—apart from Montgomery's trademark use of octaves which, along with right-hand thumb technique (necessary in the absence of a pick), Metheny tried hard to expunge from his early playing because they were too close to his hero's distinctive soundworld. Another guitarist, Bobby Broom, pointed out that the seminal Montgomery album triumphantly demonstrated how guitar and piano could, in the right hands, work supremely well together in a small ensemble.[61] This was a possibility of which many guitarists were skeptical, though Metheny and Mays were also to prove them wrong.

The other two albums of Metheny's chosen three have both been criticized for their seemingly commercial stance, reflected in their unabashed tunefulness and use of backing arrangements for large ensembles. Both were recorded in 1967-8, when Metheny was still a teenager. Metheny felt listeners who rejected Montgomery's recordings on the CTI/A&M label in this period as overly commercial 'are missing some of the most profound playing that Wes ever did, exactly because it was so simple'.[62] This trait was beautifully demonstrated by Montgomery's interpretation of 'Georgia on My Mind' on *Down Here on the Ground*, the second album Metheny mentioned, as well as by

---

59 *Ibid.*
60 Quoted in Aaron Cohen, 'Still Smoldering: Guitarists Marvel at Wes Montgomery's *Smokin' at the Half Note* 40 Years after Its Recording', *Down Beat* 72/7 (July 2005): 50.
61 *Ibid.*
62 Barth, *Voices in Jazz Guitar*, 318.

'A Day in the Life' from Montgomery's album of the same name (also dating from 1967). Such simplicity of utterance—especially as a contrast to compositional sophistication—was to become a vital element in Metheny's work. Metheny also singled out Kenny Burrell's *Blues—The Common Ground* for its performer's rich timbre and subtle placing of the beat, and his own playing occasionally came to echo the blues licks and dyadic riffs characteristic of Burrell's style in, for example, the album's rendition of Horace Silver's 'The Preacher'. Metheny's fondness for these jazz albums with wide popular appeal was not surprising, given his contemporaneous interest in bossa nova (see Chapter 4) and, above all, the guitar-dominated pop and rock music exemplified by the Beatles, which Montgomery had celebrated in his version of 'A Day in the Life' (the final song on *Sgt. Pepper's Lonely Hearts Club Band*). Metheny recalled: 'I come from the middle of the generation that viewed the guitar almost as an icon of some sort of youthful revolution . . . [The Beatles] brought to my mind a consciousness concerning the guitar that wasn't there before.'[63] The Beatles were important for other reasons, too: Burton remembers being fascinated by their music, which for him embodied an exciting stylistic eclecticism, harmonic freshness, and structural inventiveness that were otherwise sorely lacking in popular rock in the mid-1960s.[64]

An important common feature in both Montgomery's and Burrell's approaches to improvising is the way in which their solos clearly demonstrate the narrative quality favoured by Metheny. Kenny Mathieson defines Montgomery's ability to 'tell a story' in purely musical terms as the 'ability to build an extended solo in logical but never predictable musical fashion'.[65] Chris Vandercook commented that, in *Blues—The Common Ground*, Burrell's solos also 'tell a story':

> They tend to simmer before they build to a great heat, and they build with clarity. Wherever he goes he makes sure to take the listener with him—and although his work has its share of signature phrases, he seems to reach for new discoveries in each solo.[66]

---

63 *Ibid.*, 311. On the early influence of both Montgomery and the Beatles, see also Moira Stuart's interview with Metheny, 'Jazz Guitar Greats', BBC Radio 2, September 3, 2013.

64 Burton, *Learning to Listen*, 166.

65 Charles Alexander, *Masters of Jazz Guitar: The Story of the Players and Their Music* (London: Balafon Books, 1999), 70.

66 Chris Vandercook, liner notes to Kenny Burrell, *Blues—The Common Ground* (Verve CD 589 101–2), 2001.

Again, these remarks sound uncannily like a description of Metheny's playing. Metheny recalled that he was most influenced by Montgomery's phrasing (which suggested that of a melodious horn player rather than a note-picker), melodic development, his adaptation for his own instrument of ideas pioneered by saxophonists Sonny Rollins and John Coltrane, his joyful spirit, and his ability to make 'a perfect jewel of a statement' in just a few bars of music.[67] Montgomery's 'story-telling quality that let ideas unfold over time in a way no guitarist had done before'[68] was crucial to the success of his solos and remained an important model for Metheny who, in response to a question about the challenge of playing simply, replied: 'It all depends on the story you want to tell. . . . It is the atmosphere that you create on a narrative level that separates musicians that are improvisers who can manifest images as opposed to just notes.'[69] Metheny also identified a narrative approach in the seminal style of improvising developed by Charlie Christian, the pioneer of bebop guitar-playing in the early 1940s, and once more related this to the melodic influence of Young.[70]

After immersing himself in the music of Montgomery and Burrell, Metheny discovered the playing of Jim Hall and soon came to regard him as the 'father' of all jazz guitarists of his own generation.[71] He felt that Hall 'took the guitar, harmonically, to a point where maybe he was the first guitar player who could function in a rhythm section without a piano and really make it speak', and this was especially true in his recordings with Rollins.[72] Another groundbreaking feature of Hall's playing was his structural use of dynamics, something that came to be equally important in Metheny's work. In 1998, Metheny and Hall made a duet recording together,[73] and they gave a joint interview in which Metheny highlighted this aspect of Hall's playing:

> One of Jim's major breakthroughs in what he offered the instrument
> was a way of increasing the apparent dynamic range of the guitar
> as a line instrument by picking softer and letting the amp do part

67 Metheny's views were published in Jim Ferguson, 'Portrait of Wes', *JazzTimes* (July/August 1995): 35, 38.
68 *Ibid.*
69 Barth, *Voices in Jazz Guitar*, 319.
70 Brodowski and Szprot, 'Pat Metheny', 38.
71 Andy Aledort, 'Pat Metheny: Straight Ahead', *Guitar Extra!* (Spring 1990): 60.
72 Brodowski and Szprot, 'Pat Metheny', 38.
73 *Jim Hall & Pat Metheny* (Telarc CD-83442), 1998.

of the job. Jim says by using the amp he could play softer and my interpretation of that is that he doesn't have to pick as hard to get the sound out of the instrument, and then when he does pick hard, it's bigger. Like, if you are picking really hard and you are hanging up here all the time [shows hand high up from the guitar], and you only have that much higher to go, you can't really pick any higher than that. What Jim does is, by picking in this certain range, by letting the amp do the thing, he has that much further to go. So, you increase the apparent difference from the softest note to the loudest note. And he will do that with this incredible shading dozens of times in the course of a single line. With so many jazz guitar guys, it's like hearing a monotone conversation, but Jim's thing has got this very natural and very continual rise and fall to it dynamically. And that breakthrough opened a door that myself, John Scofield, Bill Frisell, Mick Goodrick, John Abercrombie, and many others have taken to find our own thing. Yet to me it can all be traced to Jim.[74]

Another revelatory influence was jazz-rock guitarist Larry Coryell who, like Hall, had played with Metheny's soon-to-be mentor Burton. Metheny's playing occasionally echoes certain of Coryell's licks, such as arpeggiated triads cutting across the metre and the use of dyadic passages by way of climaxing a solo, both of which devices can be heard in Coryell's playing in the funky blues-based 'June the 15, 1967' on Burton's album *Lofty Fake Anagram* (1967). The latter also featured Steve Swallow on bass and Bob Moses on drums, two sidemen with whom Metheny would frequently perform in the following decade.[75] Both Coryell and Moses played for a time with the group Free Spirits, which mixed jazz and rock elements, and Coryell's stylistic eclecticism was a significant influence on other emerging guitarists at the time, notably Abercrombie.[76]

Metheny's interest in composition intensified during his late teens, but it was not until he went to Florida at the age of 18 that he began to learn

---

74 'Study Hall: Pat Metheny analyzes the Hall phenomenon', in Ken Micallef, 'Jim Hall and Pat Metheny: mutual admiration society' (1998). Formerly available at http://www.guitar. com/articles/jim-hall-and-pat-metheny-mutual-admiration-society (August 15, 2012). See also Barth, *Voices in Jazz Guitar*, 351.

75 For a detailed profile of Swallow's work in the 1970s, see Rosenbaum, 'Steve Swallow: Renegade Jazz Bassist'.

76 Coryell and Friedman, *Jazz-Rock Fusion*, 122. See also Bob Blumenthal's liner notes to *Gary Burton: Artist's Choice* (RCA Bluebird ND 86280), 1987.

theoretical terminology. Enrolled on a scholarship at the University of Miami, he abandoned his course after a matter of weeks, disillusioned by an ill-fated attempt to learn classical guitar, but he was retained on the institution's books as a jazz guitar instructor for a year. Six months after arriving in Florida, Metheny's rediscovery of his neglected Gibson ES-175N marked a turning point in his search for a distinctive personal sound, and he would continue to use this instrument as his primary vehicle for lyrical soloing until 1995, when it became too fragile and was reluctantly retired. Metheny's version of this classic electro-acoustic guitar, which was launched in 1949 and quickly became beloved by mainstream jazz players such as Herb Ellis and Joe Pass in the 1950s and 1960s, and also by Hall and many others, was made in 1960 and bought 'as new' in 1968 from a father who had lost his son to the Vietnam War.[77]

Metheny's spell in Miami also introduced him to bassists Jaco Pastorius and Mark Egan, and drummer Danny Gottlieb, all of whom were to play crucial roles in his early ECM recordings. Gottlieb played with Metheny in the faculty/student group Kaleidoscope, with pianist Dan Haerle, and elsewhere, including inventive duetting for just guitar and drums which would later occasionally feature in Metheny Group gigs.[78] Egan was studying trumpet at the University of Miami but switched to bass during his time there.

THE FOLLOWING CHAPTERS chart the development of Metheny's music—and the striking consistency of his creative preoccupations throughout the ECM years—with particular reference to three concepts: first, the fundamental notion of 'a new paradigm' capable of keeping jazz relevant to the musically diverse tastes of contemporary listeners, and the way in which this aim was achieved not only by absorbing an unusual plurality of influences but also by the music's refusal to subscribe fully to either of the then prevailing mainstream styles of bebop or jazz-rock; second, the increasingly symbiotic relationship between improvisation and composition, as manifested both in the studio albums and in live performances on the road; and third, the various strategies through which a linear model for musical narrative was constantly varied. The eleven ECM albums are also seen as

---

77 Adrian Ingram, *The Gibson ES175: Its History and Players* (Ely: Music Maker Books, 1994), 22–3. Metheny provided a foreword to this volume (vii).
78 Personal communication from Danny Gottlieb via email, July 9, 2014.

embodying a gradual shift away from the early 'documentary' manner of on-the-spot studio recordings, which were mostly accomplished rather rapidly, towards a more creative application of technology that permitted both significant timbral experimentation and the development of more challenging musical structures. Additionally, the origins of the distinctive sleeve artwork for these releases is investigated, shedding light not only on the label's general artistic preoccupations at the time but also on the specific metaphors of travelling and the natural world which are reflected in much of Metheny's most vividly characterised music.

Chapter 2 explores the background to ECM and its distinctive manner of record production, and considers its roster of seminal recording artists, which included Eberhard Weber, Chick Corea, Keith Jarrett, and Metheny's early mentor Gary Burton. Burton, like many American performers, found the label's explorations of European jazz and alternative types of improvised musics revelatory, and it was with his group that Metheny first recorded on the label at the age of 19. The chapter charts the first part of Metheny's career as both sideman to Burton and as a newcomer to the small body of talented guitarists who recorded for ECM, and his more experimental playing with Paul Bley and Jaco Pastorius. Metheny's debut as a leader on ECM, with the trio recording *Bright Size Life* (1976), showcased early compositions that embodied specific harmonic and rhythmic challenges and which were designed as otherwise orthodox vehicles for improvisation. Metheny's subsequent creative collaboration with Lyle Mays (the nature of which is further explored in Chapter 4) was first documented in the quartet album *Watercolors* (1977), analysis of which here includes a detailed comparison of Metheny's solos on the title track, as performed in the studio and at a contemporaneous live gig.

Chapter 3 recounts how Metheny and his group's punishing tour schedules resulted in an increasingly widespread fan base in the late 1970s, when the awareness that the musicians were on something of a crusade to pursue their own stylistic inclinations—belonging neither to bebop nor to fusion—became truly palpable. The Pat Metheny Group's eponymous debut album (1978), which sold in huge numbers, featured tracks of extended length that effectively balanced improvised and pre-composed material in their more ambitious narrative trajectories (notably 'San Lorenzo'), and one guitar solo in particular ('Phase Dance') became the first of Metheny's improvisations to be widely transcribed and studied. The two albums that followed in 1979 revealed Metheny's extraordinary diversity to an even greater extent. The solo guitar project *New Chautauqua* explored the sounds of country and pop music, long influences on Metheny but here emerging for the first time in recorded form, as well as creative overdubbing; what emerged was a fresh kind of 'pastoral' jazz of considerable cultural significance. By contrast, the group album *American Garage*, recorded in the United States and Metheny's first venture as his own producer, revelled in explicit and sometimes raucous rock associations—which disturbed some critics—and experimented with electronics while continuing to explore extended structures. The most notable of these was 'The Epic', with which the recording concludes, and which achieves its strong narrative quality in no small part from the seamless integration into the pre-planned whole of substantial improvisations based on limited but strategically selected harmonies from the pre-composed sections.

In Chapter 4, the quasi-country elements of *New Chautauqua* are seen to come into what (at the time) seemed a startling conjunction with both straight-ahead and experimental jazz in the shape of the album *80/ 81* (1980), featuring fine saxophone performances from Michael Brecker and Dewey Redman and bass playing from Charlie Haden, a performer who shared both Metheny's Missouri background and his admiration for the music of Ornette Coleman. The surprising appearance of Coleman's music as an entirely plausible element in the emerging 'pastoral' jazz aesthetic was nothing short of revelatory. Meanwhile, Metheny's and Mays's shared commitment to sonic experimentation through the exploitation of increasingly elaborate electronics and their bold structural initiatives were both to culminate in their joint album *As Falls Wichita, So Falls Wichita Falls* (1981), in which synthesizers and overdubbing techniques came to the fore in an atmosphere of theatrical and at times quasi-cinematic drama that reflected the vivid stage presentations (including novel lighting effects) of all Metheny's gigs, whether with his regular group or trios. This chapter also investigates the seminally important influence of Brazilian popular music on Metheny, not only in harmonic and melodic terms but in inspiring him to include wordless vocals in his music as a means to humanize his increasingly technology-driven soundscapes.

Technological capabilities were to increase still more in the music examined in Chapter 5, which is characterised by Metheny's espousal of the Roland guitar synthesizer and hugely capable Synclavier. Both were at the cutting edge of what was possible in the early 1980s: the Roland company's device at last offered a way of playing synthesized music from a guitar controller with the suppleness and flexibility formerly only possible on a conventional instrument, while the Synclavier was not only a wondrously capable sonic resource but also a powerful compositional tool. At the same time, the advent of acoustic bass in the music recorded by the Pat Metheny Group allowed more straight-ahead jazz playing to be incorporated into the band's increasingly eclectic stylistic mix, vividly represented by the boldly conceived album *Offramp* (1982). In addition to investigating the various stylistic elements on this disc, the chapter includes a detailed analytical comparison of two guitar-synthesizer solos on 'Are You Going with Me?': one from the *Offramp* sessions, and the other performed live on the double album *Travels* (1983), an important document of the group's still gruelling and wide-ranging tours at a time when their fan base was continuing to burgeon impressively. Cracks were, however, by this time beginning to show in Metheny's relationship with ECM, particularly over what he regarded as their disappointing handling of the recording sessions for the trio album *Rejoicing* (1984), a project which ought to have been a thoroughly rewarding experience given the intimate performing relationships between the musicians and their deep respect for the repertoire they were recording.

Metheny's association with ECM came to an end in 1984, but not before his group recorded one final and critically acclaimed album on the label. *First Circle* increased the size of the ensemble and, in its intricate title track in particular, its music marked the culmination of the interest in long-term structural control which had already been evident in most of the preceding projects. Chapter 6 explores two new influences on Metheny's composing which are directly reflected in this final album: an inspirational encounter with film composer Jerry Goldsmith (and the growth of Metheny's own film-composing career at this time) and the minimalism of Steve Reich. Metheny regarded *First Circle* as the finest of the seven group albums he recorded during the ECM years, and the significant structural and stylistic breakthroughs it embodied were to be further developed in the two Geffen albums *Still Life (Talking)* (1987) and *Letter from Home* (1989), released after his break from the German label. At the same time, his acclaimed and boldly experimental album with Coleman, *Song X* (1985), his first recording after leaving ECM and his debut with Geffen, demonstrated that the equal commitment to exploratory improvisation in a small-ensemble context and to substantial formal conceptions with larger forces—a seminal and consistent duality throughout the ECM period—was set to remain undiminished.

CHAPTER 2

CONTEXTS
AND COLLABORATORS

I was invited to make a record for ECM, which was an unbelievable
honor and incredibly distinctive opportunity for me as a young musician.
ECM at that time was the most important and interesting label in jazz.[1]

EDITION OF CONTEMPORARY MUSIC (ECM) was founded in Munich
by bassist Manfred Eicher and businessman Karl Egger in 1969. This
small, independent label from the outset strove to improve recording
standards in the field of jazz in a concerted attempt to bring them up
to the level routinely expected in the classical-music industry (Eicher
had prior personal experience of both fields), a goal quickly achieved by
sound engineers Martin Wieland and Jan Erik Kongshaug, who worked
respectively in studios at Ludwigsburg (Germany) and Oslo (Norway).
Eicher's attention to sonic detail—described as 'fanatical' by Keith
Jarrett—sat rather oddly alongside the label's relaxed dealings with
its musicians, who were not bound by conventional contracts.[2] Three

1 Niles, *Pat Metheny Interviews*, 34.
2 Lake and Griffiths, *Horizons Touched*, 1–2. For a vivid illustration of Eicher's fastidious-
ness in controlling timbral subtleties in the studio, see his input into a recording session

notable stylistic avenues of exploration for which the label soon became renowned were various meldings of free jazz and jazz-rock, and of free jazz and world music, and the exploration of other improvisation-based idioms in which the (often European) performers explored their own musical cultures and freed themselves from what some perceived to be the shackles of the traditional formulae of North American jazz.

These strategies were boldly exemplified by Norwegian saxophonist Jan Garbarek's ECM debut album *Afric Pepperbird* in 1970, with its adventurous free-jazz spirit—and ethnically tinged use of such unusual instruments as xylophone and African thumb piano, plus metallic-sounding electric guitar—all very different from the label's later fondness for gently folk-nuanced Scandinavian acoustic jazz and an associated sonic imagery suggestive of 'The Idea of North'.[3] For many, Garbarek's subsequent, prolific and easier-going melody-based output came to typify an immediately identifiable ECM 'house sound': sometimes criticized for an alleged superficiality, Garbarek and others recording on the label arguably 'proved that it is possible to create convincing jazz with scant reference to the African-American tradition'.[4] The label's early albums were in fact strikingly varied, and in particular the work of German bassist Eberhard Weber (who was briefly to play with Metheny in 1974–7, on ECM albums led by Burton and with Metheny's own *Watercolors* quartet) quickly demonstrated a refreshing creative eclecticism and refusal to be typecast. Weber's *The Colours of Chloë* (1974), for example, brought together an orchestral cello section with Garbarek on saxophone and Rainer Brüninghaus on (sometimes overdubbed) piano and synthesizer to play music which John Fordham has described as 'a cut-and-paste compositional minimalism in which [Weber] took fragments of music [he] had heard and liked and turned them into engaging new melodies or repeated them as loop-like ostinatos'. Weber reportedly allowed his band to play whatever they wanted, 'as long as it doesn't sound like jazz'.[5] Weber's Colours ensemble, which recorded three further albums for ECM (*Yellow Fields,*

of the 2010 album *Llyria*, by Nik Bärtsch's Swiss group Ronin, in Peter Guyer and Norbert Wiedmer (directors), *Sounds and Silence: Travels with Manfred Eicher* (DVD; ECM 5050), 2011.

3 This musico-geographical concept is discussed by Michael Tucker, 'Northbound: ECM and "The Idea of North"', in Lake and Griffiths, *Horizons Touched*, 29–34.

4 Alyn Shipton, *A New History of Jazz* (New York: Continuum, 2007), 701. See also Stuart Nicholson, *Jazz: The 1980s Resurgence* (New York: Da Capo Press, 1995), 325–8.

5 John Fordham, 'ECM and European Jazz', in Lake and Griffiths, *Horizons Touched*, 14.

1976; *Silent Feet*, 1978; and *Little Movements*, 1980) featured soprano saxophonist Charlie Mariano, one of a number of American musicians who were attracted to the creative possibilities offered by the label, and these came to include John Abercrombie, Paul Bley, Gary Burton, Don Cherry, Chick Corea, Bill Frisell, Keith Jarrett, Ralph Towner, and of course Metheny and his collaborators.[6]

At the opposite end of the timbral spectrum from Weber's collages were spare and restrained solo-keyboard performances by Corea and Jarrett, whose solo and group work for ECM has been described by drummer Peter Erskine as 'music that asked as many questions as it seemed to answer', and which was notable for its keen sense of space.[7] Paul Bley also recorded an unorthodox solo-piano album for ECM, *Open, to Love*, in 1972, when on his own admission he was 'trying to be the slowest pianist in the world'.[8] Jarrett's album *The Köln Concert*, recorded live in front of Cologne Opera House in January 1975, was the first ECM release to achieve massive international sales: by 2008 the total number of copies sold had reached some 3.5 million, making this not only the best-selling solo jazz album in history, but also the best-selling solo-piano album in any idiom.[9] Its phenomenal and immediate success prompted Leonard Feather to write in 1977: 'Are we about to enter a brave new world of acoustic music to which young, rock-reared audiences can relate?'[10] Jarrett explored lengthy improvised forms incorporating elements of jazz, rock, country, and classical music, and thus archetypally 'crossed over' a number of formerly discrete consumer demographics. In a not dissimilar manner, the Pat Metheny Group's eponymous 'white' album (1978; see Chapter 3) quickly reached a large audience by selling around 150,000 units in under two years and propelling the group into the international limelight. And, importantly, both Jarrett and Metheny differed from many of their ECM colleagues

---

6 For the background to ECM's unique position within the growing attractiveness of Europe to experimentally inclined US musicians, see Markus Müller, 'ECM in Context: Independent Record Companies and the Self-Determination of Musicians in the 1950s, '60s, and '70s', in Okwui Enwezor and Markus Müller (eds.), *ECM: A Cultural Archaeology* (Munich, New York and London: Prestel Verlag, 2012), 54–62.

7 Lake and Griffiths, *Horizons Touched*, 159.

8 *Ibid.*, 251.

9 Corinna da Fonseca-Wollheim, 'A Jazz Night to Remember', *Wall Street Journal* (October 11, 2008). http://online.wsj.com/article/SB122367103134923957.html (July 18, 2012).

10 Quoted in Elsdon, *Keith Jarrett's The Köln Concert*, 39.

in wholeheartedly embracing distinctively American rather than European soundworlds.

A notable feature of ECM's manner of working was that albums would be completed in a maximum of just two or three days of recording, followed by one or two days of mixing. This led to a productive intensity amongst the participating musicians. Sound engineer Kongshaug paid tribute to both the professionalism of the performers with whom he worked and the consistent personal vision of producer Eicher, and denied that the distinctive 'ECM sound' was artificially created: 'you're dealing with very competent musicians who are mostly controlling the dynamics when they play. It's not like the pop world where the dynamics are often invented afterwards.'[11] (Compositional strategies involving dynamic growth and contrasts are encountered many times in Metheny's music. As Paul Wertico recalls, Metheny was committed to the concept of 'dynamics within the phrase' as a means to ensure that the music was 'always going somewhere'.)[12] Metheny described his ECM recordings as 'documentary records, as most jazz records are. You record for a day or two and mix for a day, and that's it.'[13] Later in his career, however, he was fully prepared to use the recording studio 'as a musical instrument' in order to achieve the effects he desired, declaring that too many jazz musicians still had a 'macho' desire to record perfect first takes:

> How somebody gets to the musical result that they hear in their head that matches that as closely as possible, that is what I care about. I have many tracks that were done totally as documentary tracks, where the best way to do it is to go in the studio, play it two or three times and pick the best one and that is that. The first three records that I made were like that, that is the way you did records if you were on ECM.[14]

11 Lake and Griffiths, *Horizons Touched*, 323.
12 Paul Wertico, interview with the author, July 19, 2014.
13 Mr Bonzai, 'Pat Metheny: Jazzing It Up', *Mix* 19/3 (March 1995): 88.
14 Sam Pryor, 'An Interview with Pat Metheny'. http://www.enjoythemusic.com/magazine/music/0402/methenyinterview.htm (May 17, 2014). For a discussion of the historical and cultural reasons why jazz musicians feel under pressure to record efficiently in the studio—and why they 'tend to take a more compositional approach to improvisation' when working in this artificial environment—see Matthew W. Butterfield, 'Music Analysis and the Social Life of Jazz Recordings', *Current Musicology* 71/3 (2001/2): 330-2.

Burton, who was responsible for introducing Metheny to the ECM catalogue (see below), summed up his own feelings about the significance of the company, which he had himself joined after much heart-searching owing to the risks that he feared might be attendant on his decision not to renew his contract with the major US label (Atlantic) with which he was already well established:

> I used to be an American-centric musician who believed everything important in the jazz world took place in New York or Los Angeles . . . But my outlook underwent a major change on this after becoming part of the ECM family of artists in the 1970s. My first ECM record was a duet recording with Chick Corea [*Crystal Silence*, issued in 1973], but soon after Manfred Eicher suggested I check out the music of Eberhard Weber . . . And I soon became aware of many more European jazz musicians, who were creating very original music. This was quite a discovery for me, because up to that time European jazz musicians were not heard in America. No record company had managed effectively to cross the Atlantic going from east to west . . . until ECM. Not only did ECM raise the level of technical production quality for jazz recording in general, but the label also introduced European players to American audiences, and to American musicians, as well.
>
> Soon, people in America were talking about the 'ECM sound'. A phrase meant to describe the thoughtful, highly evolved improvisational styles of the musicians who emigrated to ECM. For the first time in my experience, influences in jazz were crossing the Atlantic in both directions, for the benefit of all.[15]

Metheny commented of his own personal situation at the time he joined the label:

> Of course, for anybody getting to make your first record is a significant occasion and certainly, in my case, it was magnified by the fact that it was going to be on ECM, which at that time [1976] was probably the most exciting music label as far as presenting new musicians and new artists of that era. To be picked by them to do a record and they had

---

15 Lake and Griffiths, *Horizons Touched*, 161–2. On his momentous move from Atlantic to ECM, see Burton, *Learning to Listen*, 248-9.

very few guitar players at all, to get that opportunity was a huge thing for me and very exciting.[16]

He also felt that the opportunities the label presented to him at a young age—he was still a month short of his 20th birthday when he made his first ECM recording as a member of Burton's ensemble—meant that he was able to record a sizeable series of albums as a leader, which 'may have been difficult to make in America, given the corporate mentality that exists in record companies'.[17] These positive views of the label were shared by fellow American guitarists Abercrombie and Towner, both of whom recorded on ECM before Metheny's debut with the company. Abercrombie praised ECM's lack of commercially motivated pressure on their artists, while Towner appreciated the company's long-term commitment to nurturing the development of an individual's artistic goals.[18]

GARY BURTON

A major turning point in Metheny's early career, and the experience that was directly to result in his recording contract with ECM, was his spell as a sideman to vibraphonist Gary Burton, which began in 1974 and (overlapping with the first of Metheny's own ECM recordings as leader) ended in 1977. Metheny had known and admired the music of Burton's quartet since his early teens, when he was impressed not only by its creative tapping of the guitar's potential as a modern-jazz instrument but also by its open-minded attitude towards rock music and its informal dress codes:

> It was around 1967; I was just starting to become totally immersed in jazz. And most of the jazz musicians were older guys, they wore suits and ties, they were very straight ahead. But Gary's band was revolutionary in a bunch of ways. They didn't wear suits; they had long hair; the band used an electric guitar. And they were fearless about playing music with a rock feel to it.[19]

16 Anon., 'A Fireside Chat with Pat Metheny' (2003).
17 Brodowski and Szprot, 'Pat Metheny', 43.
18 Coryell and Friedman, *Jazz-Rock Fusion*, 123, 175.
19 Quoted in Neil Tesser's liner notes to Gary Burton, *Reunion* (GRP 9598-2, 1990), 3. Burton discusses his group's informal dress code at the time, which club owners tolerated mainly because 'our outfits qualified as stage costumes', in *Learning to Listen*, 171.

At the Wichita Jazz Festival in 1973, Metheny first had the opportunity to play alongside Burton during what the then 18-year-old guitarist later described as the 'scariest 25 minutes' of his life. Burton was sufficiently impressed by Metheny's interpretation of the two numbers they played on this occasion—Burton's own blues 'Walter L' and Mike Gibbs's 'Blue Comedy'—that they did a gig together; Burton then suggested Metheny move to Boston in order to broaden his horizons by playing with experienced local musicians there, and also by teaching at Berklee. In May 1974, Metheny joined Burton's group as second guitarist, becoming a member of what was now the Burton Quintet and which also included Mick Goodrick (guitar), Steve Swallow (bass), and Bob Moses (drums). Thus began what Metheny came to regard as 'by far the most important period of my life, musically . . . every night I would get a two-hour critique of every note that I played for the first six months I was in the band'.[20]

Two significant elements of Metheny's playing and composing were refined as a result of the influence of Burton and his experienced sidemen. First, the concept of improvisation as narrative was gradually honed as Burton time and again told him that his solos were not yet 'telling the story' he wanted to express: in addition to advice on general shaping of solos, the vibraphonist gave highly specific technical guidance (e.g., not to utilize the third degree of the scale to excess) and also persuasively demonstrated his own ideas through the medium of his own refined soloing.[21] Second, Burton's virtuosic command of a complex vocabulary of chord changes inspired Metheny to write harmonically and rhythmically demanding tunes which were later to be a core part of his compositional repertory (see, for example, 'The Whopper', analysed below). Metheny recalled that Burton was inspirational about 'the way you analyze music, the way you look at chords, the way you fit into situations dynamically, texturally, in terms of how much activity is required in order to achieve this or that effect', and offered rigorous criticisms of the guitarist's own tunes. He also gave his protégé invaluable practical advice on the business side of running a successful band.[22]

---

20 Carr, 'Bright Size Life', episode 1.
21 *Ibid.* Burton's advice on 'how to develop a solo on a narrative level over time' is also discussed by Metheny in Barth, *Voices in Jazz Guitar*, 322.
22 Niles, *Pat Metheny Interviews*, 30.

The other members of the Burton Quintet inspired Metheny by the restraint they demonstrated in deploying their formidable creative talents economically: 'To see them have all of this "fire power" available and willfully not use it is impressive'.[23] Swallow, a notable pioneer of the electric bass, encouraged him to compose at the keyboard in order to shed himself of guitarists' clichés, and the bassist's command of displaced harmonies and a particular method of using arpeggiated chord inversions in his solo playing came to leave their mark on Metheny's later compositions—for example, in 'Uniquity Road' and elsewhere on *Bright Size Life*.[24] Goodrick's fluent command of his instrument motivated Metheny to take his own improvisational powers to a higher level, but the very existence of two guitarists in the quintet also forced him to contribute something fresh and distinctive to the group: this was a challenge akin to that which famously confronted the young Louis Armstrong when he joined the front line of Joe 'King' Oliver's Creole Jazz Band as a potentially redundant second cornettist in the early 1920s. Metheny's response was to turn to an electric 12-string guitar in the pursuit of timbral contrast, a decision that would have a notable impact on his later work. In addition to the challenge of trying to keep his 12-string in tune with the vibraphone, the instrument proved somewhat demanding to play, until he replaced his initial Fender Coronado model with the Guild Starfire that he would continue to use into the 1980s.[25] Metheny almost exclusively played his 12-string while Goodrick remained as a member of the band, and only returned to six-string after his colleague left in 1976 and the lineup reverted to its original quartet format, with Metheny now as the sole guitarist. The distinctive sound of the electric 12-string was something of a rarity at the time, although acoustic equivalents were used in country and folk music. The instrument was nevertheless memorably exploited in the ECM catalogue on Towner's album *Solstice*, recorded in December 1974 with a quartet including Garbarek and Weber, notably in its opening solo on the track 'Nimbus'; and Towner had previously showcased its timbre when guest-soloing on the track 'The Moors' from Weather Report's 1972 album *I Sing the Body Electric*. In a blindfold listening test for *Down Beat*, Metheny praised Towner

23 *Ibid.*, 134.
24 Carr, 'Bright Size Life', episode 1. The track listing in *Bright Size Life* uses the spelling 'Unquity Road', but 'Uniquity Road' appears in Pat Metheny, *Pat Metheny Song Book* (Milwaukee, WI: Hal Leonard, 2000), 21, 438.
25 Forte, 'Pat Metheny—Jazz Voice of the 80's', 98.

for his improvising on the 12-string, which he described as 'one of the most cumbersome instruments, very difficult to play'; he also stated his admiration for Towner's compositional skills, which resulted in 'little gems of musical logic'.[26]

Metheny's early work with Burton is documented on three ECM albums: *Ring* (recorded in July 1974), which added Weber to the group; *Dreams So Real: Music of Carla Bley* (December 1975);[27] and *Passengers* (November 1976), which lacked Goodrick but again featured Weber, and on which the drum chair was now occupied by Danny Gottlieb. Only in the third of these recordings, made nearly a year after Metheny's debut as an ECM leader on *Bright Size Life*, are Metheny's own compositions featured. He later described Burton's music as 'very laid back by my standards',[28] and found other outlets for his more adventurous creative tendencies in this period, notably with Paul Bley and Jaco Pastorius (see below). Laid back his music might have been in some respects, but Burton was determined to capture complete live takes without recourse to patching, with the result that (as Gottlieb recalls) the *Passengers* sessions involved between six and eight complete takes on certain numbers, with the loss of much fine soloing in the rejects.

In *Ring*, Metheny's solo work is heard exclusively in the second half of 'Intrude' (one of three compositions by Gibbs on the album), from which Goodrick and Weber sat out; the track commences with an introduction from Moses making evocative use of multiple cymbals, later to be a prominent characteristic of the percussion playing in Metheny's ensembles. Here, as in Goodrick's quintuple-time tune 'Mevlevia' (featuring a fine example of its composer's incisive and economical guitar soloing) and Gibbs's 'Unfinished Sympathy' (based on the additive rhythm 4 + 3 + 2), Metheny faced the kind of stimulating rhythmic challenges that would later be a prominent feature of his own work (see, in particular, Chapter 6). A refined, dissonant, and (in places) near-atonal harmonic language characterized Gibbs's 'Tunnel of Love', while the quintet's interpretation of Weber's 'The Colours of Chloë' (the eponymous composition from the bassist's own album, recorded in December 1973) seemingly looks ahead to the soundworld of some of Metheny's music in both its modal harmonic idiom and distinctive

26 Leonard Feather, 'Blindfold Test: Pat Metheny', *Down Beat* 48/2 (February 1981): 47.

27 A photograph of the recording sessions for this album is reproduced in Enwezor and Müller, *ECM: A Cultural Archaeology*, 134.

28 John Alan Smith, 'Pat Metheny: Ready to Tackle Tomorrow', *Down Beat* 45/13 (July 13, 1978): 24.

texture of lyrical melody doubled at the octave by guitar and bass and set against a quasi-minimalist ostinato backdrop from the 12-string and vibraphone.

More solo playing from Metheny is heard on *Dreams So Real*, where the varied set of Carla Bley compositions presented him with a rich and strongly directional harmonic language, and the opportunity to improvise in a post-bebop experimental vein with strong, if occasional, echoes of the music of Ornette Coleman and Thelonious Monk, and spirited double-time flourishes ('Doctor'). The most substantial track is a medley of three tunes ('Ictus', 'Syndrome', and 'Wrong Key Donkey'), of which the first exhilarates in near-atonal and frenetic time-no-changes playing.[29] The second incorporates a Metheny solo replete with characteristic dyadic riffs, sometimes cutting across the metre. 'Vox Humana' showcases Goodrick's shapely soloing, and its chordal patterns are typical of many 1970s ECM recordings (including parts of Metheny's) in their slow harmonic rhythm and distinctive shifts to minor harmonies and Lydian-inflected major modality above pedal points.

Passengers sees Metheny taking a more dominant role, acting as solo guitarist alongside the drummer (Gottlieb) and bassist (Weber) with whom he went on to make his quartet album *Watercolors* a few months later. Of the three Metheny compositions on the album, two set out to explore harmonic unpredictability. The first of these, 'Nacada', was composed during a Burton gig in Vancouver and described by its composer as an attempt to create 'unexpected modulations in a short form ballad'.[30] 'The Whopper', dedicated to Weber, was on the other hand designed 'with a lot of rhythmic accents and an active harmonic scheme—the kind of things that Gary Burton was especially great at soloing over'.[31] Example 2.1 gives the head, together with Weber's introduction and supporting bass line.

29 A technique, refined in brands of 1960s experimental jazz that retained bebop rhythmic and improvisational characteristics, by which the rhythm section continues to play in a recognizably coherent jazz manner ('time'), though conventional harmonies ('changes') are abandoned and both the walking-bass line and solo improvisations pursue their own freely evolving courses. Later in his career, Metheny honed his expertise in this idiom by working with bassist Charlie Haden, a renowned exponent of time-no-changes bass lines.

30 *Pat Metheny Song Book*, 438.

31 *Ibid.*, 439.

Metheny's compositional and improvisational voices emerge already fully formed in 'The Whopper'. The head melody is circular, in that it can—via the ritornello-like vamp bars—theoretically be performed seamlessly ad infinitum, owing to the constant avoidance of any solid cadence, even after the melody and harmonic field have both begun to stabilise somewhat in the second half of the tune. (Circular forms of this kind were increasingly explored in the 1960s and formed part of Burton's repertoire, notably in the shape of Swallow's 'Falling Grace', which Metheny and Burton performed as a duo encore in their 1989-90 reunion performances.) The harmonic language is a mixture of modal passages and sudden chromatic shifts in more rapid harmonic rhythm, these shifts made still more unexpected by being allied to strong metrical displacements in all the rhythm-section parts. The tonal solidity of the introductory 10 bars of two-chord vamping, providing B♭ Mixolydian support for Weber's solo and serving as a dominant preparation for the first 3 bars of the melody, which are in E♭ Aeolian, quickly evaporates and in fact has otherwise little to do with what follows. Thereafter isolated, roving cadential patterns are presented in irregular durations—seven quavers (F minor), eleven quavers (A minor), and six quavers (Gmaj7)—before the music settles temporarily into E major/A Lydian, this region prolonged for 6 bars before another shift which appears to be taking us back to G but is instead truncated by the return of the B♭ Mixolydian vamp by way of interlude. In the E/A Lydian section (bb. 17-22), the contrasting diatonicism coincides with a hook-like melodic idea which is developed in sequence (bb. 19-20 and 21-22): the combination of solid diatonicism and catchily syncopated melody here aids the memorability of the head as a whole, and pleasingly offsets the harmonic and rhythmic instability of the first half of the tune.

Metheny's three-chorus solo (transcribed in Ex. 2.2, which also indicates the continuation of the metrical dislocations in the rhythm section) comes after a characteristically fluent and resourceful solo of the same duration from Burton. The guitarist's playing here exemplifies many mainstream jazz techniques. There are occasional allusions to three motivic patterns from the head: the turn-like figure at the opening (Ex. 2.1, bb. 11-12; reworked in Ex. 2.2, bb. 16-22 and 45); the falling and rising perfect fifth following the turn (Ex. 2.1, bb. 12-13; compare Ex. 2.2, bb. 27 and 31, and the dyadic patterns of 35-42); and falling triadic patterns (Ex. 2.1, bb. 14 and 16; compare Ex. 2.2, bb. 4-5 and 60-61). There is a sparing but effective use of sequential construction in bb. 4-5, 8-9, 19-20, and 53-5. Ideas sometimes overlap the underlying phrase structure, most notably in the early arrival of the climactic dyadic riffs in bb. 35-6,

EX. 2.2 'The Whopper' guitar solo (AT).

PAT METHENY: THE ECM YEARS, 1975–1984

(cont.)

(cont.)

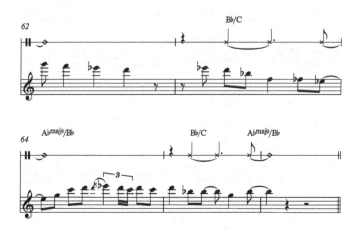

which are continued into the ensuing vamp-interlude. The playing here demonstrates two of Metheny's natural tendencies: basing improvised ideas on triad-derived patterns (with a fondness for emphasising the third degree of the scale), rather than obfuscating the implied harmonies; and, in the longer term, aiming for strategically placed 'target notes'.[32] The mid-term target notes constitute strong arrival points, rising in register in turn, at bb. 15, 35, 53, and 60-62. Strategies such as this help aid the storytelling quality of the improvisation, as do expectantly rising scales (especially at the start of the first and third choruses), the sparing use of hook-like melodic phrases (bb. 48-9), and the compelling climaxes based on emphatic riff-like intensification: all three vamp-interludes take this form, using repeated notes in the first (bb. 15-22), powerful dyadic fifths in the second (bb. 35-42), and elaborated triadic patterns in the third (bb. 59-61). The last of these three signifies a gradual unwinding of tension into the recapitulation of the head that follows by way of conclusion, with the climax of the solo having occurred somewhat earlier when the metrically displaced falling figures in bb. 53-5 (marking the solo's registral peak) occur over static harmonies similar in effect to those of the vamp-interludes. General characteristics of Metheny's playing which may also be observed here include occasional pentatonic flourishes and plentiful hammered-on but essentially lyrical acciaccaturas.

32 See his comments in an interview with David Mead, 'Open Secret: Pat Metheny', *Guitarist* 9/4 (September 1992): 44-52; and Jon Garelick, 'Pat Metheny: Making Melodies with Jazz's Favorite Guitar Wizard', *Boston Phoenix*, March 2-9, 2000.

The third Metheny piece, 'B & G (Midwestern Nights Dream)', had already been recorded on his own album, *Bright Size Life* (see below). Its unusual title was derived from a temporary label which had merely described the tune's principal chords (Bmi9 and Gmaj9) in the absence of any more imaginative title from the guitarist, who generally found naming his pieces difficult.[33] Metheny's solo on Weber's 'Yellow Fields' (a composition from the bassist's eponymous ECM album, recorded in 1975) has been transcribed by Jacques Panisset and Claude Moulin,[34] who comment on the basic outline shape of a monophonic beginning leading to a dyadic climax before a return to single notes, a widespread use of pentatonic figurations, and arpeggio patterns suggested by the physical characteristics of the instrument. The examples of idiomatic guitar fingerwork noted at bb. 7 and 17 of their transcription (see Ex. 2.3) may be directly compared with bb. 30–31 and 57–8 of Example 2.2.

Metheny left Burton's group in the spring of 1977, at a time when he was confident enough to want to make his own way as a leader and was beginning to resent his mentor's fastidious criticisms. At this stage, Metheny was improvising with a degree of freedom and sense of spaciousness that 'really pissed Gary off . . . he almost fired me',[35] and tensions came to a head when Burton forgot to take Metheny's new amplifier rig on a tour of Canada. Burton's account of Metheny's departure also recalls that the

EX. 2.3   'Yellow Fields' motifs (after Panisset and Moulin, *Pat Metheny*, 13–16).

33 Burton, *Learning to Listen*, 256.
34 Jacques Panisset and Claude Moulin, *Pat Metheny: Improvisations. Concepts et techniques* (Paris: HL Music/Editions Henry Lemoine, 1993), 13–16.
35 Carr, 'Bright Size Life', episode 1.

guitarist was taking 'too long with his solos, sometimes playing too loud'.[36] The breach between them lasted for the next decade; but Metheny later likened their relationship to those between a father and son, or an elder and younger brother. They were not to play again until a collaboration at the Montreal Jazz Festival in 1988 led to the album *Reunion* (recorded in May 1989) which, like *Passengers*, included three of Metheny's compositions. Interviewed for the recording's liner notes, Burton enthused:

> I was stunned at what Pat had developed into. I am now deeply impressed by the clarity of his improvising. It represents all the ideals that I have always preached to myself and to my students. It's consistent, controlled, easy to follow and to understand, and absolutely right for each piece.[37]

The *Reunion* project also provided the opportunity for a long-lost Metheny tune from the ECM years, written in 1983 at around the time of the *First Circle* repertoire, to receive its premiere recording. Now given the title 'The Chief' in honour of Burton's nickname, this breezy up-tempo melody—which had not fitted comfortably with the group's thinking at the time it was penned—proved to be ideal as a vehicle for the vibraphonist.[38]

Years later Metheny recorded the album *Like Mind*s (1998) with a Burton quintet including Corea, the keyboard player with whom Burton had made his very first ECM disc (*Crystal Silence*) in 1972. The new project numbered among its tracks two types of jazz that had been conspicuous by their absence from Burton's and Metheny's albums from the 1970s: a slow, swinging blues number (Burton's own 'Country Roads', included here at Metheny's request, which was memorably recorded by Burton in 1968 with guitarist Jerry Hahn, Swallow (co-composer) and drummer Roy Haynes); and straight-ahead bebop improvising on a standard (Gershwin's 'Soon'). Metheny's occasional blues playing on his own ECM albums had reflected the strong influence of Coleman, whose tune 'Turnaround' was featured on *80/81*, and whose example had previously shaped 'Broadway Blues' on *Bright Size Life*. Critics, who were sometimes perplexed by the guitarist's stylistic versatility and willingness to experiment, were always pleased to see him (as one put it) 'wring pure honest feeling out of the blues' (see p. 158).

36 Burton, *Learning to Listen*, 263.
37 Tesser, *Reunion*, 4.
38 *Pat Metheny Song Book*, 441.

Bob Moses, whose playing was a vital component of the *Bright Size Life* project, was the first East Coast drummer with whom Metheny worked. Moses' remarkably free spirit 'messed' with Metheny (as the guitarist put it himself) and never let him be complacent—precisely what he felt he needed as he emerged from Burton's group.[39] Metheny later summed up Moses's importance to him at this time:

> He was the first drummer I played with who had that wild, you-never-know-what's-gonna-happen-next sort of groove. At first I didn't know what to do with it, but as I played more and more, those kinds of drummers became my favorite. You'd be playing along with him and all of a sudden he'd start beating on the tom-toms [*laughs*], real loud. At first I thought, 'What is he *doing* over there?' Then I realized that drums aren't necessarily where you play your solo on top of; at their best they're part of the music, a commentary.[40]

Throughout his career, Metheny was to pay detailed attention to specific methods of drumming and choice of percussion instruments that were appropriate to the musical identities of the various groups with which he worked.

The prodigious electric-bassist Jaco Pastorius, the third member of the *Bright Size Life* trio, had already been a close friend of Metheny's during his time with Burton, and they both benefited from a relationship founded on mutual respect, frankness, and a sense of common creative goals. Later to be tragically wasted by a self-destructive lifestyle, Pastorius in these early years had much in common with Metheny: both were self-taught; both felt their respective instruments had been insufficiently exploited in contemporary music; both admired an unusually wide range of musical styles (including jazz, rock, pop, and classical music); both had started out by teaching themselves to play Beatles tunes by ear; and both had cut their teeth playing in local organ trios—a format that sometimes gave them room in which to experiment. In Pastorius's case the locality was Florida, and Metheny met him there in 1972, two days after the guitarist took up his scholarship at the University of Miami; they played on many occasions together before Metheny left for Boston, including gigs on Miami beach and after-gig

---

39 Carr, 'Bright Size Life', episode 1.
40 Forte, 'Pat Metheny—Jazz Voice of the 80's', 100.

jam sessions in the bassist's apartment in Hollywood, Florida.[41] In the process, they both learnt much from the lack of musical prejudices and preconceptions which Pastorius singled out as a vitally important characteristic of the current Florida scene. Indeed, it was this free atmosphere that helped him to develop his own 'new paradigm' in the shape of what he liked to term 'punk jazz'.[42]

Metheny and Pastorius were able to give free rein to their experimental impulses in an album recorded in New York in the summer of 1974 with Paul Bley on electric piano and Bruce Ditmas on drums, based almost exclusively on compositions by Paul and Carla Bley and particularly notable for its astonishingly energized bass-playing from Pastorius. Paul Bley recalled the month-long gig at Greenwich Village of which this album was the sole documentary record:

> We'd play continuous hour-long suites, which gave us a chance to incorporate some of the written material while inventing transitions from one piece to the other. Conceptually, it was just a simple translation of the acoustic music to an electric setting. But to electric musicians at the time, it was earth-shattering.[43]

Given the liberal doses of free jazz on the quartet's album, it comes as no surprise to learn that when Pastorius and Metheny later joined forces with Moses to form a trio at the Zircon Club near Berklee—where Metheny was by then teaching—the compositions of Coleman (who had briefly played in Bley's band in Los Angeles in 1958) were part of their repertoire.[44]

The Metheny-Pastorius-Moses trio performed together during breaks from the guitarist's and drummer's schedule with Burton, appearing in New York, Boston, and across New England, from 1974 until the end of 1976. The combination of Pastorius and Moses as

---

41 See Bill Milkowski, *Jaco: The Extraordinary and Tragic Life of Jaco Pastorius* (Milwaukee, WI: Backbeat Books, 2005), 50.

42 Coryell and Friedman, *Jazz-Rock Fusion*, 40–41.

43 Milkowski, *Jaco*, 67. Milkowski recounts (68) how Bley ran into legal difficulties in 1978 after he had issued the recording two years earlier under the title *Jaco*, evidently in an attempt to cash in on the bassist's meteoric rise to fame as a member of Weather Report. (The album's original title was *Pastorius/Metheny/Ditmas/Bley*.) A later attempt was made to exploit Metheny's name in connection with the same recording: see Luigi Viva, *Pat Metheny: Una chitarra oltre il cielo* (Rome: Editori Reuniti, 2003), 44.

44 Viva, *Pat Metheny*, 51. See also Shipton, *A New History of Jazz*, 564.

rhythm section was described by Metheny as 'completely wild',[45] though it has been argued that this is not especially evident from *Bright Size Life* (recorded in December 1975, more than two years after the possibility of such a project had first been discussed), which was the trio's sole recorded legacy.[46] Moses recalled significant tension in the group during the sessions, which he felt was caused by Metheny's desire for refinement conflicting with the bassist's wild and unpredictable musical temperament:

> Jaco's shit was too strong, and the truth of it is Metheny did try to suppress it. I actually had to referee between those two cats. I mean, they loved each other, but they were also at each other's throats. And I could see both points of view. First of all, it wasn't Jaco's music; it was Metheny's gig ... But at the same time, when you have a group like that it kind of has to be an equal thing ...
>
> [Jaco would] do stuff like turning a waltz into a reggae in the middle of the tune, and Metheny would get pissed ... And when we'd do some rave-up shit, some killer, loud, crazy Afro-Cream shit, Jaco's spirit would take over. Metheny would always come back afterwards with the lightest, most gentle bossa nova. He'd completely take it back to Jim Hall or Wes Montgomery, just to regain control of the band.[47]

Moses felt the album was not a true representation of the group's capabilities when performing live, describing the outfit as 'like a power trio' and again comparing it to Eric Clapton's British group Cream,

> but with a lot of 16th-notes and a million chord changes, because Metheny's music was really complex. That shit was loud, and we were funking, too ... But the ECM vibe kind of squelched all that energy. They didn't want it to be too ballsy and grooving. To me, the album is really lightweight compared to what we were doing on the gigs.[48]

45 Carr, 'Bright Size Life', episode 1.
46 The making of *Bright Size Life* was enabled by one (literally) unsung contributor. After recording his own album *Dreams So Real* for ECM, Burton had stayed in Germany to oversee Metheny's debut on the label, which was recorded in the same studio immediately afterwards. But Burton's seminal role as the de facto producer of the guitarist's first ECM project was obscured by the absence, to his disappointment, of any credit to him on the sleeve when the album was released: see Burton, *Learning to Listen*, 258–9.
47 Quoted in Milkowski, *Jaco*, 83–4.
48 *Ibid.*, 84.

These remarks may be compared with Gottlieb's recollection that what he thought had been his dynamic drumming on Burton's *Passengers* was surprisingly subdued in ECM's final mix: 'It felt like the impact of the drums was literally taken "out of the mix". Nice, polite, no impact. "I was slammin' on those tracks", I thought to myself. And I guess it was somewhat characteristic of the ECM type of sound ... very open, clear and beautiful, but it was not the intense, jazz-rock type of drum sound.'[49]

Metheny was, nonetheless, making something of a stand in persuading ECM to include Pastorius in his debut lineup, since Eicher did not empathise with many electric-bass players—with the notable exception of Swallow—and tended to prefer either acoustic bass or Weber's uniquely customized upright electric bass, its playing technique and appearance both close to those of its acoustic cousin. So great was Pastorius's subsequent fame that it is perhaps necessary to stress that at the time he recorded *Bright Size Life* he was virtually unheard of, and Metheny's album was an important step in bringing the bassist's phenomenal talents to wider attention. Metheny had considered hiring Dave Holland on acoustic in deference to Eicher's preference and had gone so far as to try out some of the *Bright Size Life* repertoire with Holland before making his final decision on the personnel for the recording. Electric bass would continue to figure prominently in the early music of the Pat Metheny Group, until Steve Rodby's acoustic playing became a key feature of the band after 1980 (see Chapter 5), but in his trio and the other keyboardless music Metheny went on to record for ECM he was to showcase the formidable expertise of Charlie Haden on the acoustic instrument.

Metheny's own recollections of the *Bright Size Life* trio's recording were far more positive than Moses's, and in a 2002 interview he singled the album out as representing the best of his early work:

I had saved up a lot of, basically my whole life into making a statement about what I wanted to say. I had many opportunities to make records up until that point; from the time I was 15 or 16 years old. I really wanted to wait until I felt that I had something that was mine stylistically. That was very important to me. The other good thing about *Bright Size Life* is that myself, Jaco and Moses really were a band ... We had very similar ambitions. We were on a mission to rethink the roles of our instruments as improvising vehicles for

49 Personal communication from Danny Gottlieb via email, July 9, 2014.

ourselves. There wasn't anything quite like that. That record does a fairly good job of capturing what the trio was about.[50]

Elsewhere, Metheny reflected that his early style of leadership (alluded to by Moses) was influenced by Burton's strictness, and that a firm hand was equally necessary when he came to shape the early course of his subsequent quartet, 'because there was a danger of it becoming just another group, and I wanted it to have its own sound. I'm sure that all the effort I put into molding and pushing it into certain directions had an influence on the way it came out.'[51] The *Bright Size Life* trio's gradual honing of ideas and compositions through many live performances undertaken during sustained touring also set a pattern later adopted by the Pat Metheny Group in its various incarnations—at least until the pop-influenced album *We Live Here* in 1995, the first group project for which the music was not initially developed during live gigs.[52]

Metheny was keen that his first recording as leader should be with a trio since he felt there were few precedents and this would also help to ensure its individuality.[53] Furthermore, all the tracks bar one on *Bright Size Life* were his own compositions, and he later recalled that his motivation in devoting himself increasingly to writing was the desire to create raw material suited to the specific manner in which he wished to improvise: 'if I played "All the Things You Are", or standards, or bossa novas or something, I always ended up sounding more conventional than I really wanted to sound, so I thought if I wrote music that set up this other vibe, maybe it would help.'[54] (Several years later, in 1982, with considerable compositional successes behind him, Metheny was still modest about his aspirations as a composer, and stressed that his own songs and manner of soloing were almost always fully integrated.)[55]

---

50 Sam Pryor, 'An Interview with Pat Metheny'. Metheny confessed elsewhere that he was not able to listen to the album for some seven years after it was released: see Goins, *Emotional Response*, 78.

51 Forte, 'Pat Metheny—Jazz Voice of the 80's', 100.

52 Jesse Hamlin, 'Pop Quiz: Q & A with Pat Metheny', *San Francisco Chronicle*, February 19, 1995.

53 Jay Trachtenberg, 'Pat Metheny Trio Blows into Austin', *Austin Chronicle*, October 6, 2000. http://www.austinchronicle.com/music/2000-10-06/78850 (September 1, 2013).

54 Aledort, 'Pat Metheny: Straight Ahead', 62. 'All the Things You Are' was nevertheless sometimes featured in Metheny gigs, for example, in a performance with Jimmy, Percy, and Albert Heath at Cannes on January 28, 1983.

55 Tim Schneckloth, 'Pat Metheny: A Step beyond Tradition', *Down Beat* 49/11 (November 1982): 15.

All the pieces on *Bright Size Life* are therefore conceived as vehicles for improvisation and generally follow the traditional head–solo(s)–head format that mainstream jazz performers inherited from bebop; but they are notably fresh in their harmonic thinking.

If there is little evidence in *Bright Size Life* of the more ambitious compositional aspirations manifested in the structures of his later work, in all other important respects—chiefly harmonic idiom, rhythmic character, occasional textural experimentation, and memorable soloing—Metheny's compositional and improvisational voices emerge here fully formed. As at every stage of his career, he shows a willingness to set himself specific creative challenges. In the opening (title) track, for example, he consciously set out to exploit large intervallic leaps and use basic diatonic triads, which he generally found to be lacking in jazz standards; and he followed the same approach, this time in a minor key, in 'Unity Village'.[56] Some of this music had in fact originated with a consciously didactic intent, since certain tunes were conceived as studies for Metheny's guitar pupils at Berklee. 'Bright Size Life', for example, which is a 32-bar tune in the familiar AABA pattern, was originally entitled 'Exercise No. 2'.[57] As with all good studies, however, the technical challenges involved are merely the creative starting points for satisfying musical conceptions.

Many years later, Metheny demonstrated ways of improvising on the basic motivic and harmonic patterns of this title track and commented that the player 'can just keep soloing in the style of the melody and it sounds fine'.[58] As the transcribed examples from this interview demonstrate, part of the coherence of the playing derives from imaginative reworkings of the tune's basic intervallic pattern, involving perfect fifths: compare the opening of the head (Ex. 2.4a) with the sequential extension of the pattern in the demo improvisation (Ex. 2.4b).[59] Metheny followed this simple variation with a far more elaborate and melodically shapely solo, in which the fifth-based pattern still appeared but was reserved for the bridge of the second and final chorus (Ex. 2.4c). On the album, the anacrusic bar of quavers (Ex. 2.4a)—which is one of the

56 *Pat Metheny Song Book*, 438.

57 Mark Small, 'Pat Metheny: No Boundaries'. http://www.thescreamonline.com/music/ music4-3/metheny/metheny.html (July 17, 2012), first published in *Berklee Today* in 2004; cited in Ken Tretheway, *Pat Metheny: The Way Up Is White* (Torpoint: Jazz-Fusion Books, 2008), 22. On the original title of 'Bright Size Life', see http://interact.patmetheny. com/qa/questionView.cfm?queID=3987 (April 1, 2013).

58 Niles, *Pat Metheny Interviews*, 129–32; 129.

59 *Ibid.*, 130.

delights of the theme, since it can be heard as either the first or last bar of the A strain, and this gives the tune's shape a distinctive fluidity—becomes a helpful point of reference throughout the track, being picked up by Pastorius at the start of his solo and sometimes doubled by both guitar and bass. The final 2 bars of the head, terminating in a gently dissonant clash between leading note and tonic, also recur as a punctuating device.

Other compositions on the album also present melodic challenges based on specific intervals. The through-composed tune 'Unity Village' explores angular but lyrical patterns based on sevenths (Ex. 2.5a), not dissimilar to the wide leaps in the bridge of 'Bright Size Life' (Ex. 2.5b), and in its final bars incorporates a shapely sequential development of material, of a kind familiar in Metheny's improvising. 'Missouri Uncompromised', a modified song form with 12-bar A sections and an 8-bar improvised bridge, commences with a pattern of ascending perfect fourths which is then transposed up a semitone to create harmonic tension over a tonic pedal (Ex. 2.6a). Patterning in fourths is also a feature of parts of the melody 'Omaha Celebration' (Ex. 2.6b). In 'Midwestern Nights Dream', sixths predominate, generally as the upper dyads in triadic patterns spanning a tenth. The opening gesture (Ex. 2.7a) is subsequently prolonged as a vamp accompaniment to the

soloing, and in the second half of the tune the pattern is expanded with metrical displacement (Ex. 2.7b). Arpeggiated figures of this kind are the building blocks for 'Uniquity Road', where their regular contours are also enlivened by a metrical disruption in bb. 4-5 (Ex. 2.7c).

In contrast to all these strongly profiled intervallic patterns, 'Sirabhorn' begins with simple descending scales, richly harmonized.

Named after a Berklee alumna, the guitarist and vocalist Sirabhorn Muntarbhorn, the piece shows how the experience of working with 12-string tunings in the Burton band had left its mark on Metheny's own music. Here he lays down a 12-string accompaniment over which he dubs a solo on his six-string to create a quartet texture. The 12-string is also featured in 'Midwestern Nights Dream', which he later adapted for six-string tuning when recording the piece for Burton's *Passengers*. There are suggestions here of the personal significance of Metheny's Missouri background, with the overdubbed guitar duet 'Unity Village' celebrating a place close to his hometown where he spent enjoyable summers, and other titles ('Missouri Uncompromised' and 'Omaha Celebration') reflecting the region and its history; these geographical associations were to become more musically explicit in his solo album, *New Chautauqua*, recorded in the summer of 1978 (see Chapter 3). Metheny's and Pastorius's shared passion for Coleman's music is celebrated in the closing track, 'Round Trip/Broadway Blues', which delights in buoyant bebop-style head melodies played in octave unison by guitar and bass, and free soloing above a time-no-changes walking bass. This approach is far removed from the refined and carefully controlled harmonic language of the remainder of the album. Metheny described this track as his only recorded example of a 'straight-ahead kind of jazz playing' prior to *80/81*, made some four years later (see Chapter 4), and characterized Coleman's tunes as 'just a short little head, and then the rest is free'.[60]

Characteristic harmonic fingerprints in the Metheny compositions on *Bright Size Life* include well-balanced contrasts between prolonged chords and dynamic harmonic progressions within a single piece ('Midwestern Nights Dream', 'Sirabhorn'), a further contrast between a rich chordal vocabulary exploiting added notes and appoggiaturas ('Sirabhorn', 'Unity Village'), and a diatonic language owing relatively little to jazz precedents: 'Missouri Uncompromised', for example, was conceptually inspired by the 12-bar blues but is based on diatonic triads and inversions, and avoids the dominant-seventh harmony that is the lifeblood of the traditional blues. There is little suggestion of the complex metres which were to become a feature of Metheny's work after the mid-1980s, although in 'Uniquity Road' he interrupts the triple-time metre with 2 quadruple-time bars to disrupt both harmonic and rhythmic expectations, and does the converse in 'Omaha Celebration' by inserting 2 triple-time bars into the prevailing quadruple metre. Written during a tour with Burton earlier in the year *Bright Size Life* was recorded, 'Omaha Celebration' stands apart from the other tracks for its easygoing tunefulness (albeit with a melody constructed with notable motivic rigour), catchy rhythms, and pop-music feel: all these appealing characteristics would occasionally resurface in later albums.

Metheny summed up the significance of *Bright Size Life* by stating that it reflected his and Pastorius's joint need to

> find a way to present our instruments in an improvisational environment that expressed our dissatisfaction with the status quo at the time. It is funny because our take on things, as reflected on that record and particularly in the trio as it existed around that time, which the record somewhat represents, but doesn't fully capture, was quite a departure from the sound of jazz at that moment in time . . .
>
> In Jaco's case, it was the same thing. We were really interested in dealing with a harmonic territory that hadn't really been dealt with

60 Forte, 'Jazz Voice of the 80's', 110.

much at all. The general reaction to that record when it came out at the time was kind of blasé. People noticed it a little bit, but it seems like every year that goes by, that record has a higher standing. It is interesting to see how long it takes for the message that you are trying to communicate to trickle down.[61]

In a later interview, he recalled that when it was first released the album received 'kind of a snide review' in *Down Beat* and 'sold a thousand records the first year . . . [but] there were many things about it that I felt were new territory . . . it's been gratifying over the years to watch the complexion of that record, the way it sort of fits into the whole music scene [which] changed pretty rapidly'.[62] The review mentioned here had lukewarmly described Metheny's guitar playing as 'intelligent embellishment'; while noting that the album had allowed him to record a sizeable body of his own compositions for the first time, the results were summarized as 'some excellent, some superfluous, yet nearly all so restrained as to be soporific'. Moses was praised for injecting some 'verve' into the trio's playing in 'Missouri Uncompromised' and 'Round Trip/Broadway Blues', both of which tracks were compared to hard bop, and 'Midwestern Nights Dream' was singled out as the high point of the album, the 'most stunning, and ominous, performance', which was 'somber' and 'masterfully executed'.[63] In his concluding remarks, the reviewer attributed the album's 'dynamic suppression' to both Eicher and Metheny, seemingly in a swipe at what was by this period widely (if often unfairly) seen as a weakness of an ECM-specific aesthetic. Looking back on the album a few years later, a different reviewer reflected that the project had 'clearly affirmed an incisive understanding of melody and harmony, and the ability to go beyond technique'.[64]

QUARTET

The band which made its recording debut with Metheny's next ECM album, *Watercolors* (1977), featured acoustic piano, bass, and drums alongside the lead guitar. The project was born directly from Metheny's

---

61 Anon., 'A Fireside Chat with Pat Metheny' (2003). See also Barth, *Voices in Jazz Guitar*, 320.

62 Niles, *Pat Metheny Interviews*, 35.

63 Mikal Gilmore, review of Pat Metheny, *Bright Size Life*, in *Down Beat* 43/12 (December 2, 1976): 22, 24.

64 Frank-John Hadley, review of Pat Metheny, *80/81*. *Down Beat* 48/1 (January 1981): 31.

desire to work with Weber—whose musicianship seemed ideally suited to the kind of music the leader had in mind for the project, and whose playing would be featured alongside Metheny's in both solos and duets. Furthermore, as he had already achieved with Pastorius, Metheny was again able on this occasion to introduce a relatively unknown player to the label in the shape of pianist Lyle Mays. Although at the time it was uncertain how Metheny's later bands might be constituted— in particular, Metheny was playing a great deal at this time with Gil Goldstein, whom he was also considering as a pianist who might have much to offer him in the future—the music performed by the *Watercolors* quartet laid down clear pointers towards his later creative development. '[S]o much of what the [Metheny] group has been about right from the start', he recalled in 2002, 'has been this whole idea of expansion and taking the fundamental sound that we made as a quartet and continuing to find ways to develop it, through dynamics, through texture, through orchestration, through formal structures.'[65]

Metheny had known of his new keyboard player since both were teenagers, and first heard him in 1976, when Mays performed with a combo representing North Texas State University (which also included bassist Marc Johnson) at the Wichita Jazz Festival, where Metheny was playing with Burton. After a brief spell performing with Woody Herman's band, Mays was first hired by Metheny for a gig with Swallow and Gottlieb at a Boston club in July 1976. Metheny then hired Mays again for 10 concerts in Chicago and Kansas City, with bassist Mike Richmond and Moses, and they toured the Midwest and East Coast in January the following year, with Richmond and Bill Evans's drummer Eliot Zigmund. Gottlieb had been tied up with his commitments as the drummer of Burton's group (in which he had by this time replaced Moses), but played with Metheny for the subsequent *Watercolors* album, which was recorded in Oslo in February 1977. Gottlieb had toured with Weber's Colours ensemble earlier that year, and while with them had visited the Paiste factory in Switzerland where he acquired new cymbals which would feature memorably in the *Watercolors* sessions.[66]

Weber, whom Metheny esteemed for his sonic individuality (always a crucial factor in his choice of collaborators),[67] had recently performed

---

65 Metheny, interviewed by Gary Walker (WBGO, Newark, NJ) for Nonesuch Records promotional disc for *The Way Up* (2005).

66 Personal communication from Danny Gottlieb via email, July 9, 2014.

67 For Metheny's comments on Weber's individuality of sound, see Barth, *Voices in Jazz Guitar*, 324.

alongside Metheny, Swallow, and Gottlieb on Burton's album *Passengers*, and the German bassist typified a crucial characteristic shared by all members of the new Metheny quartet: a refreshing absence of partisan allegiances to either of the then prevailing, and sharply contrasted, stylistic poles of bebop and fusion. This same virtue had also attracted Metheny to the work of Mays. Metheny's attitude towards the concept of 'fusion' was explored in detail in Chapter 1, and in 1978 even one of its leading exponents, guitarist John McLaughlin, stated that contemporaneous jazz-rock 'bores me to tears; it just doesn't go anywhere'.[68] By this period, however, it could be argued that bebop had also grown potentially moribund in the hands of performers whose own displays of technical prowess, like their fusion counterparts, seemed more important than memorable musical substance or compositional originality. Metheny was deeply distrustful of young jazz players' ambitions to play fast for its own sake, for example, and commented in an interview in 1981, in terms that again stress the importance of 'breath' in improvising:

A guitar is one of those instruments that's easy for some people to learn how to play quickly—to play a lot of notes and stuff—but sometimes that can be deceiving because you can tell that there are players that don't really *hear* everything they're playing. They're just kind of letting their fingers do the work without really letting their head or their feelings get involved. On a horn you can never really do that, because the notes come from inside you. You have to actually breathe the note out, so that tends to give horn players a certain kind of focus that guitarists, drummers, or pianists sometimes don't have.[69]

Weber's involvement in *Watercolors* was fortuitous, since certain of his own compositional tendencies were similar to Metheny's creative preoccupations at the time. The name of Weber's band Colours suggested parallels with the visual arts—an increasingly important aspect of ECM's album packaging, on which more is said in subsequent chapters—and Weber's artist wife Maja painted the cover art for their albums. This seemed to intensify the narrative strategy of much of the music, and Michael Tucker notes that the watershed album *The Colours*

---

68 Coryell and Friedman, *Jazz-Rock Fusion*, 165.
69 Forte, 'Jazz Voice of the 80's', 91.

of Chloë (1974) drew the attention of both Burton and Towner to 'the mythopoetic, or story-telling, potential of both the soulful new sound and rhythmic implications of what Weber calls his electrobass'.[70] Tucker assesses that 'the chief impact of the *Chloë* material lay in the floating treatment of time and phrase which introduced the sort of reflective, distinctly European note that would come to characterise a good deal of the music on ECM', echoing Weber's own description of how, following this album's great success, he wondered how he might develop the idiom and perform the music live: 'There were various aspects to the session, from the reflective European or chamber music side of the writing to some jazz-rock and a kind of pictorial play with minimalism'.[71] In particular, the album's extended structures, evocative orchestration (including synthesizer), wide dynamic range, a finely judged alternation between harmonically static minimalist procedures and strongly structured harmonic progressions (some serving as the backbone for improvised solos), and the foregrounding of both a solo string instrument (here bass rather than guitar) and acoustic piano are all features to be found in the work of Metheny and Mays, although they did not emerge fully until their joint album *As Falls Wichita, So Falls Wichita Falls* in 1981 (see Chapter 4). The later trilogy of Colours recordings included multi-tracking and ethnic instruments (*Yellow Fields*, 1976), acoustic piano solos building in intensity over an extended timespan (*Silent Feet*, 1978), and additive rhythms and harmonic displacements sometimes not too far removed from the spirit of Weather Report, an identification especially noticeable when the ensemble featured Mariano's soprano saxophone (*Little Movements*, 1980).

At the time of *Watercolors*, Metheny's compositional aspirations were comparatively modest, and tunes serving as the basis for improvisation were still the order of the day; but the later Metheny Group albums were to involve increasingly substantial doses of structural experimentation, as outlined in subsequent chapters. Mays proved to be an ideal assistant in this process.[72] In many respects, his accomplishment and stylistic

---

70 Michael Tucker, 'Hearing Colours', booklet notes to Weber's *Colours* (ECM 2133–35, 2009), 11. The 'electrobass' was a customized electric bass, played vertically like an acoustic bass, which had been Weber's principal instrument since 1974: see Lake and Griffiths, *Horizons Touched*, 65.
71 Tucker, 'Hearing Colours', 10–11.
72 Mays gave a detailed account of his influences and musical views in an interview with Mike Brannon (May 2001), formerly available at http://www.allaboutjazz.com and http://www.jazzreview.com/articledetails.cfm?ID=657.

interests broadly paralleled those of Weber's regular pianist Brüninghaus (whom Mays was temporarily to replace on the bassist's ECM album *Later that Evening* in 1982). Both possessed flawless keyboard technique and a thorough knowledge of classical music from Baroque counterpoint to French impressionism, Skryabin, and modern composers; the jazz pianists by whom both were most influenced were Evans and Jarrett, both texturally and harmonically; both foregrounded acoustic piano solos in spite of their simultaneous interest in electric piano and the rapidly developing capabilities of synthesizers (notably, at this stage, the Oberheim polyphonic models); and both played acoustic piano with a sensitive manner of agogic phrasing that resulted in subtly expressive rubato.[73] This last characteristic was ultimately to lead to memorable duets between Metheny and Mays in which the two performers' seemingly spontaneous rubato effects were perfectly matched, even when playing live at opposite ends of a large concert-hall stage: see, for example, the discussion in Chapter 4 of their interpretations of 'September Fifteenth', the memorial to Evans on *As Falls Wichita Falls*. The strikingly similar timbres and atmospheres at times produced by Mays and Brüninghaus in their work for ECM were naturally strengthened by the use of the same sound engineer (Kongshaug), studio (Talent Studio, Oslo), and instrument, and are testament to Eicher's commitment to preserving predominantly acoustic soundscapes in vibrant tones of often considerable beauty.

A vivid foretaste of Mays's composing, arranging, and performing talents may be gleaned from a Grammy-nominated album he masterminded with the North Texas State University (One O'Clock) Lab Band at Denton in 1975. *Lab '75!* presented three original compositions by the 22-year-old Mays, together with his arrangement of Corea's 'What Was': all are substantial extended works, ranging from around eight to 13 minutes in length. Mays's assured playing on Fender Rhodes electric piano, clavinet, and acoustic piano is showcased throughout the record, though only in the Corea arrangement do his solo passages undulate in intensity as they were later to do when he played with Metheny. 'F.M.' commences in a funky stomp style, alternating with passages of harmonic and rhythmic displacement typical of his later work with Metheny;

---

73 For comment on these aspects of Brüninghaus's playing, see Tucker, 'Hearing Colours', 12–14. The German pianist's keyboard style, and its similarities to certain aspects of Mays's playing, is well demonstrated on his ECM album *Freigeweht* (1981), a quartet project featuring flugelhorn (Kenny Wheeler), double reeds (Brynjar Hoff), and drums (Jon Christensen).

an interest in counterpoint is later revealed in the canonic trading of the main theme between instrumental sections before the climactic layering of various melodic ideas. Contrapuntal superimpositions also characterize 'Overture to the Royal Mongolian Suma Foosball Festival', with catchy octave melodies alternating with bubbling electric-bass riffs (à la Pastorius), and the arranged sections alternating with solo improvisations accompanied by riffs which animate essentially static chords. In this piece, the witty parody of non-Western soundworlds—an eccentric (quasi-Mongolian?) saxophone duet, and ethnic gong stroke by way of conclusion—show both a sense of humour and an interest in non-standard timbres and textures. The Corea arrangement is notable for its resourceful instrumentation and two substantial solos on acoustic piano, the first demonstrating a firm grasp of Corea's dynamic manner of right-hand passagework, the second (unaccompanied throughout) at first based on two repeated chords in the left hand, then moving into freer improvising characterized by considerable rubato and atmospheric exploitation of the entire range of the keyboard. Virtuosic flourishes on the diminished (octatonic) and anhemitonic pentatonic scales suggest the influences of Liszt, Skryabin, Ravel, and even early Messiaen, while the solo's impressionistic harmonies and light, classically influenced keyboard touch both recall the example of Evans, whose characteristic techniques Mays had taught himself exhaustively while in his teens.[74] The harmonic language in this arrangement alternates between modality and rich chromaticism, Mays's idiomatic textures serving as sonically imaginative ways of sustaining and elaborating strong harmonies; there is a compelling sense of structural architecture, with carefully controlled dynamic growth and appealing contrasts. The concluding suite, 'The Continuing Adventures of Supertonic', alternates an easygoing tunefulness with the funky-riff style of parts of 'F.M.', but here reaching an impressively virtuosic level of intricate activity.

While the big-band arranging techniques evident on this album were put on hold during Mays's early work with Metheny's band, they were later to resurface in certain tracks on the keyboardist's second album as leader, *Street Dreams* (1988); and the appearance of Bob Curnow's big-band arrangements of twelve Metheny Group pieces on the album *The Music of Pat Metheny & Lyle Mays* in 1994 (which spawned a sequel in 2011), including the watershed composition 'First Circle' (discussed in Chapter 6), showed how 'the dynamic and coloristic range of the

---

74 Pawel Brodowski and Janusz Szprot, 'Lyle Mays', *Jazz Forum* 97/6 (June 1985): 37.

Metheny Group was not that far removed from the directions [Curnow] had pursued with the Stan Kenton band.[75] (Curnow had played trombone in the latter during the 1960s.) Interviewed in 1995, shortly after the release of the initial Curnow album, Metheny himself commented that the manner in which his band had evolved compositionally 'does set up improvisation in a different way', and continued:

> Both Lyle and I have done a fair amount of big band writing over the years, and we kind of think like that anyway. There are certain aspects of our group that I have often compared to a big band in the sense that we often have an ensemble section or some kind of an orchestrated-out chorus or something, but we've always tried to do it using our own vocabulary. Certainly, there is a conceptual connection to writing for a large ensemble like a big band.[76]

The same comparison was made by Metheny when discussing *American Garage* (see Chapter 3), and Wertico recalls Mays describing the Group as 'like a modern big band'.[77]

Mays's keyboard style was initially influenced by Evans and Oscar Peterson, followed by pianists as diverse as Corea, McCoy Tyner, and Cecil Taylor. Mays strenuously made the effort to expunge bebop clichés from his playing, and also found 'the bebop sort of jazz theory that you get from the summer camps' to be 'real detrimental; it doesn't give you the whole picture'.[78] Although Metheny was also distrustful of the more formulaic qualities of improvising in bebop style, he admitted that he had started out as 'a bebop snob kind of guy' and never ceased to be aware of the 'intimate relationship with harmony and rhythm' that learning to play in this manner could engender if tackled intelligently:

> Somehow you are actively involved with all the elements; you're not just playing a part. You can play bebop *a cappella* and you can hear

---

75 Bob Blumenthal, liner notes to Bob Curnow's L.A. Big Band, *The Music of Pat Metheny & Lyle Mays* (MAMA 1009, 1994), 3.

76 Mr. Bonzai, 'Pat Metheny: Jazzing It Up', 88.

77 Paul Wertico, interview with the author, July 19, 2014.

78 Dan Forte, 'The Pat Metheny Group—Jazz's Foremost Garage Band', *Musicians' Industry* 2/2 (15 March 1980): 32-41. It has not proved possible to locate an original copy of this publication, and subsequent references to the article have therefore been taken from an unpaginated transcription. I am grateful to Mr Forte for his advice on both this source and several other related matters

all the parts and all the chords, everything. The only other music you can say that about is real good classical music, most notably Bach. Bebop has a lot in common with Bach.[79]

In later years, he would stress that, even though bebop-style playing was 'probably never, ever going to come right out' in the setting of his regular band, it was necessary to 'find guys who are capable of playing high level bebop but are never going to do it, who have the maturity and sensibility to draw from it without actually coming right out and doing that thing [which] is almost impossible'.[80] He also noted that bebop expertise was an important common ground in his collaboration with Mays, since they both had

> learned to improvise almost exclusively from a bebop point of view. I mean, everything I do I still relate to Charlie Parker. Even if I'm playing with David Bowie, I'm comparing that constantly to the music that I know best, which is bebop. But on the other hand, neither one of us has a particular need to prove that we can play bebop. It's just always there. It's kind of ironic that neither one of us has ever recorded in that style. It's just a common ground.[81]

Apart from Evans, another potent influence on Mays's keyboard playing and harmonic thinking was Jarrett, whose music also had an impact on Metheny: the latter was particularly impressed by Burton's and Jarrett's duo album (released by Atlantic in 1971, and supported by a rhythm section including Swallow on bass),[82] which used electronic and funk elements typical of the time but less common in their later work. A continuing interest in Jarrett's music was shown by the inclusion of 'The Wind Up' in the Metheny Group's live gigs in the 1980s, as David Ake notes.[83] In terms of acoustic-piano textures and harmonic vocabulary, Jarrett's example opened Mays's ears to unorthodox ways of rhythmically animating harmonies, notably in conjunction with a folk-like modality and strong echoes of country music. Peter Elsdon

79 Peter Mengaziol, 'Pat Metheny: Classic to the Core' (subtitled 'No tricks, no fads, just straight-ahead bebop on a happy groove thing'), *Guitar World* 6/3 (May 1985): 30-31.
80 Barth, *Voices in Jazz Guitar*, 329.
81 Bill Milkowski, 'Pat Metheny's Digital Manifesto', *Down Beat* 52/1 (January 1985): 19.
82 John Milward, 'Wandering Minstrel', *Boston Globe Magazine*, August 23, 1992.
83 David Ake, *Jazz Matters: Sound, Place, and Time since Bebop* (Berkeley: University of California Press, 2010), 176 n. 47.

has categorized Jarrett's substantial solo improvisations as bringing together elements of three clearly defined idioms, all of which were echoed in Mays's playing: the ballad, which involved expressive rubato; the folk-ballad, promoting melodic directness with simple harmonies and an aura of folk-rock; and lastly the blues vamp.[84] Elsdon also draws attention to critics who found Jarrett's repeated blues and country vamps monotonous, a viewpoint that perhaps reveals a lack of sympathy not only towards the minimalist tendencies that were to become important in some ECM recordings and the music of other performers keen to break away from bebop harmonies, but also an aversion to the notion of a pop-influenced visceral sense of groove as a 'physical, bodily experience'.[85] Jarrett-like vamps were also a characteristic of some of Brüninghaus's playing—for example, on the title track of Weber's *Silent Feet*.

A significant aspect of Metheny's quartet was its relatively unusual pairing of lead guitar and piano. In an interview in 2002, the guitarist— whose solo playing was always highly resourceful in its harmonic explorations and chord voicings—commented that playing with a piano can mean that

> the guitar's power as a chordal instrument is compromised. A piano player can play a chord that might have only four or five notes in it, but is something that's quite impossible to play on a guitar. The piano has set a harmonic precedent so that even if you can duplicate that chord on a guitar, it just doesn't have the same harmonic weight. As a result I find that when I play in the group I very rarely play chords; if I do, it's only one or two notes that can sit in with what the piano's doing.[86]

When able to voice chords more fully in the absence of a keyboard, the influence of the harmonic thinking of pianists such as Evans, Jarrett, Paul Bley, Herbie Hancock, and classical performer Glenn Gould nevertheless remained paramount, and Metheny tried to emulate the strengths of keyboard voice-leading within the limitations of guitar technique; in a rarefied setting, such as guitar and bass duo playing, he might 'use just a single note or two to define an entire chord and then

---

84 Peter Elsdon, 'Style and the Improvised in Keith Jarrett's Solo Concerts', *Jazz Perspectives* 2/1 (2008): 56-61. See also Ake, *Jazz Matters*, 95 and 176 n. 47.

85 Elsdon, 'Style and the Improvised', 62-3.

86 Metheny interviewed in Julian Piper, 'Time to Re-group', *Guitarist* (May 2002): 126.

follow that later with more full kinds of voicings to create the sense of orchestration'.[87]

A notable feature of the quartet's textures was Gottlieb's sensitive deployment of various cymbal sonorities, which was to remain a conspicuous feature of all Metheny's later ensemble work. This had been a preoccupation of Gottlieb's since his high school days, when he was influenced by the playing of Mel Lewis and Tony Williams, and intensified after he had observed Moses, Airto Moreira, and Roy Haynes exploiting the distinctive sound of flat (i.e., bell-less) cymbals, which he felt were particularly well suited to accompanying electric guitar. Coupled with this attention to fresh textures was Gottlieb's firm belief in the importance of exploring a wide dynamic range, a feature of classical music which Metheny felt had been ignored in jazz, rock, and pop, and which he set out to resuscitate in the quartet's playing.[88] Unlike the metronomic rock- and funk-influenced drumming of the early fusion bands, Gottlieb's contribution paralleled that of Elvin Jones in his work with John Coltrane by providing an organic commentary on the music, with the three other players often maintaining a firm pulse so that the drum rhythms could remain flexible.[89]

WATERCOLORS

Watercolors was issued in a sleeve designed by Dieter Bonhorst, who had previously created the cover for *Bright Size Life*, and it incorporated a photograph by Lajos Keresztes (see Fig. 2.1).[90] The album's title, and those of some of its tracks, had a personal significance for Metheny, since he revealed that 'Sea Song'—perhaps the project's most unusual composition—was written in Miami in 1972 and had been directly inspired by his first seeing the ocean there on his arrival from Kansas City.[91] Pastorius told *Down Beat* in January 1977, the month before Metheny's album was recorded:

> There's a real rhythm in Florida. It's because of the ocean. There's something about the Caribbean Ocean; it's why all that music

87 http://www.patmetheny.com/qa/questionView.cfm?queID=4551 (September 6, 2014).
88 Forte, 'Garage Band'. Information in this paragraph is also derived from personal communication with Danny Gottlieb via email, July 9, 2014.
89 *Ibid.*
90 Lars Müller, *ECM: Sleeves of Desire* (Baden: Lars Müller, 1996), 277, 280.
91 *Pat Metheny Song Book*, 438.

PAT METHENY
WATERCOLORS

ECM

827 409-2 ⎘

FIG. 2.1 *Watercolors* sleeve art. Design by Dieter Bonhorst; photograph by Lajos Keresztes. © ECM Records, 1977. Used by permission.

from down there sounds like that. I can't explain it but I know what it is. I can feel it when I'm there. The water in the Caribbean is much different from other oceans. It's a little bit calmer down there. We don't have waves in Florida, all that much. Unless there's a hurricane. But when a hurricane comes, look out! It's more ferocious there than anywhere else. And a lot of music from down there is like that—the pulse is smooth even if the rhythms are angular, and the pulse will take you before you know it. All of a sudden, you're swept away.[92]

92 Milkowski, *Jaco*, 80.

In addition to its specific appropriateness for Metheny's album, the *Watercolors* sleeve was also a reflection of the growing prominence of such imagery in ECM's refined packaging, which increasingly carried metaphorical overtones. Eicher, referring to Charles Lloyd's album *The Water Is Wide* (recorded in 1999), explained his thinking:

> It's almost a line for ECM: the water is wide. In my mind, I often bring the music we do together with water music. I see a sea, a big ocean. And it's extremely calm. Then, two and a half minutes later, the waves start moving and it becomes a storm. It changes, and the tide changes. That is inside ECM, I think. A continuous movement of undercurrents and unexpected drifts, winds coming from different directions to become a central storm. But sometimes the sea is tranquil, and stays tranquil. We had a period when there was a certain sameness, maybe, or weakness even, but it was needed—as in the Keith Jarrett solo concerts, his great concerts, where you hear all these long waves, and you hear the parts where he needed to reload his energies to fly into the storm.[93]

Thomas Steinfeld, describing water as 'absolutely present and beyond reach', expanded further on the metaphorical significance of aquatic imagery in the sleeve designs:

> It is this metaphysical quality of water that makes it so attractive for ECM album covers: it changes all the time, in color and shape, but it is not changed by anything, not even by the seasons. It builds up to a huge mass, but can divide itself into infinitely small portions: it forms waves, is shaped into grooves and ridges, filaments and panicles, swells and withdraws, breaks in ever new, ever-different foam-topped crests; and finally, it washes over stones, pebbles or sand . . . One can become almost mesmerized while looking at water, and it is easy to fall into a small, ruminant rapture while watching the sea, and time stands still.[94]

The fluidity of water was, above all, a potent symbol for improvisation. Steve Lake suggests that the golden romantic sunset on the sleeve of

93 Steve Lake, 'The Free Matrix: An Interview with Manfred Eicher', in Lake and Griffiths, *Horizons Touched*, 222.
94 Thomas Steinfeld, 'When Twilight Comes', in Müller, *Windfall Light*, 36-7.

Burton's and Swallow's ECM album *Hotel Hello*, released in 1975, had dated by the time it was reissued on CD in 1993 (for which release it was rendered in starker monochrome, because 'this is a bleaker, tougher, lonelier time for the creative musician'); water imagery was both more ambiguous and enduring, yet the label at times avoided the obvious by, for example, issuing Terje Rypdal's album *Waves* (recorded seven months after *Watercolors*) in a sleeve depicting 'trees whipped by the winter wind'.[95] The significance of watery images in Metheny's later music was raised by an interviewer in relation to his hard-hitting album *Zero Tolerance for Silence* (1994), which she felt was part of a broader series of recordings that 'look at [a] river from a different angle, or with different filters on the lenses', with *Zero Tolerance* giving an impression of being 'immersed inside the river'— and he readily agreed.[96]

The opening (title) track on *Watercolors* was composed by Metheny in early 1976 and was first performed at the guitarist's very first gig with Mays at Zircon, Somerville, in July that year, with Swallow on bass and Gottlieb on drums.[97] The head melody embodied what the guitarist described as the 'simple, but open-ended changes' on which he particularly enjoyed improvising, and these involve harmonic shifts syncopated in a generically similar manner to those in 'The Whopper' (with the change from one chord to the next mostly occurring on the last quaver of a group of four); yet the ensuing improvised solos are all based upon simple repeating patterns of two chords with roots a semitone apart, each maintained for 2 bars: A♭maj7 and Gmi7 alternated for 8 bars, then D♭maj7 and Cmi7, alternated for another eight. (Metheny's interest in building a solo form independent from, but growing out of, a tune's principal material has been a career-long preoccupation, already in evidence as early as 'Midwestern Nights Dream' and 'Bright Size Life', and also to be heard in *Watercolor*'s 'Lakes'.) In 'Watercolors', a 4-bar codetta to these solo changes alludes to the harmonic language of the head, functioning in a similar way (and similar rhythm) to the vamp-interludes in 'The Whopper'.

Metheny's three-chorus solo in the studio recording can be compared with his longer solo from a live performance given by the group— now with Mark Egan rather than Weber on bass—in San Francisco

95 Steve Lake, 'Looking at the Cover', in Müller, *ECM: Sleeves of Desire*, 253-4, 258.
96 Barth, *Voices in Jazz Guitar*, 331.
97 *Pat Metheny Song Book*, 439.

on August 31, 1977, some six months after the *Watercolors* sessions.[98]
Egan's bass-playing and his interaction with Gottlieb on drums are
incisive and look ahead to the dynamism of the group's rhythm section
in its next incarnation (explored in Chapter 3). In the studio, the head
is performed three times before the solo: the first statement in free time
as a rhapsodic duet for guitar and piano, joined by brushed cymbal
and bass only in the closing phrase; the second and third in strict time
and in a faster tempo, with full rhythm-section support. Live, the third
statement of the head was omitted but, as if to compensate, the guitar
solo extends into an extra chorus. With one notable exception, the solos
have little direct connection with either the melody or the harmonies
of the head and do not engage with the metrical changes in the closing
phrase (which lilts its way first through 3/4 and then 3/8): the solos are in
4/4 throughout and, as noted above, based on different changes.

For ease of comparison, the two solos are here directly superimposed,
with Example 2.8a transcribed from the studio version and Example 2.8b
from the live gig. A number of details recall hallmarks already
encountered in 'The Whopper' solo analysed above: the idiomatic
semiquaver figure identified as a Metheny lick by Panisset and Moulin
(Ex. 2.3) is used sparingly, occurring only once in each solo and in
entirely different locations (Ex. 2.8a, bb. 35–6; Ex. 2.8b, bb. 52–3), and
the syncopated descending scale beneath an inverted pedal note
(Ex. 2.2, b. 14) becomes a more prominent feature in the live performance,
where it traverses a complete descending octave (Ex. 2.8b, bb. 97–8)
and immediately initiates a climactic ascent in staggered octaves
(Ex. 2.8b, bb. 99–102) which culminates in the solo's registral peak.
A similar inverted-pedal figure is embedded in the syncopated two-part
counterpoint which rounds off a lengthy dyadic passage at the start of
the third chorus in the live solo (Ex. 2.8b, bb. 85–6). Both solos make
use of dyadic riffs as intensifying or punctuating devices, though again
the location of these moments differs significantly from one solo to the
next. Dyads are more liberally deployed in the live version, including
a memorable chromatic-thirds motif (Ex. 2.8b, bb. 16 and 82), and this
solo also makes a more sustained use of high tessitura and prominent

98 The date of the San Francisco concert, and its venue (the Great American Music Hall), are
given in Trethewey, *The Way Up Is White*, 28. As Trethewey notes, the performance has
been circulated on an unauthorized CD, and at the time of writing is similarly available
on the internet. The reader is directed towards Metheny's substantial and thought-
provoking statement on the vexed question of the many bootleg releases of his music at
http://interact.patmetheny.com/qa/questionView.cfm?queID=317 (August 8, 2013).

(cont.)

(cont.)

(cont.)

(cont.)

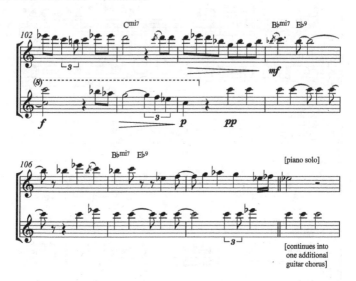

flat-five blue notes (Ex. 2.8b, bb. 55-6 and 67) not exploited in the studio version; for all these reasons, the studio take seems somewhat more laid back than the live performance.

Structurally, the two solos differ significantly, although they both share a basic strategy of beginning with relatively short-breathed phrases in order to allow room in which the 'story' can develop. In the live example, the first chorus uses plentiful rests for this purpose, whereas in the studio performance the simplicity of some of the melodic ideas (particularly the plain crotchet rhythms in Example 2.8a, bb. 9, 11, and 15) creates the economical effect. The solos also share a few similar phrase shapes, albeit again located in different positions within the pattern of changes: compare, for example, Example 2.8a, b. 16 with Example 2.8b, b. 14; and Example 2.8a, bb. 16-17 with Example 2.8b, bb. 20-21. The studio solo demonstrates Metheny's fondness for arch-like melodic construction, with an ascending phrase often immediately followed by a descending one (e.g., Ex. 2.8a, bb. 17-20, 21-3, 24-6, etc.). A longer-term sense of direction is achieved throughout the second chorus, with increased phrase lengths and a climactic passage offering an excellent example of intensification through varied sequential repetition leading to a high target-note peak followed by a gradually relaxing descent (Ex. 2.8a, bb. 55-67). In two places, a melodic idea is repeated at a later stage in varied form (Ex. 2.8a, bb. 9-11 and 39-42), with the two statements again located in quite different parts of the chorus. The principal difference in the approach taken in the live solo is a more rigorous manner of motivic development throughout, with a good deal of the material being derived from the three-note falling pattern which pervades the head. The most prominent developments of this idea occur in Example 2.8b, bb. 33–6, 37–9, 57–60, and 91–2, whereas in the studio version it appeared only at the very beginning of the solo, in decorated and sequential form (Ex. 2.8a, bb. 2–8). With its occasional unpredictability in registral leaps (e.g., Ex. 2.8b, bb. 24–8), the live performance has a paradoxical combination of spontaneity and motivic coherence which lends it a compelling intensity. The additional fourth chorus in this performance (not transcribed here) is unusual in the way it begins by prolonging and elaborating the *pianissimo* monotone Cs introduced at the end of the third chorus (Ex. 2.8b, bb. 104–9) in a most effectively understated manner, linking delicately to the beginning of the ensuing piano solo.

'Icefire' is an improvised solo on the Guild Starfire 12-string electric guitar, animated by understated chordal punctuation and strumming, and inhabiting a metallic, glacial soundworld featuring a telling use of multiple harmonics (a Metheny hallmark). Predominantly modal at the start, and again tending to alternate between two simple chords, the music then explores parallel triadic harmony over pedal points and settles into quasi-minimalist riff patterns. The instrument's tuning is unorthodox, and notably different from the regular tuning used on this guitar in Burton's *Dreams So Real*. Metheny explained:

> I've always been interested in what you can make the guitar be by forcing it into different registers and tunings. To get that sound from Icefire you'd have to buy an electric 12-string, take off all the strings and restring it with all unwound strings except for the lowest, then tune it in fifths to a diatonic major pentatonic scale. That piece was built around not only an odd tuning but also a major restringing.[99]

In this respect the conception of the piece looks ahead not only to the use of modified 12-string tunings in 'San Lorenzo' (*Pat Metheny Group*, 1978) but also to the performer's endless fascination with custom-made instruments in his later work.

99 Piper, 'Time to Re-group', 128. See also http://interact.patmetheny.com/qa/questionView. cfm?queID=1162 (March 31, 2013), where Metheny comments in response to a fan's disbelief that the piece was improvised: 'the piece was in fact totally improvised with a few preplanned signposts along the way—but, there was not a lot of room to move harmonically within that tuning's vocabulary'.

Further textural experimentation for strings alone is heard in the third track, 'Oasis', also composed in 1976 and 'conceived as a melody for Eberhard Weber to play over a whole bunch of overdubbed 15-string harp guitars'.[100] Metheny had purchased a GEWA harp guitar while playing in Germany with Burton, and had tried it out during his January 1977 tour with Zigmund and others.[101] The instrument added nine bass strings below the standard six strings of the orthodox guitar, a resource which Metheny used (sparingly) for 'added texture'.[102] In 'Oasis', freely arpeggiated and slowly changing chords in the harp-guitar overdubs provide a *bisbigliando* backdrop for a single statement of Weber's ethereal alto-register melody. The harmonic language is predominantly modal, with the melody entirely in E♭ Aeolian apart from a single chromatic inflection; as a result, the richer guitar chord at the mid-point (C♭13♯11) provides a considerable if temporary harmonic frisson, which appears to be heading back to the tonic via B♭9sus4 but instead is further diverted to C♭mi9—in support of the single chromatic deviation in the melodic line—before the home root is finally reached. This progression is shown schematically in Example 2.9 and is a microcosmic illustration of Metheny's finely honed harmonic-temporal sensibilities. Also notable in this track is the free pulse in which melody and accompaniment are performed, providing an expansive feeling not only appropriate to the waterscape suggested by the title but also looking ahead to some later soundscapes in his music. Characteristic, too, are the subtle gradations of dynamic level.

In the greatest possible contrast to 'Oasis', the next track—'Lakes'—is replete with liberally rich harmonic changes, to the point where *Down Beat* reviewer Neil Tesser likened its release section (i.e., bridge) to Coltrane's infamous 'Giant Steps'.[103] In fact, there is no bridge: the melody is simply an 8-bar theme played three times, with variant harmonies on the second and third statements; Tesser presumably had in mind the different changes underpinning the ensuing solos, where the roving perfect-cadence patterns moving rapidly through D, F, D♭, E, G, B♭, G♭, and C majors challenge the improviser's resourcefulness in a manner akin to the notorious Coltrane standard, which Metheny once likened to a picture by M. C. Escher.[104] The harmonic and metrical dislocations

100 *Pat Metheny Song Book*, 439.
101 Viva, *Pat Metheny*, 62.
102 Forte, 'Jazz Voice of the 80's', 107.
103 Tesser, review of *Watercolors*.
104 Shipton, *A New History of Jazz*, 547.

of the head are a continuation of the strategy evident in both 'The Whopper' and 'Watercolors'. Whereas 'The Whopper' had been intended to stimulate Burton's imagination at his mallet-played keys, Metheny recalled that 'Lakes' had originally been conceived for James Williams's two-piano quartet in 1968, and in this case the music's keyboard origins had been directly responsible for its emphasis on active harmonies; the piece was later performed by Metheny's quartet with Goldstein and Gottlieb.[105] Weber's bass line in the *Watercolors* performance of the head is transcribed in Example 2.10, commencing after 4 bars of diatonic introduction in D major on a tonic pedal, which—as in the introduction to 'The Whopper', also featuring Weber— are deceptively stable. At several points the bass line moves through simple chromatic scale segments in contrast to its many moments of unpredictable side-slipping, in which single chromatic steps initiate local-level movement through segments of the circle of fifths. The chord progressions are made still less predictable by the frequent occurrence of dissonant slash chords whenever bass and melody are harmonically out of synchronization, these many moments of surprise effectively reinforced by equally unexpected metrical dislocations. With aurally

105 *Pat Metheny Song-Book*, 438.

EX. 2.11 'Lakes': scalic patterns in guitar solo (AT). © 1977 Pat Meth Music Corp. All rights reserved.

comprehensible motivic logic, Metheny's solo steers the listener through the complex blowing changes with a purposeful linearity, as shown by the passage from the opening of the second chorus transcribed in Example 2.11, which uses simple descending scale segments—some necessarily involving enharmonic shifts—as a cohesive device. Similar strategies, involving ascending scale segments and short motifs developed sequentially, are used in Mays's piano solo.

'River Quay' (named after a district of Kansas City) was written in the summer of 1976 for Metheny's first tour with Mays, Richmond, and Moses, when they gigged in Chicago and KC.[106] Its easygoing tunefulness, even quavers and rock-like feel, complete with gentle backbeats, is typical of certain later Metheny tracks which unashamedly

106 *Pat Metheny Song Book*, 439.

tap pop resonances. As Tesser put it in his *Down Beat* review, the piece is characterized by 'the sliding-chord pop-song lope (effectively used on the hit *Midnight at the Oasis* some years back)'. The reference is to the 1973 song composed by David Nichtern and recorded by Maria Muldaur, though Metheny's tune demonstrates only the most superficial of similarities to this particular antecedent, which had already received funky instrumental treatments from trumpeter Freddie Hubbard and flutist Hubert Laws. In 'River Quay', the solos (of which Mays's is notably Jarrett-like in its figurations) are improvised above the same strong changes as the tune. This foreshortened song form comprises a repeated 8-bar minor-key phrase followed by a contrastingly bright 8-bar bridge in the major which, instead of leading to a recapitulation of the opening strain, instead links into the first chorus of the ensuing solos, thus preserving the circular feeling of typical song forms but avoiding formulaic predictability at the same time as promoting an ongoing sense of momentum. The piece ends with a double statement of the bridge in order to clinch the major key.

Two shorter pieces are linked as a 'suite' in the album's sixth and seventh tracks. The outgoing and sunny 'Florida Greeting Song' is typical of the spontaneous duets for guitar and drums that are occasional features of Metheny's live gigs, and which he and Gottlieb had enjoyed performing during their earliest days in Miami. The tune comes from the same stylistic stable as *Bright Size Life*, but the metric freedom of its central improvised solo is an intriguing glance ahead to its composer's keyboardless work on several later projects. 'Legend of the Fountain' is a guitar solo distinguished by a wonderfully ringing, clear tone, and deep bass notes. Its overall texture, in which a lyrical melody is punctuated by well-projected bass notes and accompanied by mid-register chords—sonically varied in places by the use of harmonics—is characteristic of Metheny's unaccompanied playing when in reflective mood, and can instructively be compared with the much later solo album *One Quiet Night* (2003).

Finally comes 'Sea Song', the composition inspired by the Miami ocean in 1972 and written originally for Florida sextet Kaleidoscope, led by pianist Dan Haerle with Gottlieb on drums. The piece was designed to be 'played rubato, and the idea was to improvise on the form while staying out of time'.[107] The six short lines of the published version of the melody are on the album transformed into a highly evocative soundscape lasting over 10 minutes, providing a substantial and

107 *Ibid.*, 438.

reflective conclusion to the project as a whole.[108] The overall conception of the performance recalls Tucker's assertion that 'the chief impact of [Weber's] *Chloë* material lay in the floating treatment of time and phrase which introduced the sort of reflective, distinctly European note that would come to characterise a good deal of the music on ECM'. The parallel with Weber's own music is intensified by the bassist's distinctively ethereal processed timbre, which makes this track to some extent a sonic companion piece to 'Oasis'. Vital to the wave-like textures are Gottlieb's cymbal washes, in which considerable dynamic contrasts were crucial to the effect: as Metheny commented, the drummer 'had to keep the dynamics going without playing time, which he was always good at'.[109] (Something similar was attempted in the second half of the concluding track 'Joanna's Theme' on Wayne Shorter's *Native Dancer* (1975), an album which was a favourite of Metheny's: see Chapter 4.) After Weber's initial statement of the 'Sea Song' theme, Metheny improvises lyrically with rhapsodic support from Mays across the full range of the keyboard, and this is the first of their recorded duets to demonstrate their astonishing empathy in a highly rubato-shaped environment. Metheny drifts into and out from the background at times, leaving Mays's lightly fingered arabesque textures occasionally foregrounded, and both merge into accompanimental patterns as Weber re-enters for his solo, once more supported by the cymbal washes from the opening and compellingly shaped by dynamic swells and contrasts. In the closing third of the piece, including the recapitulation of the head, all four performers ebb and flow in the shimmering texture as equal partners. Gottlieb recalls that Mays's piano part was overdubbed because Eicher was dissatisfied with the sound of the first take, and the microphones were moved very slightly for a second attempt: the fact that Eicher was pleased with the new take but none of the musicians 'could really tell the difference' is testament to the ECM team's characteristic attention to sonic detail.[110]

Watercolors achieved a finely judged balance between impressionistic pieces in free time and solidly structured chord changes with catchy melodies and traditional chorus-based improvisation, thereby establishing the distinctive pattern maintained in many of Metheny's later group projects; as yet, however, no large-scale innovative structural ambitions were in evidence. For his part, Metheny felt that *Watercolors* 'didn't turn

108 *Ibid.*, 13.
109 Rick Mattingly, 'A Different View: Pat Metheny', *Modern Drummer* (December 1991): 82.
110 Personal communication from Danny Gottlieb via email, July 9, 2014.

out to be such a great record, because I really didn't think that album through'.[111] Considering the album as a whole to be not especially impressive in its standards of playing, he nevertheless continued to retain a personal fondness for 'Sea Song'. The preference for this particular track was not shared by Tesser, however, who in his otherwise favourable account of the album found the concluding piece not only 'problematic' and cast in a 'shapeless rhythmic format', but also felt 'it succumbs to the pejorative charges of "impressionism" sometimes leveled at the ECM line'.[112] Earlier in his review, Tesser had mentioned that some commentators at the time felt Metheny was

> a symbol of the ECM controversy. Critics of the label, its producer, and its distinctive sound point quickly to Metheny (along with his former employer Gary Burton and a few others) when they start moaning about white middle-class jerkwater jazz and suburban soul. He is written off as being too clean, sounding too pure; even his song titles come under icy fire.

The guitarist's highly personal timbre as displayed in *Watercolors* nonetheless came to have an enormous impact on a younger generation of performers. As Tesser put it, Metheny's 'round, pure winter-sun tone (enhanced further by discrete use of a digital sequencer [*sic*]) is among the most captivating voices in modern jazz'. The sound of the Gibson 175 had been enhanced through the use of a Lexicon digital delay during the mixing process, this modification having arisen almost by accident, as Metheny once explained:

> I was living in Boston at the time, but I was in a studio in Oslo and saw a Lexicon there, noticed that the company was in Boston and said, 'Can you put it on the guitar and see what it sounds like?' It was supposed to be used for vocals, for ADT [automatic double tracking, used to enrich the timbre], and the guy said, 'Oh, yeah.' So when I got back to Boston I thought, 'God, there must be a way to do this live,' so I called up Lexicon and said, 'I'm this guitar player . . .' and they gave me one!
>
> I messed around with it and got into this thing of splitting up the amps because I always thought that the guitar was a bit flat in mono.

111 Barth, *Voices in Jazz Guitar*, 323.
112 Tesser, review of *Watercolors*.

It seemed like when I heard a saxophone player like Sonny Rollins the sound seemed to come from all over the place—it didn't come from this one little spot. So I tried it and that was it.[113]

From these relatively simple beginnings, Metheny's use of digital delays and amplifiers over the following years was to become far more sophisticated, but always with the principal aim of dispersing the sound of any electronic or electric elements so that the richness of the overall effect was comparable to an enhanced version of unamplified acoustic playing.[114]

113 Mead, 'Open Secret', 46.
114 Metheny described his later onstage technical setup (c. 1981) in fine detail in Forte, 'Jazz Voice of the 80's', 108-9.

CHAPTER 3

TAKING THE LEAD

Watercolors is a pretty laid-back album
by my standards. The next album will be
practically a rock record. Very powerful.[1]

IN THE TWO albums which followed *Watercolors*, Metheny's new
quartet maintained its unorthodox combination of electric guitar,
electric bass, acoustic piano, and drums, collectively feeling that they
had embarked on a mission to play (as he put it) an 'alternative thing',
which was neither bebop nor fusion.[2] Now with a new bassist, and
all members still in their early twenties, they toured extensively for
three years (1977–9), initially as a supporting act to established jazz
and rock artists, and played a great deal in Europe. First rehearsals
were held in May 1977, and an initial gig followed on June 28, at Club
Axis in Soho, New York. A word-of-mouth reputation steadily grew

---

1 Pat Metheny, interviewed in John Alan Smith, 'Pat Metheny: Ready to Tackle Tomorrow',
  Down Beat 45/13 (July 13, 1978): 53.
2 Carr, 'Bright Size Life', episode 2.

as the group appeared in San Francisco, Seattle, Chicago, New York, and Boston, and punishing touring schedules were endured in order to secure the best-paid gigs. A typical example cited by Metheny was a Thursday night performance in Seattle followed by appearances in Dallas on the Saturday and Quebec the following Monday; they drove all night, sleeping in turns on mattresses laid on top of their instruments, and notching up literally hundreds of thousands of miles in their Dodge camper van (bought from Metheny's father, who was a car dealer), spending as much as 300 days a year on the road in the process. When interviewed in 1982, Metheny cited the group's almost ceaseless live gigs as the single most important factor in their unwittingly having secured a widespread fan base.[3] Danny Gottlieb recalls:

> We would show up, and the club or concert hall would think that we were the road crew ... and then we would set up and play and it turned out to be the band! I loved playing in front of an audience that didn't have a clue [who we were], and we would win them over with the great songs written by Pat and Lyle, amazing solos, and sensitive playing, while also being able to rock out. It was a pretty unique combination of acoustic music, with real tunes and difficult chord changes, and electric music. Winning over the audience was a fun challenge.[4]

The new bassist, Mark Egan, had been suggested by Gottlieb, with whom he went on to found the group Elements in the early 1980s, after their departure from Metheny.[5] Egan was in any case already well known to Metheny, as they had played together during the guitarist's time in Florida. The bassist was in some respects a logical successor to Pastorius, with whom he had studied in Miami during the summer of 1973, and (in Metheny's words) 'could play both the things that Jaco did on *Bright Size Life* and what Eberhard [Weber] did on *Watercolors* and because we had

---

3 Schneckloth, 'Pat Metheny: A Step beyond Tradition', 15.

4 Personal communication from Danny Gottlieb via email, July 9, 2014.

5 The Elements initiative was partly a reflection of Egan's and Gottlieb's need to find more room for solo work than was possible in some of Metheny's music at this time: in live gigs, they might take one or two solos, but the studio recordings gave the lion's share of the soloing to guitar and piano. (Personal communication from Mark Egan via email, July 14, 2014.)

done just the one album, we had to fall back on the material of those two albums as well [in live gigs]'.[6] Egan recalled:

I had been listening a lot to Stanley Clarke and was very impressed by what he was doing with Return to Forever. But Jaco's approach was much more advanced harmonically, and he played with such frightening intensity and attitude. That's one thing he taught me when I studied with him—just by playing with him, just by being in the same room with him—he taught me to play with a kind of conviction I never knew before.[7]

Like Pastorius, Egan felt maintaining a firm groove was an essential foundation for the kind of experimental flights of fancy in which his teacher had excelled.[8] For Metheny's group, Egan adopted a fretless bass on which Pastorius had been working: this was a customized Fender Precision instrument made in 1958 which had originally been fretted but now, in addition to losing its frets, had also been furnished with a jazz-bass pickup. Egan felt his introduction to this instrument and its potential was a creative 'awakening'.[9] Metheny, who owned the instrument, felt that the fretless bass

somehow blends better when there's that nebulous intonation. I always enjoyed playing with Steve Swallow, who plays a fretted bass, but he's always sort of slopping it up. I can't get in between the frets, and I rarely bend strings, so if Mark is playing fretless it gives it a little more mystery, which I like.[10]

Like Metheny and many of his associates (including former collaborators Burton and Swallow, and Mays), Egan had previously been a wind player, studying trumpet in his youth and much admiring the playing of Chet Baker; all such players felt this experience had been invaluable in encouraging their melodic conceptions to breathe expansively.

6 Barth, Voices in Jazz Guitar, 325.
7 Milkowski, Jaco, 92–3.
8 Ibid., 294–5.
9 Viva, Pat Metheny, 67.
10 Forte, 'Garage Band'. In this article, Egan discusses the technical setup for his bass-playing at this time, including details of the pedal volume control, custom-made amplifier, and use of Metheny's MXR digital delay 'to give it some phasing and slight pitch-bend'. The delay was not used constantly, and triggered by a foot switch when required.

The group's first seven months of intensive touring were to result in their eponymous debut album, recorded in Oslo in January 1978. The release stunned both ECM's management and the participating musicians by quickly selling more than 100,000 copies instead of the roughly 15,000 typically achieved by contemporary jazz albums, and by staying on the *Billboard* jazz chart for more than a year. The recording was issued in a starkly simple white sleeve (see Fig. 3.1), which resulted in its later being habitually referred to by those involved as 'the white album': this was perhaps the boldest example of the design philosophy of ECM's Barbara Wojirsch, who noted that 'the sheer quantity of things and messages day in and day out make[s] me want to remove as much as possible

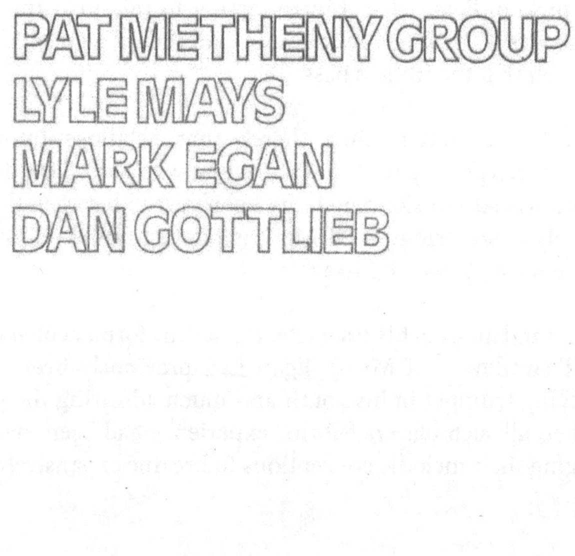

PAT METHENY GROUP
LYLE MAYS
MARK EGAN
DAN GOTTLIEB

ECM

FIG. 3.1 *Pat Metheny Group* sleeve art. Design by Barbara Wojirsch. © ECM Records, 1978. Used by permission.

from my designs until only something essential, only a thought or gesture, remains'.[11] Wojirsch later designed the evocative sleeves for *80/ 81*, *As Falls Wichita, So Falls Wichita Falls*, and *First Circle*, the last of which was almost as minimalist in conception as the stark white of *Pat Metheny Group*.

The developing collaboration between Metheny and Mays resulted in the inclusion of more arranged material on the Metheny Group's debut album. Their (as yet fairly modest) experimental outlook included Metheny's adaptations of Nashville and 12-string tunings on the tracks 'Phase Dance' and 'San Lorenzo', and Mays's growing interest in the Oberheim modular four-voice synthesizer and autoharps, which the leader had secured for him with specific musical effects in mind. Autoharps are a form of zither in which pre-set chords are played by depressing button-operated damping bars, and when not amplified these instruments produce a characteristically tinny sonority that had long been associated with bluegrass and folk music, but not jazz. As used in the Metheny band, they were described by Mays as having

> the bars taken off, tuned to open chords—one is a big open D chord, which I use on 'Phase Dance'; the other I use on 'San Lorenzo' in conjunction with the tuning Pat has on his 12-string. We put a hockey puck pickup on each one, which I think is like a submarine detector or something.[12]

'San Lorenzo', the first Metheny–Mays co-composition to be recorded, was written in June 1977, and its basic structure as performed on the album is summarized in Table 3.1. The piece was felt by Mays to be a good example of how their creative ideas developed through numerous gigs on the road.[13] Metheny compared the piece to 'Icefire' (*Watercolors*), since both began with electric 12-string tunings

> with all the strings replaced with very light-gauge strings and tuned in a pentatonic '5th-y' kind of system, very high. I ended up with a few melodic phrases that I liked (the opening five-note phrase, the 'harmonics section' that recurs throughout the tune, etc.). With Lyle, over the course of a few days, we wrote the basic arrangement, using

11 Müller, *ECM: Sleeves of Desire*, 9–10.
12 Forte, 'Garage Band'.
13 Mike Brannon, interview with Lyle Mays (May 2001).

TABLE 3.1   Structure of 'San Lorenzo"

Bars	Thematic/textural material	Harmony
A (ritornello)		
1–7	Guitar chordal motif (Ex. 3.2)	Fmi7–E♭maj
B (theme 1)		
8–43	Electric-bass melody (Ex. 3.3), stated 3 times	E♭ Ionian
C (riffs)		
44–75	Syncopated 2-bar pentatonic motifs with supporting harmony (Ex. 3.4), 4 × 8 bars (3rd and 4th with synthesizer countermelody)	D♭maj7/Cmi7 A♭maj7/Gmi7 (×4)
76–7	Organum fifths linking to:	G♭maj7
A′ (ritornello)		
78–82	= bars 1–5	Fmi7–E♭maj
D (theme 2)		
83–90	Electric-bass variation of **C**, as intro. to:	E♭ Ionian
91–114	Homophonic chordal theme (Ex. 3.1a), 3 × 8 bars	
115–38	Riffs derived from chordal theme (Ex. 3.1b)	
139–54	Homophonic chordal theme (Ex. 3.1a), 2 × 8 bars, with improvised fills	
C′ (riffs)		
155–86	= varied form of bars 44–75	D♭maj7/Cmi7 A♭maj7/Gmi7 (×4)
187–90	Organum fifths linking to:	G♭maj7
A′ (ritornello)		
191–5	= bars 1–5	Fmi7–E♭maj
E (piano solo)		
196–273	19 × 4 bars, plus 2 bars (in half-time)	E♭ pedal

TABLE 3.1   Continued

Bars	Thematic/textural material	Harmony
F (theme 3)		
274–89	Half-time development of elements from B and C (including Ex. 3.5)	E♭ Ionian
C″ (riffs)		
290–319	= varied form of bars 44–75 (minus 2 bars)	D♭maj7/Cmi7 A♭maj7/Gmi7 (×4)
320–23	Organum fifths linking to:	G♭maj7
A″ (ritornello)		
324–26	= bars 1–3	Fmi7–E♭maj

* This chart is based on the published lead sheet in *Pat Metheny Song Book*, 54–60, replacing rehearsal letters with letters denoting the components of the formal structure. Bar numbers reflect the actual lengths of sections notated using repeat marks in the score. Detail in the solo section is based on the studio recording released on *Pat Metheny Group*.

those few phrases as the basic materials, with Lyle adding a lot of new melodic material. The form of the long improvised piano solo evolved tremendously over the course of the next year from getting played each night (sometimes twice; we often played two shows a night in those days).[14]

On this album, Metheny plays an Epiphone electric 12-string guitar, its idiosyncratic tuning having originated during a tour of Austria with Burton. Metheny later commented that another 12-string, made by Ibanez, was a particularly fine instrument for sustaining the harmonics that are a notable feature of the piece.[15] In this tuning, the harmonics may be played easily across the seventh and twelfth frets; Metheny was in due course amused to discover that one of his fans had not realised this, and had laboriously managed to recreate them on a 12-string in orthodox tuning by using Lenny Breau's artificial-harmonics technique.[16]

14 *Pat Metheny Song Book*, 439.
15 Forte, 'Jazz Voice of the 80's', 106.
16 Forte, 'Garage Band'.

In an interview conducted in 1989, Metheny himself identified the perceptible influences of Weather Report and Cannonball Adderley on the tune's central section.[17] The passage in question is reproduced in Example 3.1: the syncopated pentatonic bass line is a feature of the composition as a whole, and it here supports a catchy sequence of diatonic chords (Ex. 3.1a) which are then distilled into a simple riff based on a major-seventh harmony (Ex. 3.1b). In later years, the echo of Weather Report in the bass line of 'San Lorenzo' became something of an embarrassment to Metheny, not least because Joe Zawinul liked to remind him of it.

The Weather Report connection was picked up by critic Neil Tesser, who wrote somewhat unappreciatively of Metheny's growing interest as a bandleader, and in terms that suggest a lack of sympathy with an (undefined) concept of 'fusion' and a preference for more traditional jazz values. Describing 'San Lorenzo' as 'the Metheny–Mays nod to Weather Report', which 'falls within the now-conventional concept of fusion', he continued:

> at the same time, in concert the band often jams [in 1979], and very convincingly, on standard changes, such as All The Things You Are or There Will Never Be Another You. In both cases, of course, white compositional traditions are involved; again, jazz meets the All American boy.[18]

Tesser also noted that Metheny

> has even weathered the band's first major artistic crisis with admirable maturity: to balance the heavily arranged, solo-deficient epics he and Mays have been tending to (such as *San Lorenzo*), he has added a couple [of] wide open stompers to the show.[19]

'Solo-deficient' is a strange epithet to apply to a number that showcased a substantial and constantly evolving piano solo, and is perhaps indicative of a tendency on the part of certain critics to undervalue Mays's solo contributions when set alongside Metheny's.[20] Chip Stern,

---

17 Viva, *Pat Metheny*, 70.
18 Tesser and Bourque, 'Pat Metheny: Musings on Neo-Fusion', 12.
19 *Ibid.*, 15.
20 See, for example, Richard Cook and Brian Morton, *The Penguin Guide to Jazz on CD, LP and Cassette*, 1st edn. (London: Penguin, 1992), 735.

EX. 3.1a 'San Lorenzo': nod to Weather Report (SB, 56).

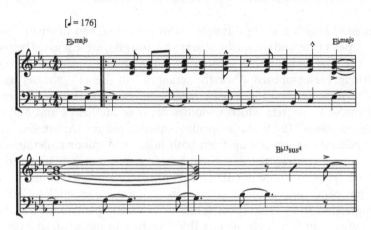

EX. 3.1b 'San Lorenzo': riffs (SB, 57).

however, praised the manner in which Mays's 'ringing tone' blended with the electronic timbres in 'San Lorenzo', and commented more generally:

> Mays is about due for some recognition as a major figure on piano, and hopefully he won't have to be saddled with comparisons with Keith Jarrett. There are similarities, but Mays has what could best

be characterized as an American sound on piano; gospel chording, blues inflections, and major voicings are prevalent.[21]

Three of Mays's solos in different performances of 'San Lorenzo' (one recorded in the studio, and the other two at live gigs) are discussed below.

The first half of this substantial (10-13 minute) piece is indeed entirely pre-composed ('heavily arranged', in Tesser's phrase) and well demonstrates the close integration of melodic motifs and harmonic characters which underlies many of Metheny's and Mays's collaborations. The guitar's opening chordal gesture (A: see Ex. 3.2) is predominantly made up from both major and minor anhemitonic pentatonic clusters, the first three based on F minor pentatonic; the fourth (passing) chord is a diatonic dominant link into the climactic E♭ major pentatonic chord on the upbeat. The strong circle-of-fifths progression from Fmi7 (pentatonic) to E♭ major (pentatonic) via the B♭ cluster—in fact, a classic jazz ii-V-I gesture in modernized garb— at once shows an interest in functional harmonies and non-functional modality, and these two contrasting facets are worked out in the ensuing thematic material. The initial theme on electric bass (B: see Ex. 3.3), played with the mellow delay Egan favoured for such melodic material, fluctuates between a pentatonic outline (first 2 bars), carrying with it the first hint of the soundworld of Weather Report, and segments which include the missing seventh degree of the diatonic major scale (third and fifth bars); the whole passage is pandiatonic and, in tonal terms, therefore static. The approach changes in the next section (C), the various components of which are shown schematically in Example 3.4. The syncopated riffs in the upper texture (lines 1 and 2) are all dyadic pentatonic formulations based on the first three melodic notes of the opening guitar chords (x), now announced as bell-like harmonics. They are given a strong tonal direction not by any inherently functional tonal properties, since all four patterns remain strictly within the diatonic E♭ major scale established at the beginning, but by a sequential bass line (line 5) elaborating, via descending chromatic neighbour notes, a V-I cadence in C minor, the relative of E♭, with the D♭ inflection imparting a Phrygian tinge. After two statements, a slowly moving countermelody is layered at first between the existing strata, on synthesizer (line 4) and, after the 'Weather Report' central section (Ex. 3.1) and just before the piano solo, an octave higher in the guitar (line 3); at the end of each of

---

21 Chip Stern, review of *Pat Metheny Group*, in *Down Beat* 45/12 (December 21, 1978): 30.

these segments, the harmony unexpectedly shifts to G♭ major beneath a suggestion of the opening pentatonic chords, now reduced to organum fifths, followed by a punctuating recapitulation of the opening guitar gesture in full. The third and final statement of this material rounds off the piece as a whole.

As with many improvised solos integrated into the compositional direction indicated by the bandleader during this early formative period, the (half-time) piano solo abandons the harmonies of the pre-composed material. In their stead, it is based entirely on an E♭ pedal, and of indeterminate length: the solo is marked 'open' in the published lead sheet, and terminated by a cue from the performer. Also typical of Metheny's early band concept is what he saw as an imperative need for the solo to be shaped dynamically, the performer being instructed to build the dynamic level gradually but then to decrescendo in the last 4 bars before the terminal nod. Apart from this feature, which in any case would have evolved during performances on the road rather than having been prescribed, the soloist is therefore entrusted with a considerable degree of freedom. Three performances featuring Mays's soloing are available at the time of writing: the studio recording on *Pat Metheny Group*, a

EX. 3.4 'San Lorenzo': riff patterns superimposed (AT). © 1979 Pat Meth Music Corp. and Lyle Mays, Inc. All rights reserved.

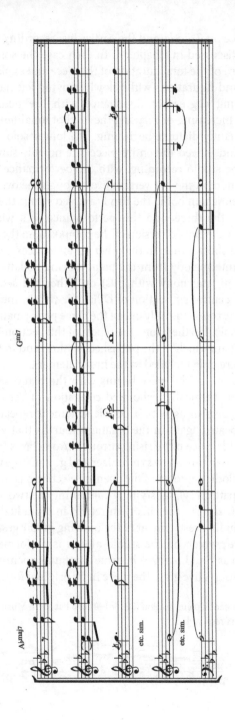

live performance on *Travels*, and the earlier live recording from the San Francisco gig discussed in Chapter 2. In each case the solo amounts to around one third of the total duration of the piece and explores relatively simple right-hand figurations while slowly moving left-hand harmonic shifts, of varying degrees of dissonance with the pedal point, are responsible for increasing or relaxing the level of tonal tension after the solo's predominantly diatonic beginning. The longer solo in the *Travels* performance, and indeed the entire piece, are notably slower in tempo compared to the studio recording, with the performance lasting a full three minutes more in the live version even though the overall structure (Table 3.1) is identical in both. The San Francisco solo is the shortest and most regular of the three, and this performance as a whole seems to reflect a less fully developed version of the composition: the opening bass melody is 2 bars shorter than in the other performances, and there is no syncopated countermelody from the piano during its latter half (which prolongs the Fmi7 harmony with fills) on either the second or third statements. The central riff section of D has the riffs in the piano with a guitar solo above: this is the only one of the three performances to feature a (brief) guitar solo. Furthermore, the repeat of this section is full-length, including the 8 bars which in the published version (and in the other two performances) are only included in the first statement.

The final section of the piece begins with the piano segueing from its solo into a rhythmically elaborated conflation of the first two riffs in Example 3.4, beginning with a double statement repeated an octave higher, then repeated again in the organum fourths that were a feature of the original riffs, once more rising through two octaves (F: see Ex. 3.5), the piano doubled in unison by synthesizer and guitar. This variation also relates to the melodic contours of the opening electric-bass theme (Ex. 3.3) in its cadential pattern (*y*), satisfyingly combining the two ideas. In their less active, original form the riffs then return in a gradual deceleration before the concluding restatement of the opening guitar gesture.

'Phase Dance', which on the studio album is performed in exactly the same tempo as 'San Lorenzo', became a popular opening number in the Metheny Group's live gigs. The piece in its original form was written

EX. 3.5 'San Lorenzo': closing section (SB, 60). © 1979 Pat Meth Music Corp. and Lyle Mays, Inc. All rights reserved.

in 1976 by Metheny, who tried it out first with his brother Mike and then with Burton. An experiment in applying Nashville tuning to a jazz idiom, it was esteemed by Metheny as an early example of a number that would work well in live performance and 'clearly define what we were looking for.'[22] In *Pat Metheny Group*, the instrument used was a Guild D-40C, a classic acoustic dreadnought much favoured by country and blues players, Metheny's example of which was furnished with a Bill Lawrence pickup.[23] Interviewed in 1990, Metheny singled out 'Phase Dance'—along with later compositions such as 'Are You Going with Me?' (*Offramp*), 'Last Train Home' (*Still Life (Talking)*), and the title tracks of *First Circle* and *Letter from Home*—as an example of a highly personal tune that provided him with seemingly endless potential for improvisation: 'There's a kind of resonance between the three chords, and the way they modulate from one to the next.'[24] The three chords are essentially B minor, B♭ major, and G major, with extensions, organized in the pattern shown schematically in Example 3.6. In the central improvised solos, each chord is prolonged for 4 bars. As Douglas J. Noble points out, the characteristic use of B♭ major with added seventh and sharp eleventh directly recalls 'Bright Size Life'.[25] In the earlier piece, the chord was also juxtaposed with a G major harmony, but in an overall tonal context of D major rather than B minor. The same basic harmony is also a feature of 'Phase Dance': see Example 3.7 below.

The title 'Phase Dance' seemingly alludes to the minimalist techniques of Steve Reich, a composer with whose music Metheny became involved in the 1980s (see Chapter 6). Jazz riffs and the ostinato patterns of minimalism—and, indeed, earlier 20th-century styles heavily based on ostinati—have much in common, and the distinctive textures of 'Phase Dance' derive from superimposed patterns in which the metrical dislocations alternately converge and diverge: see Example 3.7, from the introduction (in which, when performed in Nashville tuning, the lower part of the upper guitar strand sounds an octave higher). The dyadic guitar ostinato echoes an accompanying

22 *Pat Metheny Song Book*, 439. In Nashville tuning, the lowest four strings of a six-string guitar are replaced with strings of a lighter gauge (e.g., from a set of strings intended for a 12-string guitar), which sound one octave higher than they do in the orthodox tuning. Nashville tuning was also used effectively in several tracks on *New Chautauqua*, discussed later in this chapter.

23 Forte, 'Garage Band'.

24 Aledort, 'Pat Metheny: Straight Ahead', 62.

25 Douglas J. Noble, 'Pat Metheny: Guitar Techniques', *Guitar Magazine* 2/5 (August 1992): 78.

EX. 3.6 'Phase Dance': harmonic reduction (AT).

EX. 3.7 'Phase Dance': introduction (SB, 42; repeat marks added).

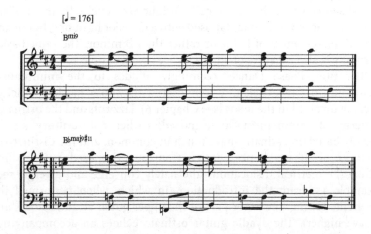

pattern briefly sounded by Metheny immediately before he starts his solo on the Burton Quartet's recording with Weber of the latter's 'Yellow Fields' (*Passengers*).[26] The substantial coda to 'Phase Dance', based on this same syncopated pattern, is a fine example of the gradual process of

26 Panisset and Moulin, *Pat Metheny: Improvisations*, 13.

intensification which characterizes much music by the Metheny Group, with the ostinati—which can be made to fit any prevailing harmony with ease—recommencing in low tessitura and crescendoing through a strong chord progression that touches on various harmonic areas not yet explored (including C major, F major, D minor, D♭ major, B♭ minor, G♭ major, and E major); the ostinati also rise in tessitura until this protracted journey towards the luminous terminal F major is clinched by a quadruple repetition of a climactic synthesizer melody (Ex. 3.8). The rising fifths and fourths of this Oberheim theme are an unexpected but nonetheless satisfying expansion of a motif hinted at by the keyboards earlier in the piece.

Given the popularity of both the piece and the album on which it was featured, it comes as little surprise that Metheny's solo in 'Phase Dance' was one of the first to be transcribed and appear in print. Of the several (rather different) early transcriptions, that by Mark L. Small is prefaced by a brief commentary outlining some of the performer's characteristics.[27] A later, uncredited transcription of the guitar part of the entire track offers considerably more detail of rhythmic subtleties and guitar techniques, and presents the music in tablature beneath the staff notation, but without any supporting commentary.[28] In his remarks, Small identifies a number of orthodox jazz techniques in the solo: anticipation of the beginnings of bars by a semiquaver, fluent phrasing across barlines, playing variously ahead of and behind the beat, introducing a chord change early, and concentrating on upper extensions of the chords ('tension' notes). To Small's list might be added double-time flourishes (some are of the generic type identified in Ex. 2.3), and the use of riffs, dyads, and triads as intensifying devices. At the conclusion of the solo, these last two features are combined with a climactic allusion to the opening ostinati: see Example 3.9a.

Although marked 'open' in the published version, the guitar and piano solos on the album, and at the Travels and San Francisco gigs, each last for three choruses. In all three performances, the introduction, theme, and coda follow an identical plan, but there is considerable variety in the

---

27 Mark L. Small, 'Pat Metheny: Solo in "Phase Dance"', Guitar Player (December 1981): 92–3. Small's transcription of the solo was published well before the appearance of the Pat Metheny Song Book, and adopts a different metre from the published lead sheet.

28 The transcription was appended to an interview Metheny gave to Andy Aledort in Guitar Extra! (spring 1990): 56–75. It is incorrectly described as the live version on Travels, and is in fact based on the studio performance on Pat Metheny Group. The opening section of the Travels performance, but not the solo, were transcribed by Noble in 'Pat Metheny: Guitar Techniques', 78–80.

central improvisations; the interpretation on *Travels* is at a somewhat sprightlier tempo than the other two, though it slackens a little in the second half of the coda when the dynamic level drops at rehearsal figure D before the final build-up. Two readily comprehensible compositional strategies help articulate the overall structure. First, in several of the solos the ostinati from the introduction are reintroduced as a ritornello-like linking device during the final 8 bars: this occurs exclusively in the piano solos on both the studio album and San Francisco performance (and, since the piano solo always follows the guitar solo, it neatly paves the way for the recapitulation of the theme which follows), but in *Travels* the ostinati reappear at the end of both guitar and piano solos. Second, in the two later recordings (but not at the early San Francisco gig) a slowly rising scale is sounded by the synthesizer during the third chorus of the guitar solo for added textural interest. Example 3.9a shows the scale as it appears in the studio recording, where its effect is that of a slowed-down reminiscence of the faster ascent previously used by Metheny as a 4-bar lead-in to the beginning of his solo, as shown in Example 3.9b.

EX. 3.9a AND 3.9b 'Phase Dance': rising scales (AT). © 1979 Pat Meth Music
Corp. and Lyle Mays, Inc. All rights reserved.

(cont.)

'Jaco' was written for same 1976 gig with Mike Metheny as 'Phase Dance' and owed its title to the fact that the main chordal lick of the melody is coincidentally like the horn line in Pastorius's funky tune 'Come On, Come Over' (the second track on his debut album, *Jaco Pastorius*). The introduction and coda—or intro and outro, in jazz parlance—hailed from a different piece, dating from 1971, which Metheny and Mays 'spruced up harmonically' during the Metheny Group's first year of touring.[29] The structure is relatively simple and arch-like: the

29 *Pat Metheny Song Book*, 439.

riff-based intro and outro frame a main theme and two straight-ahead solos based on its changes, for guitar then bass, each lasting for two choruses. Metheny's solo is accompanied discreetly by Mays on piano, who lays out for the bass solo, which is supported by guitar; Gottlieb's restrained backbeats maintain rhythmic tautness throughout, and the chordal lick returns as punctuation between each principal section. Egan here plays his bass close to the bridge for an incisive delivery, in contrast to the mellow lyrical manner he demonstrates elsewhere. Gottlieb recalls the recording of 'Jaco' as an early example of tension growing between Metheny and Eicher, since the allotted day-and-a-half of recording time had come to an end before Metheny had found an opportunity to play the piece: Eicher allowed the group strictly one additional take only, which was in the event used (even though Gottlieb now cheerfully admits to having dropped a stick during Metheny's solo and 'you can hear me sloshing round on the cymbals for a few beats while I picked up another one').[30] But the tensions may have been symptomatic of the essential difference between Metheny's recordings for ECM and the other artists with whom Eicher worked. Metheny had already perfected what he wanted his band's music to sound like on the road and could simply record 'documentary' takes, which allowed relatively little room for creative input from a producer.

The main theme's changes coincidentally preserve some commonality with those of 'San Lorenzo', since they are coloured by successive semitone descents of roots from D♭ to C, and A♭ to G. Another audible link with 'San Lorenzo' is the prominent use of parallel fifths, which occur immediately after the chordal lick and return more obsessively at the beginning of the outro. At the opening, the guitar's syncopated riffs are characterized by cross-metre shifting accents, with more than a hint of minimalism, and both these and the high bass melody they accompany are pandiatonic, being exclusively made up from white notes (C major in the guitar and F pentatonic in the bass); the effect is folk-like. After the sudden shift into C minor when the chordal lick first appears (b. 18), the music remains in this key after the main theme and solos have run their course. The guitar licks from the opening therefore reappear in the outro based on E♭ rather than C, but with the piano and bass harmonizing them with strongly directional jazz chords held over from the main theme and now rotating in the pattern Cmi7 – A♭maj9

---

30 Personal communication from Danny Gottlieb via email, July 9, 2014.

– D♭maj7 – G+7 – (Cmi7, etc.). This is a deft and readily comprehensible mechanism for uniting two bodies of material which were derived from independent compositions with little in common.

The track listing of the next two items, 'Aprilwind' and 'April Joy', is rather confusing. The former is not the composition Metheny later published under the title 'April Wind' but rather a short overdubbed guitar introduction to the eight-minute track labelled 'April Joy'. The second part of the latter, however, is in fact the composition 'April Wind' as it appears in the *Pat Metheny Song Book* (34–5). 'April Wind' differs from the other repertoire on the album in not having originated in live performances: it was written specifically for the recording 'as a kind of reprise to the "Phase Dance" motif that was such a part of the group's early identity'.[31] The syncopated riffs from 'Phase Dance' (see Ex. 3.7 above) are reintroduced beneath the solos and continue without resolution into the piece's fade-out ending; they are related rhythmically to the oscillating diatonic sixths which open 'April Wind' and accompany its melody, the latter characterized by what Metheny termed 'a kind of simple diatonic harmony that was popular in the pop music of the time and that I still really love to play over.'[32] Metheny praised Gottlieb's drumming in this track, especially his rendering of its 'little rock vamp'.[33]

The first half of the track 'April Joy', later published as an independent piece with this same title,[34] is a particularly early work, composed in 1972 for the Kansas City Jazz Festival while Metheny was still a teenager. As with another early piece, 'Bright Size Life', it features a florid up-beat pattern at the start of the melody, which is slightly truncated in the recorded version. Like many of his first compositions, the theme's main purpose was to serve as a vehicle for improvisation; less typically, however, it had already been recorded before its ECM outing, on *Winter Love, April Joy* by vibraphonist David Friedman and flutist Hubert Laws in 1975.[35] Introduced by Friedman's 'Exercise #5', the rendering of Metheny's tune by Laws's flute, Friedman's parallel fourths, and the general air of bubbling virtuosity all combine to suggest the soundworld of Corea's contemporaneous music with Return to Forever—an association which Metheny is unlikely to have intended, however, in spite of

31 *Pat Metheny Song Book*, 439.
32 *Ibid.*
33 Mattingly, 'A Different View', 82.
34 *Pat Metheny Song Book*, 12.
35 *Ibid.*, 438.

the Corea-like shift from modality to a *tierce-de-picardie* major at the end of the theme's first strain. Metheny later commented that he felt this was his first successful tune as an improvisation-oriented composer.[36] For the Metheny Group recording of 'April Joy', Metheny wrote a fresh solo to showcase Egan's fretless playing, now locating this prominently as the introduction rather than (as had been the case on the road) featuring an improvised bass solo in the middle of the piece. The solo was written in Oslo on the night before the recording session, with Egan practising it overnight and subsequently doubling the live recording for added lushness.[37]

The album's final track, the samba 'Lone Jack', is another tune from the 1976 gig with Mike Metheny which Metheny updated with Mays in June 1977 by giving it a new interlude and coda (a variation on the interlude).[38] Described by Metheny as an 'easy, fun tune to play', this is the most conventionally structured composition on the album: the tune is essentially a 32-bar song form (notated in 64 bars of rapid tempo) following the orthodox AABA pattern, and was likened by *Down Beat* to a hard-bop number.[39] There is a notable contrast between the stable, predominantly modal, harmonic language of the A strain and the far more active harmonic progression in the bridge (B), in which the bass ascends rapidly by step. Guitar and piano solos are based on the tune's harmonic changes, although once more Mays's solo sets out from a leisurely pedal point. The most prophetic feature of the piece is the interlude, in which even more propulsive harmonic motion, featuring parallel slash chords, is allied to sharp and catchy metrical displacement: see the scored-out realisation of the passage in Example 3.10. Writing of this kind, which was to be encountered again in several later Metheny Group pieces, arose here from an out-take on *Bright Size Life* in which Metheny moved a single grip of sus4 chords around the neck of the 12-string guitar; this was later transformed into a synth

36 Niles, *Pat Metheny Interviews*, 146. During the course of these interviews, Niles suggested that 'April Joy' reflected the 'feel' and 'phrasing' of Wes Montgomery's 'Windy' (*ibid.*, 19).

37 Personal communication from Mark Egan via email, July 11, 2014. In his notes on the published version of 'April Wind', Metheny states that the tune was intended to showcase the Pastorius-like sound of Egan's bass playing, but the bass melody serves as the introduction to the composite piece recorded under the title 'April Joy' and does not appear in the *Pat Metheny Song Book* versions of either 'April Joy' or 'April Wind'.

38 *Pat Metheny Song Book*, 439.

39 Stern, review of *Pat Metheny Group*.

version using four-voice technology to generate a roving interval stack with single fingers on the keyboard. 'Lone Jack' was recorded many years later on Metheny's album *Trio 99→00* (2000), where the guitarist supplies more chordal playing—notably in the interlude—in the absence of a keyboard part, thereby restoring the harmonic parallelism to its original incarnation.

After recording *Pat Metheny Group*, the band returned to North America and resumed touring, now with an album to launch: the release date had been set for July 12, 1978. Both Metheny's own trademark Lexicon-delayed sound and the freshness of his group's musical idiom garnered considerable attention, a review of a performance in Montreal in June 1978 declaring that the music could not be called jazz-rock because of its avoidance of commercial clichés, and that Metheny had in fact 'invented his own music'.[40] For his part, at around this time Metheny asserted that improvisation remained of crucial importance,

---

40 *Montreal Gazette*, June 1978, quoted (in Italian translation) in Viva, *Pat Metheny*, 75.

noting that it was avoided by many jazz-rock artists, and that his interest in arrangement and composition primarily served to create space for improvisations.[41]

NEW CHAUTAUQUA

Metheny's first solo recording, made in August 1978 after the end of a long tour with his band, is characterized by several significant stylistic developments. *New Chautauqua* for the first time embodied a prominent 'Americana' dimension, partly as a result of a fresh perspective on his homeland occasioned by having spent more than half the previous year touring in Europe.[42] In addition to its innovative reworking of musical elements that fall under the broad (and not especially helpful) label of 'country' music, rather than deriving from mainstream jazz styles, the album was also notable for its overdubbing of multiple guitar lines, a sometimes diatonic harmonic language based on simple triads, and a quasi-minimalist use of ostinato patterns. Overall, as in all Metheny's music, a sensitive balance is achieved across the album as a whole between slowly changing (and sometimes static) harmonies enriched and enlivened by surface textures of varying complexity, contrastingly dynamic and rich harmonic progressions, finely shaped and memorable melodies, and occasionally overt pop influences with a distinctly contemporary flavour.

Country elements in jazz had previously surfaced in Burton's 1966 album *Tennessee Firebird* (on the tracks 'Faded Love' and Bob Dylan's 'I Want You') and the vibraphonist had also utilized overdubbing in the same year's *The Time Machine*. In 1967, Burton was playing with Coryell, who had in the 1950s been influenced by country guitarist Chet Atkins, whose example inspired him to play 'finger style' in a mix of country, classical, and jazz techniques. Burton had spent some time in Nashville as a teenager during the summer of 1960 and he was later to draw broad parallels between jazz and country music on account of their shared rhythmic drive, improvised solos, and 'an enormous respect for instrumental skill and creativity' on the part of the players.[43] In Metheny's case, Lee's Summit had introduced him to non-jazz methods of guitar playing from a very early age, and he first heard the instrument in local amateur country and bluegrass sessions, which also featured mandolin and banjo. Lee's Summit—where players were universally

---

41 *Ibid.*, 79.
42 http://www.patmetheny.com/qa/questionView.cfm?queID=3964 (September 1, 2014).
43 Burton, *Learning to Listen*, 37. On *Tennessee Firebird*, see *ibid.*, 147.

in awe of the great mandolinist and founding father of bluegrass, Bill
Monroe—was described by Metheny as

> the centre of the country music aesthetic. Around town there were
> guitars everywhere. I remember at the local barbershop there would
> be all these guitars hanging on the walls and when there were no
> customers, they'd pick them up and all play. So, my first exposure to
> the guitar was a combination of the Beatles—the rock and roll thing,
> and the country thing.[44]

Specifically, Metheny became interested in both the strumming
techniques and strongly triadic harmonic language of the music he
heard, and later came to realize that both had been sorely neglected in
jazz guitar playing:

> I realized that one of the things I loved most about the guitar was the
> sound of strumming . . . At that point in jazz, nobody had really dealt
> much with strumming, although Gabor Szabo had a little . . . To have
> a jazz musician play music built around simple triads was somewhat
> unusual. Many jazz guys don't know how to play on very simple triads,
> without using upper extensions and tension notes, because in fact it
> is really hard. So, to do some really strongly triadic based songs was
> something that I wanted to really address. That stuff is what I loosely
> associate with the Mid-Western sound, the guys at the barbershop in
> my home town, my neighbor with his hootenannies, all those guys
> were playing triads. I always felt like, why can't that be part of the
> language? The guitar is great at those kind of sounds.[45]

The (often powerfully rhythmicized) strumming effects characterizing
his own music were a stark departure from jazz guitarists' traditional
tendency to concentrate on horizontal melodic lines and quasi-pianistic
chord voicings. And in Metheny's hands, dynamic strumming came
in some performances to be extended to considerable lengths, and in
consequence required great reserves of stamina more associated with
drumming than guitar playing.

Interviewed by his brother Mike in 1995, Metheny reflected about
the aesthetic impact on him of the midwestern landscapes in which he

44 Barth, *Voices in Jazz Guitar*, 312.
45 *Ibid.*, 326.

grew up, and stressed the importance of huge open spaces to the creative imagination.[46] In some respects, the watershed of his first encounter with the Miami ocean in 1972 may have been part of a similar liberating process. Both Metheny and Mays felt that what an interviewer once termed the 'remarkable sense of melody' which they shared was a midwestern attribute.[47] Another of Metheny's closest musical associates, Charlie Haden, shared his cultural and geographical background and described their later duo album, *Beyond the Missouri Sky* (recorded in 1996), as 'contemporary impressionistic americana'[48]—a concept broadly equivalent to what Metheny himself once termed his 'American heartland-whatever thing'.[49] In a note Metheny contributed to the booklet accompanying this recording, he placed his formative years in a wider perspective:

> Missouri. For me, as a kid growing up there, it was a place to dream. A place to sit out in the backyard and consider the possibilities of life and music while practicing as many hours as I could stay awake, staring out into those vast, midwestern spaces. But as much as I loved it there, it was also filled with a restlessness and curiosity about the whole world that I knew existed beyond that Missouri sky.[50]

The term 'pastoral jazz' has been used for certain kinds of music that seem consciously to avoid what the *Chicago Tribune* once called 'the jittery rhythms, metallic horns and surging energy of American cities'.[51] David Ake describes certain ECM recordings of the 1970s more specifically as 'Americanized pastoral jazz', and notes that this may be considered to be in part a reflection of 'the collectivist principles of the 1960s counterculture' when 'a highly visible, mostly white and middle-class, contingent of young people embraced the virtues of communal

---

46 Mike Metheny, 'Q&A with . . . Pat Metheny', *Jam* [*Jazz Ambassadors Magazine*], August/September 1995. http://www.kcjazzambassadors.com/issues/1995-08/q&ametheny.html (May 10, 2014).

47 Forte, 'Garage Band'.

48 Charlie Haden, liner notes to *Beyond the Missouri Sky* (Verve 537 130, 1997), 5. This warmly received album was partly responsible for February 25 being celebrated as Charlie Haden/Pat Metheny Day in Missouri in the late 1990s: see Goins, *Emotional Response*, 90. For further on Haden's midwestern background and its connection to Metheny, see Forte, 'Jazz Voice of the 80's', 91.

49 Quoted in Tom Moon, 'Pat Metheny Gets Serious', *JazzTimes* 23/6 (July/August 1993): 27.

50 Pat Metheny, liner notes to *Beyond the Missouri Sky*, 9.

51 Geoffrey Himes, 'Hybrid Harmony: Bill Frisell Pitches His Tent at the Intersection of Country and Jazz', *Chicago Tribune*, April 20, 2001, 3; quoted in Ake, *Jazz Matters*, 81.

agrarian living'; he also notes that some rock musicians turned from blues-based idioms to country-inspired material, this cultural shift being reflected in the folk-oriented images of their album covers.[52] Ake discusses Jarrett's contribution to the pastoral-jazz aesthetic (after setting the scene with the much later homage to it by Bill Frisell, in his 1997 album *Nashville*) before moving on to consider *New Chautauqua*. He relates the album's music to the iconography of its artwork, which includes a photographic portrait of the smiling guitarist—sitting on a wooden stool by a window, and bathed in sunlight—as 'casual, youthful, genial, and unmistakably white', in sharp contrast to the predominantly serious depictions of (urban-rooted) African American jazz musicians in album artwork from the 1950s onwards.[53] *Down Beat*'s condescending review of *New Chautauqua*, which seemingly missed the entire point of the project, cited the race factor even more explicitly by referring to the music as 'a cleanly orchestrated rhapsody in white, bearing none but the most tangential relationship to Afro-American traditions'.[54]

The genial photograph of Metheny on the rear of the album's sleeve belies the fact that the front-cover artwork caused something of a heated in-house dispute. Metheny had chosen three potential images from the portfolio of Dieter Rehm, two depicting evening cloudscapes, and the third 'the mysterious headlights of a car emerging from a dark wood'.[55] Eicher decided that the cloudscapes were 'too sweet for Pat's music' and, as a result, designers Rehm and Wojirsch replaced this concept with 'a stretch of stark and unromantic highway, while Pat floated in the sky in the form of a negative silhouette', with the resulting 'greenish picture . . . framed in shrill red'.[56] (See Fig. 3.2.) ECM staff were excited about the design, but Metheny had not been consulted—and felt the combined images, which he greatly disliked, made him look like the disembodied spirit of the victim of a fatal road accident. His attempt to have the cover altered was unsuccessful. Interestingly,

52 Ake, *Jazz Matters*, 82. See also Gabriel Solis's response to Ake's text in his book *Thelonious Monk Quartet with John Coltrane at Carnegie Hall* (New York: Oxford University Press, 2014), 153. Mark Gilbert uses the term 'rural fusion' to characterize this aspect of Metheny's and Frisell's work: see Alexander, *Masters of Jazz Guitar*, 107.

53 Ake, *Jazz Matters*, 90. For Ake's discussions of Frisell and Jarrett, see *ibid.*, 80–82 and 85–8, respectively.

54 Larry Birnbaum, review of Pat Metheny, *New Chautauqua*, *Down Beat* 46/9 (September 6, 1979): 36.

55 Lake and Griffiths, *Horizons Touched*, 179.

56 *Ibid.* On Metheny's views on appropriate cover artwork for his post-ECM albums, see his interview with Jeff Charney for *Contemporary Jazz* (February 15, 2002): http://www.contemporaryjazz.com/interviews/pat-metheny-2002 (July 18, 2014).

FIG. 3.2 *New Chautauqua* sleeve art. Design by Dieter Rehm and Barbara Wojirsch. © ECM Records, 1979. Used by permission.

Ake—who does not recount this background story—nevertheless finds the highway cover 'in keeping with the rustic setting' of the itinerant New Chautauqua movement which had inspired the album, and in his account he emphasizes the trees and green fields situated at the edge of the image, which are in reality completely dwarfed by the yawningly empty stretch of charcoal-grey asphalt road receding into the vanishing point of infinity.

In an interview recorded in 1979 to promote his ECM albums (and discussed further below), Metheny commented that he felt *New Chautauqua* to be a highly personal record that celebrated growing up in the simplicity and clarity of the countryside, with its wide open spaces; the opening title track, he said, combined country strumming with a solo which contained 'elements of development and all that kind of thing that I like to have in all my music'.[57] The strummed 'heartland' idiom is unleashed wholeheartedly in this track, which explicitly connects with the Midwest in deriving its title from the name of Metheny's great-grandfather's travelling musical/evangelical group, a branch of the still continuing Chautauqua organization who toured the region, and which was also inspired by nostalgia for Lee's Summit.[58] The piece is in the guitar's characteristically bright 'home' key of E major; the music is mostly diatonic (apart from two flat-seven Mixolydian inflections) and makes plentiful use of tonic pedals. The tune's riff-based hook suggests pop influences, and is harmonized both with a strongly directional bass line—performed by Metheny himself on electric bass as part of the multi-tracking process—and, at the end, in the alternating diatonic triads over a pedal point first heard in the introduction: see Examples 3.11a and 3.11b, respectively. The first of these passages is preceded by classic bluegrass-style pickup notes in the bass, ascending by step from to $\hat{5}$ to $\hat{1}$ in straight crotchets.

A homespun quality pervades the aptly titled 'Country Poem', which was improvised in the studio and is one of several tracks on the album conceived for a Guild DN 40C acoustic guitar strung in the Nashville manner: the effect is also to be heard on the title track and 'Sueño con Mexico'.[59] So folk-like are both the bright timbre and musical idiom, in which chords are in certain passages animated by banjo-style roulades, that one reviewer (incorrectly) deduced that the piece had been based on the Appalachian folk tune 'Cumberland Gap'.[60] Typically, even in this miniature the completely pandiatonic opening is followed by contrastingly directional functional harmonies.

The far more substantial 'Long Ago Child/Fallen Star' which follows was conceived as essentially a chord progression that could serve as a basis for overdubbing to create what Metheny termed 'a textural piece', which he recalled was an approach encouraged by Eicher at this time.[61] The concept is broadly similar to that which had prompted 'Sea Song' on *Watercolors*. A rubato delivery shapes a slow rate of harmonic change before the texture is enlivened by cross-rhythm syncopations which make the music more active than would otherwise be suggested by a

---

57 *An Hour with Pat Metheny: A Radio Special* (1979).
58 *Pat Metheny Song Book*, 439.
59 Forte, 'Pat Metheny—Jazz Voice of the 80's', 107. For a definition of Nashville tuning, see note 22 above.
60 Birnbaum, review of *New Chautauqua*, 36.
61 *Pat Metheny Song Book*, 439.

EX. 3.11a AND 3.11b 'New Chautauqua': closing section (3.11a) and coda (3.11b) (ASB, 62-3). © 1979 Pat Meth Music Corp. All rights reserved.

slow or static harmonic rhythm: the central section prolongs a single minor chord (plus ninth) in second inversion for some considerable time, with a plangent Aeolian melody improvised above. Then highly evocative *bisbigliando* textures with a ravishingly beautiful sound quality support a lyrical acoustic solo. 'Fallen Star' uses the 15-string harp guitar that had also been featured in 'Oasis' from *Watercolors*.

Both the lilting syncopations and tonic F that bring 'Fallen Star' to a close serve as audible links into the beginning of the next track, 'Hermitage' (named after a club in Austria), which develops the syncopations as an accompaniment to the new tune and prolongs the same tonal region until the second half shifts firmly down a semitone to E minor. As Metheny expressed it, the piece is based on 'a simple arpeggio and a few deceptive modulations before the minor-key hook at the end.'[62] The pop feel in this number derives as much from the syncopated parallel triads in the second half of the head as from the melodic hook, and triads are also prominent in the solo. The tune's structure is a 32-bar song form in which the 8-bar A strain is developed both melodically and harmonically on its immediate restatement, and the second 16 bars themselves embody a miniature AABA form in which each segment is 4 bars in length. Particularly characteristic twists are the unexpected shifts from E7/F to G♯mi9 in the reharmonisation of the first 8 bars, and from Cmaj7 to A/B (i.e., B9sus4) at the end of the clinching hook.

'Sueño con Mexico' is based on two simple chords and their arpeggios; Metheny pointed out that the bass is altered 'to give different meanings to the chords', and noted that this was one of the few pieces he wrote in this early period which were based on ostinati.[63] Here the multiply repeated patterns again look ahead to the interest in minimalism in his later music (discussed in Chapter 6). Typical of Metheny's harmonic and textural acumen are the strong contrast between repetitions of just two diatonic chords (Cadd2 and Gmaj7/D) and the more directional changes later in the piece, inextricably linked to an unexpected shift from the enlivening of harmonic stasis by rhythmicized textures to a strongly moving functional bass line (Ex. 3.12a). Towards the close of the solo, a haunting moment of relaxation combines the two approaches by interpolating simple bass notes into the texture to create yet further poignant reharmonisations of the basic ostinato pattern (Ex. 3.12b).

---

62 *Ibid.*, 439. The piece also appears as the opening track on Charlie Haden's *Quartet West* (Verve 831 673, 1987).
63 *Pat Metheny Song Book*, 439.

(a)

(cont.)

After its long and rhapsodic introduction, more relaxed strumming and a pop influence—in this case, the Beatles—are the driving forces behind the album's final track, 'Daybreak', though the twists and turns in the changes (and delicate echo effects in harmonics) are characteristic solely of Metheny. Here the opening of the melody (Ex. 3.13a) recalls that of 'Hermitage' (Ex. 3.13b), although the harmonisation is different, and a fleeting link into the second chorus of the last track's solo harks back to the soundworld of 'Bright Size Life' (Ex. 3.14; cf. Ex. 2.4a, which also occurs in an anacrusic position in the structure of the theme). In both the (probably subconscious) allusions to other pieces and its simple yet memorable melody, the track brings the album to a satisfying close.

New Chautauqua was released in April 1979 while Metheny's regular ensemble was again intensively touring in America, and sold 200,000 copies in just four months. This recording and *Pat Metheny Group* were both featured on a special promotional disc issued by ECM (in March 1979) for use on radio stations and entitled *An Hour with Pat Metheny*. The disc interleaved segments of a Metheny interview with the tracks 'Phase Dance', 'San Lorenzo', 'New Chautauqua', 'Sueño con Mexico', and 'Daybreak' (though the last was not included in the track listing on the label). Speaking over part of a playback of 'Jaco', Metheny began by

EX. 3.13a 'Daybreak': opening (SB, 68). © 1979 Pat Meth Music Corp. All rights reserved.

EX. 3.13b 'Hermitage': opening (SB, 64). © 1979 Pat Meth Music Corp. All rights reserved.

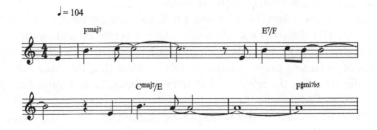

EX. 3.14 'Daybreak': fifths (AT).

discussing the balance between rock elements and improvisation in his group's music:

> obviously a lot of rock'n'roll is geared to people just entering puberty— and that's good. That music can really stimulate those old hormones, you know. Our music has elements of that sort of power and rhythmic stuff, but at the same time we try and keep the tradition of improvising in mind too; with all the emphasis on, sort of, sexual music or kind of pounding music, people have lost a lot of the possibilities of nuance and subtlety, and what we're trying to do is have both elements.

He went on to describe how he got to know progressive-rock albums at the age of 15 but found them 'just awful'; the players were not improvising, but merely 'playing blues scales up and down', just as he felt rock players always did, only for considerably longer 'and twice as boring'. He then fell under the spell of Jimi Hendrix, being especially struck by his rhythmic sense, which he could not begin to imitate on the hollow-bodied guitars that were his preference at the time. He noted that the creative potential of the guitar had been neglected in jazz until Coryell joined Burton in 1967, then it all 'exploded' with the rise of McLaughlin and others; until Metheny's own debut as leader, only Burton, Jack DeJohnette, and Chico Hamilton were actively featuring the instrument in their front lines. Metheny partly blamed a lack of technological advancement for this neglect, because the standard guitar sound was perceived as dull and always seemed like it was coming from a 'little box on the stage'. It was Coryell's 'overtone-rock-groove sound . . . in the context of a jazz group . . . that probably was what opened the doors'.

Later in the interview, Metheny predicted that commercial success might well lie ahead but was adamant that he 'never would make a change musically' in order to achieve it, and spoke appreciatively of growing signs of increasing public interest in 'subtle' music that has 'more than a few chords'. After the release of *Pat Metheny Group*, he had immediately been wary of falling into the trap of always having to top the success of his previous album, and for this reason he thought the solo *New Chautauqua* project—which Eicher encouraged—would help to prevent him from becoming typecast. Eicher's support remained crucial, but there were already signs of independent thinking on Metheny's part that would ultimately lead to his break from ECM, as he hinted in an interview he gave in 1978 which discussed the group's plans for a new album:

'If Manfred had his way, every album he did would be six ballads and a bossa nova for an up tune,' he says laughing. 'There are some problems for me with ECM, but it's still 50 times better than anything else. To me the only real fault is that Manfred tends to choose artists who don't know how to swing. This next record is going to be definitely very American, very pop—meaning, I think, the way the drums are recorded. It's something that I'm sure Manfred is capable of producing, but it's a question of whether or not he's really interested in doing it.'

Even though Metheny finds himself moving into more dynamic musical modes—away from the austere intellectuality that he feels characterizes some of the ECM output—it's not toward anything remotely related to what could be called the current jazz-rock-funk sellout.

'Many of the jazz-rock bands are not jazz bands in the sense of being improvisers. And my number one priority is to be an improviser at this point. Although, as I was telling you, I'm feeling more and more drawn to orchestrated and arranged things, I want them to be unusual orchestrations and unusual arrangements with room for improvisation.'[64]

In discussing his move towards a more American sound, Metheny singled out 'San Lorenzo' and 'Phase Dance' as reflecting his 'leaning all the time toward rock—not rock, exactly—but a more American influence'.[65]

AMERICAN GARAGE

The next album indeed proved to be 'very American', as its title boldly announced, and in places 'very pop'. As shown at the end of this chapter, however, this initiative was in some critical quarters seriously misunderstood, since the music was perceived to fall between the two stools of authentic jazz and commercial fusion rather than being celebrated on its own terms as another (rather startling) example of what the Montreal critic, as we saw above, deemed to be '[Metheny's] own music'. Given the

64 Smith, 'Ready to Tackle Tomorrow', 53.
65 *Ibid.*, 23.

vivid contemporary resonances that characterised this particular project, the album's fresh and predominantly energetic idiom was a clear and resolute reflection of the 'new paradigm' concept explored in Chapter 1.

The new album marked Metheny's first foray into production without the presence of Eicher, whom he felt (in addition to the reservations expressed in the quotation above) was interested in making albums quickly for the sake of economy. As Metheny insisted on an increased experimentation with electronics and unusual instrumentation from everyone in the band, he wanted more time in which to develop his conception of the direction in which he wanted the music to go; as a result, he produced this album himself (with Eicher billed on the sleeve as executive producer). Seeking a recommendation for a good sound engineer, Metheny called on his former student Richard Niles, who after Berklee had spent the second half of the 1970s producing records in London. Niles recalls that the guitarist at this time felt restricted by Eicher's 'purist production methods', which meant that everything was 'recorded live with superb microphones in superb studios with expensive sounding reverbs'.[66] For the first time in Metheny's recording career, the new album would feature a very different set of production techniques.

American Garage was recorded in June 1979 by sound engineer Kent Nebergall, who had been recommended by Niles and was duly hired on the strength of examples of his previous work, including an impressive recording by Rita Coolidge. The sessions took place at the Long View Farm studio in North Brookfield, Massachusetts, instead of at ECM's regular Oslo and Ludwigsburg facilities. (The Long View Farm studio was later a favourite rehearsal venue for the Rolling Stones.) Although Metheny later came to feel that the release was not entirely successful,[67] *American Garage* was significant in reflecting a more overtly American spirit in its heartland-influenced sounds, which followed on naturally from the precedent of *New Chautauqua*. The album also incorporated some tongue-in-cheek humour (a trend later to climax in the riotous 'Forward March' of *First Circle*) and an even greater degree of compositional planning than had prevailed hitherto. Metheny recalled that the initiative to record 'a record in America with a sort of American

---

66 I am grateful to Richard Niles for sharing his recollections of the *American Garage* sessions, which may be seen in full at 'Working on *American Garage* with The Pat Metheny Group (1979)', http://richardniles.com (July 30, 2014).

67 Metheny told Ian Carr in 1998 ('Bright Size Life', episode 3) that *American Garage* was flawed sonically, and represented 'the worst of the group' in both its rhythm-section playing and the inclusion of certain 'poor' tunes. See also Viva, *Pat Metheny*, 81.

'sound' and the need to play 'some more rock-out stuff' arose from a desire to document on disc a distinctively nationalistic kind of material which the Metheny band had already been playing live but had not yet recorded: 'we had to get it out of our system'.[68] The album's full-colour cover photo (a stock shot by Joel Meyerowitz, incorporated in a design by Basil Pao) was a vivid picture of shiny chrome 'Airstream' trailers in a US caravan park (Fig. 3.3), which donated their brand name to one of the album's tracks. The image on the rear of the sleeve, by Rob Van Petten, depicted the band in a typical domestic garage—sporting characteristic long hair and jeans, and

PAT METHENY GROUP

AMERICAN GARAGE

FIG. 3.3 *American Garage* sleeve art. Design by Basil Pao; photograph by Joel Meyerowitz. © ECM Records, 1979. Used by permission.

68 Forte, 'Jazz Voice of the 80's', 113-14.

with Mays's basic electric-keyboard/amplifier setup supporting a baseball glove and ball. Van Petten's original image is shown in Figure 3.4a, and as it appeared on the rear of the album's sleeve in Figure 3.4b.

Van Petten's image had originally been intended to grace the album's front cover and was significantly cropped when reproduced instead on the rear. The subtle colour tinting in the original—added in oils by the photographer's then wife, Patti Roberts, to provide dashes of yellow and green on Egan's and Mays's shirts, and to bring out a few other details—was also removed by the decision to print the cropped image in monochrome. This change of plan may well have arisen because the photograph is so unashamedly suggestive of rock music and therefore out of keeping with customary ECM styles, both in terms of musical idiom and rarefied album packaging. Van Petten, a keen guitarist himself who became good friends with Metheny, vividly remembers 'the wildness of shooting this cutting edge jazz ensemble reverting to elemental rock roots playing "Wipeout" and "Pipeline", "Louie Louie" and "Hang on Sloopy"'.[69] The live performance for the camera was ear-piercingly loud and all concerned were in very high spirits, with infectious laughter threatening to sabotage the success of the shoot. Metheny and Van Petten had conceived the idea of portraying the band 'playing in the open doorway of a typically tacky American garage scene' in the manner of 'a small time all American cover band', and during discussions Metheny mentioned his occasional frustrations when working with ECM's design team. The owner of the studio at Long View Farm suggested a neighbouring farm as the ideal location for the shoot, and whatever props happened to be to hand—including the Ford station wagon—were set up by Van Petten's assistant, Christopher Harting. Some of the lighting rigs were hidden behind the laundry hanging at the extreme right of the uncropped picture. During the deafening impromptu performance, all instruments were channelled through the single amplifier in the manner of low-budget amateur bands. As Van Petten puts it, 'We had reduced this erudite quartet to an impression of their most humble beginnings.'[70] In his 1979 promotional disc, Metheny recalled that, at the age of 13, he began to play in garage rock bands because he was disinclined to take formal grade exams on trumpet. This initiative, together with the trademark long hair, were

69 Personal communication from Rob Van Petten. I am greatly indebted to Mr Van Petten— and his friends Patti Roberts, Deborah Feingold, and Christopher Harting—for sharing their reminiscences of his various Metheny photoshoots.
70 *Ibid.*

(a)

(b)

PAT METHENY GROUP

1 (CROSS THE) HEARTLAND 6:51

2 AIRSTREAM 6:17

3 THE SEARCH 4:48

4 AMERICAN GARAGE 4:10

5 THE EPIC 12:59

PAT METHENY: 6 & 12-STRING GUITARS
LYLE MAYS: PIANO, OBERHEIM,
 AUTOHARP, ORGAN
MARK EGAN: BASS
DAN GOTTLIEB: DRUMS

℗ 1979 ECM RECORDS GMBH

ECM RECORDS
GLEICHMANNSTRASSE
10 MÜNCHEN 60

ECM   AAD
        (LC)2516

FIG. 3.4a   Rob Van Petten's original uncropped image for *American Garage*. © Rob Van Petten, 1979. Used by permission.

FIG. 3.4b   The cropped version of Rob Van Petten's *American Garage* photograph as it appeared on the rear of the ECM sleeve. © ECM Records, 1979. Used by permission.

part of a 'rebellious thing'; by the age of 14, however, he had heard both Montgomery and Burton playing in Kansas City and moved from rock'n'roll towards jazz, being drawn to instrumental jazz in particular because he thought jazz without singers was more 'vivid'.[71]

As it turned out, *American Garage* was in some respects recorded in a manner fairly close to the traditional ECM approach. Because the group had been playing much of the music on tour for nearly a year, they could for the most part record definitive versions of the tracks in first, second, or third takes. Metheny recalled that the entire second side of the original LP, for example, was 'recorded in as long as it takes to play it'.[72] The most ambitious track, 'The Epic', was at first patched together from different takes but, as Gottlieb recalled, 'we went back and played it another time in its entirety and that was the keeper'. Niles remembers that the first attempt to record 'The Epic' on the opening day of the sessions was unsatisfactory, and that rocking out on the encore tune that later became entitled 'American Garage' (and would donate its name to the album as a whole) cathartically loosened up the band and helped them recreate the formidable performance standards they had demonstrated in a live gig only the night before.[73] A few synthesizer parts had to be overdubbed 'for technical reasons', as they had been in the previous album, but all the solos on the album were recorded live.[74] Other creative studio techniques suggested by Niles are detailed in the account below.

A distinctively American soundscape is already suggested by the title of the first track, '(Cross the) Heartland'. The piece's origins lay in a number written by Mays for a gig at Ryle's in Cambridge, Massachusetts, in 1978, which was later adapted for the Metheny Group by including a bass interlude for Egan based on new harmonies penned by Metheny.[75] As in the opening of 'Jaco', a pulsating cross-metrical ostinato pattern accompanies a pentatonic folk-like melody, at first in the guitar which is then joined by the bass for a second strain, in which the theme's own metrical displacements combine with the ostinato's syncopations to create considerable rhythmic dynamism within the essentially static tonal field (Ex. 3.15). Also similar to the earlier piece is the distinctive soundworld poised between pulsating minimalism and the optimistic timbres of country music, and once more there is coincidentally a

71 *An Hour with Pat Metheny: A Radio Special.*
72 Forte, 'Garage Band'.
73 Niles, 'Working on *American Garage*'.
74 Forte, 'Garage Band'.
75 *Pat Metheny Song Book*, 439.

superficial similarity with the textures of some of Weather Report's repertoire (for example, the more ethnically coloured pentatonic synthesizer melody of the title track in *Black Market*, released in 1978). The bare fifths animated by the ostinato's syncopated rhythms were a direct reflection of the openness of American landscapes, Metheny further commenting that the album was a conscious attempt to get away not only from 'the thick, dense sound of so many jazz chords' but also to explore extended and unconventional forms.[76]

After the opening statements of the melody, the music enters a half-time feel in which the pentatonic theme is enriched by both melodic developments and the addition of strong supporting harmonies, both parameters emphasizing blue notes and plagal cadences which are alien to the melody's pentatonic scale: these two features both create a decidedly homespun quality appropriate to the album's broad concept, which at various stages in both this track and others is intensified by hot licks and effervescent glissandi on acoustic piano. The opening section is rounded off by a sequence of blunt, metrically displaced plagal cadences roving flatwards, before the opening ostinato proposition returns by way of interlude.

76 Barth, *Voices in Jazz Guitar*, 326.

The contrasting theme for Egan, written by Metheny, has something of the slow-moving and contemplative quality of certain of Weber's lyrical solos, and fluctuates between two modes (G Phrygian and G Dorian). The harmonic support here includes slash chords which echo the darker semitone patterns of the minor modes by sometimes superimposing major triads over roots which are a semitone lower (e.g., Eb/D and Ab/G). Although both harmonically and melodically this section is markedly different from the remainder of the piece, continuity is achieved by maintaining the bubbling ostinato throughout the entire minor theme, with appropriate harmonic modifications. Bass pentatonic patterns from the synthesizer steer the music back towards its opening tonal realm, eventually achieved after a trademark slow crescendo on a G pedal. Before the theme returns, however, an 'open' section (8 bars repeated ad lib.) is included for improvised solos: based on diatonic chords from the theme organized in a tightly circular pattern, this section seems intended less as a vehicle for extended bebop-like display than as a delightful pretext for a dose of high-spirited jamming in a garage vein. Segueing straight into three statements of the opening theme, the piece is rounded off by the displaced plagal cadences and pentatonic flourish which had closed the first section.

In both '(Cross the) Heartland' and the next track, 'Airstream', Mays plays a Yamaha CP-30 electric piano sparingly. Also featured on the album is the Yamaha YC-20 electric organ, which contributes significantly towards the garage mood, especially on the title track. Mays did not at this stage view electronic keyboard instruments as suitable vehicles for soloing, however, commenting in a 1980s interview that he'd 'die first' before contemplating performing solos on a synthesizer rather than his preferred acoustic piano. As Metheny wryly observed, 'It's funny, now we've got all those keyboards up there [on stage] and it looks real impressive, but the fact is, some of the keyboards he only plays, like, once a night for eight bars.'[77] Mays later explained that he felt the waveforms of the comparatively basic synthesizer sounds available at the time were far too simple to allow for the kind of emotional engagement possible on acoustic instruments such as violin or piano.[78]

77 Forte, 'Garage Band'. This source includes a detailed technical description of Mays's preferred keyboard and amplifier setup: he avoided piano pickups, which 'give the piano a real metallic, electronic sound', and preferred instead to close-mike the instrument and cover it with blankets. Mays concluded: 'I consider myself an acoustic piano player. I consider the other keyboards as orchestral devices, things to add color.' For a photograph of Mays's typical keyboard paraphernalia in the early 1980s, see Enwezor and Müller, ECM: A Cultural Archaeology, 161.
78 John Diliberto and Kimberly Haas, 'Lyle Mays: Straight Talk on Synths', Down Beat, 50/7 (July 1983): 26.

'Airstream' was based on a hook by Metheny, which he developed with Mays, later recalling that his keyboardist 'was able to help me define a context for this cool little musical idea'.[79] A pop-flavoured melodic accessibility is evident from the outset. The simple G major theme, first played by acoustic piano (in mid-register, with a gentle descant overlaid) and then repeated by guitar, begins in an amiable diatonic harmonisation but after 10 bars modulates to B♭ major. A more stately bass melody in A♭ major is then presented beneath Lydian-flavoured chordal writing for guitar and keyboards, the latter idea emerging in elaborated form as a brief statement of the hook, where the reliance on parallel triads recalls the texture of the segment of 'San Lorenzo' which Metheny compared to Weather Report (cf. Ex. 3.1). Metheny then takes a laid-back three-chorus solo on the theme's changes, now transposed into E♭, after which a linking passage ushers in a more harmonically elaborate and extended version of the hook which preserves the tertiary chord relationships of the theme (G to B♭) by now pulling from E♭ to G♭ major. After 8 bars of metrically displaced roving harmonies, the music once more stabilizes for two restatements of the principal theme, the first in E♭ and the second (after an abrupt shift) back in the opening key of G major. The latter key is quickly jettisoned, however, in favour of a fade-out ending in which repetitions of the extended version of the hook (again in its E♭/G♭ loop) serve as the foundation for solo jamming.

The reappearance of G major as the opening key of 'The Search', and indeed of the remaining two tracks on the album, might suggest that a degree of tonal consistency was planned for the project; but (as in 'Airstream') this tonality is simply a point of departure, and the music veers off into other regions, sometimes never to return. In 'The Search', a tertiary tonal relationship again prevails, this time in the shape of a shift from G to E major, the key in which the number concludes. The piece was written in response to a commission to accompany visual images for a high-school science series called 'The Search for Solutions', the nine episodes of which aired on PBS in April 1979.[80] This is another composition featuring an unconventional guitar tuning—the 12-string is tuned entirely in octaves upwards from the A below the normal lower E string, with all strings doubled an octave higher—and was also the first

79 *Pat Metheny Song Book*, 439.
80 A brief video clip from the series is available at http://www.patmetheny.com/film-scores/detail.cfm?id=67 (May 10, 2014). This clip includes footage of hot-air ballooning with a music cue including the melody of 'September Fifteenth' (later to be recorded on *Offramp*), and the end-credits sequence featuring 'The Search'.

Metheny Group item to feature Mays as a lead voice on the Oberheim synthesizer.[81] In spite of Mays's dislike of soloing on synthesizers discussed above, the Oberheim was to remain his preferred instrument for simple melodic statements until the advent of the Prophet 5, after which the Oberheim remained the instrument of choice for pads and what Metheny thought of as 'cello-like functions'.[82] The entire composition, in the album version, is dominated by the keyboards, both in the melodic passages (Oberheim) and the single solo (acoustic piano). Metheny's guitar provides bubbling quaver ostinati in the background, interlocking with the piano: the published lead sheet's simple designation 'arpeggiate chords'[83] for the 4-bar introduction gives little idea of the delicate cross-metrical patterns these arpeggiations embody in the recorded performance, and they blur the metre in a similar way to those in 'Sueño con Mexico' in *New Chautauqua*.

The distinctive texture of the closing guitar material on the album version (before Mays's second and final Oberheim melody) came about as a solution to a problematic moment in the piece—a point at which no melody was present, and at which a guitar solo might have seemed inappropriate. (In any case, as Metheny recalls, the 12-string strung in the way described above was not exactly conducive to freedom in improvisation.) Dealing with the need to find a creative solution to this structural challenge vividly demonstrated how beneficial it was to be working outside of the tight time restrictions that would have been required in a more typical ECM project and confirmed Metheny's growing view that his future recordings would need to be carried out at the pace required by the nature of the music. On this occasion, Metheny proceeded to improvise a melodic idea to tape, and he and Mays then transcribed it from the recording and harmonized it in three parts, the subsequent recording of the constituent parts taking longer than would normally have been possible on such an occasion.[84]

The version of the piece in the closing credits of the 'Search for Solutions' TV series concludes earlier, with a fade-out on the C major harmonies beneath the high inverted pedal E (which, on the album, is followed by the piano solo and a fresh melodic interlude developing

---

81 *Pat Metheny Song Book*, 439.
82 Diliberto and Haas, 'Lyle Mays', 25.
83 *Pat Metheny Song Book*, 75.
84 I am indebted to Pat Metheny for sharing his recollection of this occasion in detail with me. See also Niles, 'Working on *American Garage*', where the author comments that the resulting texture was 'a sound I've never heard on any other record since.'

the opening theme). The TV performance also features a buoyant bass countermelody, absent from the opening statement of the theme on the album, where drums and bass enter for the first time at the cadential inverted pedal.

The album's title track was developed by both Metheny and Mays on the basis of a lick for the bass line written by Metheny in 1975 for a concert with John McKee at Unity Village: 'This was another one that really kind of grew beyond the notes on the page from playing it night after night.'[85] More than any other number on the album, the resulting 'American Garage' encapsulates the sheer, noisy, energetic joie-de-vivre of Van Petten's memorable garage-ensemble photograph, to the point where Metheny told Niles (who had suggested they record it to break the ice in the studio): 'I'm not sure Manfred would want that tune on an ECM album.'[86] Asked in 1985 about the piece's 'unmistakable rock'n'roll feel', Metheny replied: 'that's about as close to out-and-out rock'n'roll as we'll probably ever get. But even in that tune, there's a big chunk in the middle that's like—O.K., we've done that and now we gotta come up with some stuff, and it's different every time.'[87] Metheny had a poor opinion of the playing in this track, however, describing it in 1989 as 'terrible' and 'truly close to maximum embarrassment'.[88] Ake feels that, for today's jazz listeners, 'the album's blithe earnestness may feel forced,' but also notes that this exuberant title track offers 'possibilities for a new kind of fusion', even a brand of 'punk jazz' (to use the term coined by Pastorius).[89]

The pounding rock beat of 'American Garage' suggests a comparison with the Beatles' energetic and chart-topping 'Get Back', released as a single in 1969—with Billy Preston contributing a bubbling solo on Fender Rhodes electric piano—a number which, perhaps significantly, began life in a heady jam session of the kind generically celebrated in Van Petten's album photo. Both the Beatles and Metheny Group tunes make prominent use of gospel-like plagal cadences: in the solo sections of 'American Garage', these punctuate the improvised line in time-honoured call-and-response fashion, and the final example rounds off the piece in a blaze of electric organ. The Beatles number lacks the backbeats of the drumming in the Group piece, however,

85 *Pat Metheny Song Book*, 439.
86 Niles, 'Working on *American Garage*.'
87 Brodowski and Szprot, 'Pat Metheny', 39.
88 Quoted (in Italian) in Viva, *Pat Metheny*, 83.
89 Ake, *Jazz Matters*, 97, 96.

which is not a feature commonly encountered in Metheny's work and an obvious sonic marker of generic pop and rock idioms. The dynamic opening of 'American Garage' (Ex. 3.16) also embodies a strong degree of humour, including a raucously shouted count-in and cheeky keyboard fills from Metheny himself. Not surprisingly, the piece was usually played (as we have seen) as an encore in live gigs. The humour was carried over into the recording studio when it was decided to augment a cymbal hit which Gottlieb had botched during the closing riffs with an overdub of the sound of glass bottles being smashed. 'It sounded like a baseball bat had been thrown through the studio window', recalls Gottlieb, and caused much hilarity; but in the final mix the effect was made considerably more discreet, to the point of being scarcely audible.[90]

At 13 minutes' duration, and aptly entitled 'The Epic', the album's final track was Metheny's and Mays's most ambitious compositional structure to date. It was literally conceived on a blank canvas, as Metheny explained:

> We laugh about this one a lot. I believe that this may be the only time we sat down with nothing, no sketches done by one or the other of us, just blank pieces of paper, and tried to write something together. It may be a feature of the piece, or maybe not, but the tune is certainly all over the map. We had the notion of expanding on the idea of having a piece that was almost like a suite in itself with lots of sections and an unusual form. I would say we learned a lot from the preparation and performance of this piece that served us well later on.[91]

Metheny later distanced himself from 'The Epic', even citing it as the worst thing his group had recorded to date and labelling it as 'totally pretentious … From the compositional point of view, it's one big pastiche.'[92] His perfectionism was nevertheless as much in evidence in recording this track as on the others, with Gottlieb recalling endless retries of a transitional 4-bar drum fill until the leader was satisfied with the results.[93]

90 Personal communication from Danny Gottlieb via email, July 9, 2014; see also Niles, 'Working on *American Garage*.' The breaking glass can be heard at c. 3m54s.
91 *Pat Metheny Song Book*, 439.
92 Quoted (in Italian) in Viva, *Pat Metheny*, 84.
93 Personal communication from Danny Gottlieb via email, July 9, 2014.

EX. 3.16 'American Garage': opening (AT). © 1979 Pat Meth Music Corp. and Lyle Mays, Inc. All rights reserved.

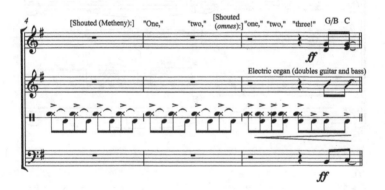

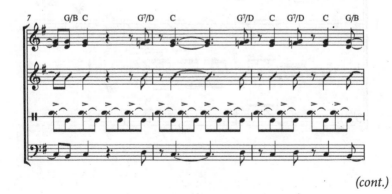

(cont.)

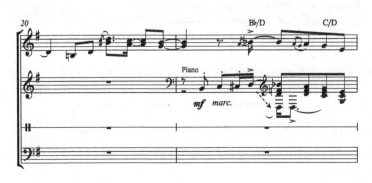

(cont.)

TABLE 3.2   Structure of "The Epic"

Bars	Thematic/textural material	Harmony
A ('intro')		
1–16	Synthesizer melody	Gmaj
B ('melody 1')		
17–51	Guitar melody	Fmaj, then Bmi7
C ('melody 2')		
52–88	Syncopated bass riff in samba rhythm beneath independent unison riff melody for guitar and synthesizer, with piano fills; 52–71 repeated (truncated) as 72–88	Dmi (Aeolian) with A♭ inflections
C' ('solos')		
89–184	Three-chorus piano solo, emerging from closing A♭ harmony of C (samba feel continues)	A♭maj7/Fmi7 (alternating for 8 bars), then roving
185–246	Two-chorus guitar solo, on same changes	
247–52	Synthesizer link to:	

(cont.)

TABLE 3.2 Continued

Bars	Thematic/textural material	Harmony
D ('interlude')		
253–60	New, metrically unstable melody in parallel chords (metre: 4+2+4+6+4+2+4+4)	C♭ (Lydian) modulating to E (Lydian);
261–8	Melody repeated in new key	A (Lydian) modulating to D (Lydian)
269–72	Chordal fill (= 13–16)	
B′ ('melody 1')		
273–92	Varied form of bars 17–36, with melody now as bass solo in 285–92 (= 29–36)	Fmaj, then Bmi7
E ('coda')		
293–310	Continuation of bass melody, ending with ascending figure in plain crotchets (307–8)	Gmaj7/F♯mi9
311–50	Guitar solo (two choruses, each 4 × 4 bars plus restatement of ascending crotchet figure)	F♯mi9/Gmaj7
351–8	D recapitulated (= 261–8)	A/D (Lydian)
359–73	C recapitulated (= 52–65)	Dmi (Aeolian);
374–85	Rhythmic augmentation of final phrase of C (= 66–71), as climactic link to:	modulation to D♭maj
A′ ('outro')		
386–404	Reworking of theme from introduction, with four-semiquaver anacrusis figure repeated as final riff	D♭maj

* This chart is based on the published lead sheet in *Pat Metheny Song Book*, 86–92, replacing rehearsal letters with letters denoting the components of the formal structure. Bar numbers reflect the actual lengths of sections notated using repeat marks in the score. Section titles in inverted commas appear on the lead sheet. Detail in the solo sections is based on the studio recording released on *American Garage*.

The structure of 'The Epic' is outlined in Table 3.2. Including repeated material, it amounts to just over 400 bars of music. With heavily sectionalized structures, length in itself is not necessarily an indication of either formal sophistication or cogency: it might be argued, for example, that the sectionalized nature of the later suites of Ellington are a somewhat disappointing characteristic given the astonishingly original approach to structure he had demonstrated in his earlier work. (Sadly, it was in all probability the muted critical reception of his groundbreaking and large-scale concert work *Black, Brown and Beige* in 1943 which discouraged him from going too much further down that particular path.) The principal difference from symphonic-jazz models in Metheny's small-group conception of large-scale structuring lies in the ongoing and crucial importance of substantial improvised sections which are integrated into the form without the slightest incongruity. This is not because the solos are necessarily based on substantial sets of changes already established in fully formed head-like melodies: more often, a harmonic suggestion from the last few bars of a pre-composed section will be adopted and developed to underpin the ensuing solo. This strategy encourages linear listening and therefore aids the narrative model which, as so often, conditions the overall conception of the music, and which is explicit in the title of the piece (a label that also suggests its epic structural proportions). Immediately after the end of the 'melody 2' section (C), for example, the piano begins its three-chorus solo by prolonging the A♭ major harmony from b. 88, then alternating it with F minor to create a simple pattern recalling the harmonies underlying a corresponding melodic passage already heard somewhat earlier (bb. 67–71). A similar alternation of two chords (now F♯mi9 and Gmaj7) forms the bulk of the later guitar solo (bb. 311–50) which, as Table 3.2 shows, are continued from the preceding bass solo. Tonal strategies such as these permit a sense of ongoing evolution—the narrative 'journey'—while at the same time, when the changes are slimmed down to just two predominant chords, allowing for moments of relaxation. As always in Metheny Group performances, the content of the solos varied considerably from night to night in live gigs. In the studio recording, Mays shows the kind of motivic logic we have already seen in some of Metheny's playing (see, for example, the excerpt from the piano's right hand transcribed in Ex. 3.17, taken from bb. 104–12), whereas Metheny's later solo on the same changes creates greater intensity through a prolonged use of heavily rhythmicized and metrically dislocated riffs (see Ex. 3.18a and Ex. 3.18b, taken from bb.

213-15 and 217-27, respectively). Again the gradual increase of motivic and dynamic intensity across the adjacent solos aids the sense of a linear journey.

Typically, solos over relatively static harmonies are sharply contrasted with other passages based on dynamically roving chord changes and snappy syncopations, most obviously to be heard in the 'interlude' (D), which may be directly compared with the example from 'Lone Jack' above (Ex. 3.10), also functioning as an interlude. The piece as a whole is framed by an exciting intro and outro, featuring the most incisive synthesizer timbres yet heard in a Metheny recording and an exhilaratingly rapid rate of syncopated harmonic change corresponding in effect to that of the interior interludes. In addition to the seamless integration of the solos into the whole, the music is in many places made coherent by the simple repetition and prolongation of riffs which serve as punctuation, for example the rippling ascending arpeggio patterns throughout 'melody 1', which are not included in the published lead sheet, and the strong bass line underpinning the samba-tempo sections. A textural enhancement suggested by Niles towards the end of the piece was created by slowing the tape to half its normal speed while Metheny

EX. 3.17   'The Epic': motivic working in piano solo (AT). © 1979 Pat Meth Music Corp. and Lyle Mays, Inc. All rights reserved.

EX. 3.18a AND 3.18b 'The Epic': guitar riffs (AT). © 1979 Pat Meth Music Corp. and Lyle Mays, Inc. All rights reserved.

played arpeggios: 'This was to give an even more epic, orchestral feel to the end. Of course at normal speed, the picking was an octave higher and sounded sparkly and bright.'[94]

94 Niles, 'Working on *American Garage.*'

American Garage achieved even greater sales than *Pat Metheny Group*. On its US release in February 1980, Metheny's first self-produced album quickly reached number one on *Billboard*'s jazz chart, and within two months had (even more rapidly than *New Chautauqua*) sold more than 200,000 copies.[95] More important, Ake argues, the project represented an alternative 'third path' to the stylistic poles of urban-oriented jazz and the emerging brands of rural-sounding jazz-rooted Americana: it offered a fresh idiom which 'runs alongside the music's traditional urban centres yet remains safely removed from them, tracing a metaphorical migration for at least one segment of jazz and its audiences: the exodus to suburbia'.[96] Ake points out that, as with the real migration of sizeable groups of Americans following the Second World War, 'this is a decidedly white flight from the city'. In its pop-influenced production methods, too, the album was a notable departure from the ECM norm. As Niles concludes: 'Even though, or perhaps *because* we had used contemporary production methods, *American Garage* was the album that first caught the powerdrive of the Pat Metheny Group live onstage.'[97]

Both of the Metheny Group albums considered in this chapter demonstrate the bandleader's commitment to exploring pre-composition at the same time as creating effective vehicles for improvisation. He outlined his thinking in this regard during an interview published in December 1981:

even within the context of our tunes that are most song-like—'San Lorenzo' or 'Phase Dance'—there are heavy arrangements, but the bulk of the song is still some sort of an improvised solo, even if the improvisation has to be in a narrower format than in an Ornette Coleman tune. When we enter that mode we become something that's more like a big band in the sense that, yes, the improvisation is still featured, but we're also interested in writing for the ensemble and using our instruments as a *common* voice as opposed to solo voices. That requires a certain amount of organization, which we're all into. I've never seen any reason why one has to preclude the other—why you can't write for an ensemble and also just turn the ensemble loose . . .

I can imagine writing tunes that are completely composed, and I can imagine doing albums where it's totally free. It depends on the musicians and what mood you're in when you're playing. At this particular time,

95 Viva, *Pat Metheny*, 90.
96 Ake, *Jazz Matters*, 98.
97 Niles, 'Working on *American Garage*.'

though, I think we're all feeling a need to stretch out more. We've always stretched out a lot, but we've got a few new tunes that are like Ornette tunes—just a short little head, and then the rest is free.[98]

The creative efforts involved were somewhat belied by *Down Beat*'s throwaway conclusion that the white album was made by 'the most amiable, accessible fusion band this side of Weather Report', or that the compositions might be 'a little too rich . . . One would hope for a little more extemporaneous space on the next album, as well as the raw power the group displays live.'[99]

But this was a moderate criticism indeed compared to the lambasting *American Garage* received in the pages of the same journal, which slammed the album's 'anemic tunes' as symptomatic of music which was deemed to be 'commercially appealing' but 'artistically disappointing'.[100] Blinded by an all-too-obvious desire to brand the music as commercial and therefore (presumably) technically deficient, the reviewer fell into the trap of taking Metheny to task for 'the simplistic nature of the melodies [which] would challenge the most inspired improviser'— seemingly oblivious that in much jazz, of all styles, the harmonic changes form the basis for the solos, not the melodic motifs of the head themes. In attempting to dismiss Mays's 'glossy piano style' as symptomatic of commercialism, she again fell into the same trap by declaring that the pianist's 'cocktail mannerisms (pampering each phrase until no melody is recognizable amid the glitter)' together with the album's 'slick compositional style combine for a frothy, forgettable product'. The review is an egregious example of the application of entirely inappropriate jazz-appreciation criteria to what was, in essence, a new type of music. This extraordinary diatribe stands on record as a vivid demonstration of how Metheny's boldness and willingness to push jazz's boundaries in surprising yet always unforced ways could easily raise the hackles of the purists, especially when the music energetically and unashamedly engaged with contemporary popular idioms as essential ingredients of the leader's new paradigm.

98   Forte, 'Jazz Voice of the 80's', 110.
99   Stern, review of *Pat Metheny Group*.
100 Elaine Guregian, review of *American Garage*, in *Down Beat* 47/4 (April 1980): 42.

CHAPTER 4

APOCALYPSE LATER

I could easily be like Keith [Jarrett] and go on an anti-electric
crusade, but I listen to a group like Weather Report and just
know that all this new technology has to be checked out . . .
I feel an obligation to give it a try. At some point I may decide
to cancel on it and just play acoustic guitar . . . But I hear
someone like Josef Zawinul, who's taken technology
and made incredible music out of it.[1]

A BRIEF RESPITE from punishing tour schedules presented itself to
Metheny when he was invited to back Joni Mitchell during her 'Shadows
and Light' tour during the summer of 1979, in a group that also included
Michael Brecker on saxophone, Don Alias on drums, and Jaco Pastorius.
The band had been hand-picked by Pastorius at Mitchell's request, as a
means of promoting three of her albums in which he had participated
(*Hejira, Don Juan's Reckless Daughter*, and *Mingus*). Mitchell's initial
idea was that the group would be an electric string band, incorporating
her own playing of her George Benson Ibanez guitars, but the texture
proved to be a little disappointing; several Los Angeles keyboard players
were then trialled before Metheny persuaded Mitchell and Pastorius to
bring in Mays instead, at a relatively late stage in the planning of the

1 Pat Metheny, interviewed in Smith, 'Ready to Tackle Tomorrow', 24.

project. Although he enjoyed the experience in general and found Joni's solo playing particularly stimulating each night, Metheny found certain aspects of the 'Shadows and Light' experience (with its comparatively leisurely tour schedule) frustrating and likened their high-powered backing group to a 'Ferrari that was limited to just driving around the block'.[2] But the gig resulted in a strong friendship between Metheny and Brecker, the latter's innovative harmonic language (not evident in his rhythm and blues work) stimulating Metheny's own compositional impulses, and the encounter soon led to the album *80/81*, which Metheny felt was one of the best of his ECM recordings.[3] In what would become a distinctive pattern underpinning his later career, this keyboard-less ensemble recording aimed to revitalize the straight-ahead jazz playing which up until this time Metheny felt he had neglected somewhat in the recording studio.

80/81

Recorded at Oslo's Talent Studio in late May 1980, *80/81* has long been considered a landmark achievement of Metheny's. He himself regarded it as not only his most pleasurable ECM experience but a vitally important culmination of his musical preoccupations in the years which preceded it. The sense of an overall trajectory conditioning the shifting musical territories of his eleven ECM albums, discussed in the opening chapter, is (with hindsight) especially palpable here: it was 'a record that took me five or six records to get to', as he expressed the immediate context to Richard Niles.[4] Whereas he felt his previous albums had all been concerned with 'very specific things' musically, *80/81* finally gave Metheny an outlet for the kind of music-making which was most familiar to him, but which had not yet been documented on record. On a personal level, too, for at least two of the participants—Metheny and Brecker—the recording constituted a 'life-changing' experience.[5]

Much of the album's special quality derives from Metheny's initiative in bringing together a number of formidable jazz talents who had not

---

2 Barth, *Voices in Jazz Guitar*, 326. For a description of the tour and Pastorius's contribution to it, see Milkowski, *Jaco*, 114–16.
3 Carr, 'Bright Size Life', episode 3.
4 Niles, *Pat Metheny Interviews*, 45.
5 http://www.patmetheny.com/news/full_display.cfm?id=81 (September 3, 2014). This source includes a substantial podcast of reminiscences concerning *80/81* from Metheny and some of his collaborators.

played with each other before. Furthermore, the individual qualities of·
these players inspired Metheny to compose music that was uniquely
suited to their playing characteristics. Tenor saxophonist Dewey
Redman and bassist Charlie Haden had already played together in an
innovative quartet with Keith Jarrett (an ensemble well represented by
the live recording *Eyes of the Heart*, made in Austria in 1976); but Haden
and drummer Jack DeJohnette came together for the first time on *80/81*,
and for his own part Metheny found working with the 'challenging'
DeJohnette thoroughly stimulating. Unusually, Brecker joined Redman
as a second tenor, and the vivid contrast between their playing styles—
both across the individual tracks in which only one of them is playing and
the moments when they play together—was not only a unique feature of
the project, but at long last reflected a successful search for horn players
who would adapt comfortably to Metheny's idiom. Although Redman
and Brecker formerly had little in common, Metheny was struck by the
intimate empathy they established when the music was toured in the
summer of 1981. Saxophone timbres were thereafter again to be absent
from Metheny's bands until he formed the Unity Group with Chris
Potter in 2012, so *80/81* provides a particularly valuable insight into a
rarely aired aspect of his creativity.

Metheny conceived the project in part as a tribute to the music of
Ornette Coleman and was delighted to be working with his old friends
Haden and DeJohnette; as we have seen, he had come to know and
admire Brecker during the recent Mitchell tour, and Redman was hired
because Metheny originally intended to include arranged material on
the album, though in the event this idea lapsed somewhat.[6] Working
at last with horn players gave him greater scope for using his guitar as
a chordal vehicle than was the case in his own regular band, given its
instrumentation.[7] Most of the music was caught in single takes, almost all
laid down on a single day (with a small amount of additional work taking
place on the following day), and to an exceptionally high level of sound
quality. So much impressive material was recorded that Eicher decided
to issue the project as a two-disc set. It was reported at the time that the
producer had first considered allocating the music to the two discs so
that one would contain only '100 proof jazz' and the other 'progressive
pop and marginal jazz',[8] this being a reflection of the two broad categories

---

6 Carr, 'Bright Size Life', episode 3.
7 Schneckloth, 'Pat Metheny: A Step beyond Tradition', 16.
8 Hadley, review of *80/81*, 31.

into which the music of *80/81* falls, though Metheny does not recall this and feels it would have been untypical of Eicher. The tracks were in fact organized in a sequence which avoided such a stark and unnecessary division of material but nevertheless grouped the content so that the outer sides (1 and 4) contained the 'progressive' pieces, and these flanked the '100 proof jazz' on the two inner sides (2 and 3). The scope was later condensed somewhat by the omission of the tracks 'Open' and 'Pretty Scattered' for the first (single-disc) CD reissue, though these items were subsequently restored in a later two-CD set. The original vinyl release, packaged in a characteristically minimalist and predominantly mauve sleeve design by Barbara Wojirsch (see Fig. 4.1), won the Jazz Record of the Year Prize of the German Record Critics' Award (Preis der deutschen Schallplattenkritik) in 1980.

The opening track, 'Two Folk Songs', occupied the entire first side in the original LP release, with a duration of almost 21 minutes and fading out at the conclusion as if it could have continued indefinitely. The

FIG. 4.1   *80/81* sleeve art. Design by Barbara Wojirsch. © ECM Records, 1980. Used by permission.

piece explores a manner of making rhythm-guitar strumming work in constant counterpoint with bass and drums, and its underlying aim was to achieve stylistic coherence in the context of the kind of modern drumming exemplified by DeJohnette's playing.[9] The simple, homely melody is a standard AABA pattern, but the bridge is improvised and the strumming style takes the listener more into the distinctive soundworld of *New Chautauqua* than mainstream jazz. Metheny's and DeJohnette's dynamic repeated patterns, further propelled by a buoyant bass line from Haden, serve as the compelling backdrop to the tune, which quickly inspires Brecker to extraordinary heights of creativity in his substantial solo, at times bordering on the avant-garde in its timbral expressionism and striking chromatic departures from the simple underlying changes (which outline a tetrachord firmly descending from tonic to dominant in Mixolydian D). One reviewer described the 'outside' elements in Brecker's playing—with its 'terrific bleats and shrieks'—as a manner of 'vocalizing very much in Redman's style'.[10] When it was suggested to Metheny that his own playing on this track was reminiscent of the Orient and India, he replied: 'Actually, I was thinking more in terms of c&w [country and western]'.[11] This heartland-inspired country feel, reflecting Metheny's and Haden's first recorded exploration together of their common heritage, perfectly complements the indefatigable energy and experimentation of the saxophonist and the powerful driving rhythms of the drummer, whose mid-point solo ushers in the second drone-based melody, the folk tune 'Old Joe Clark' interpreted by Haden and fluctuating between Mixolydian and Ionian major modes. Metheny's own brightly ringing solo is consistently diatonic at the start, exploring dyads (Ex. 4.1a), some of them folk-like parallel thirds (Ex. 4.1b), and dissonances within the strict confines of the diatonic major scale (Ex. 4.1c).

'Two Folk Songs' has been regarded by David Ake as a musical high point of the era, being especially notable—as is true of much of the remainder of the album—for its pioneering melding of rural and avant-garde elements, and allowing listeners (with the benefit of hind-hearing) to appreciate how what Ake terms 'pastoral' tendencies were already latent years before in the music by Coleman which had largely inspired the project.[12] Frank-John Hadley's *Down Beat* review, by far

9   *Pat Metheny Song Book*, 440.
10 Hadley, review of *80/81*, 31.
11 Schneckloth, 'A Step beyond Tradition', 16.
12 For Ake's analysis and discussion of this track and the remainder of the album, see *Jazz Matters*, 92–5.

the warmest the journal had yet given to a Metheny recording, hailed it as 'a triumph, a stirring blend of the traditional and the contemporary'. Echoing the narrative thrust of so much of Metheny's music, DeJohnette singled out the storytelling qualities of all the solo performances on this track for particular praise.[13]

The album's title track and 'The Bat' were both conceived for Redman. '80/81' is a mostly chordless bebop-like melody recalling the idiom of Coleman's quartet work in the early 1960s, a source also suggested by the unison rubato playing in the bridge. A modified song form of 23 bars in total, its first three sections contract from 8 bars (A) to 6 bars (B) and then 5 bars with an extra interpolated beat (C), before being rounded off by a recapitulation of the first phrase, now shortened to half its original length. Solos are here mostly of the time-no-changes variety, although the tonic Eb serves as a frequent reference point. 'The Bat', which would later reappear on the Metheny Group album *Offramp* (see Chapter 5), is another harmonically rich ballad, in this case consciously designed to exploit Redman's 'soulful and expressive' tone.[14] Both saxophonists participate in the head melody, some of which is cast in two independent voices, with DeJohnette supplying animated cymbal washes similar to Gottlieb's contribution to 'Sea Song' in *Watercolors*. The texture is a good example of how simple, three-part voicing can in this context be just as compelling as richer chord voicings in other contexts: see Example 4.2. Metheny recalled the unusual manner in which Redman negotiated the tune's challenging harmonies at short notice: he practised the changes for a couple of hours in the bathroom by constantly playing straightforward arpeggios on them, but when he emerged to perform the piece his playing bore not the slightest resemblance to what he had been practising.[15]

When the melody was reworked as 'The Bat, Part II' in *Offramp*, Naná Vasconcelos thought the piece was a direct reflection of Metheny's ongoing admiration for the music of Milton Nascimento (discussed below).[16] The mellow interpretation on the later album is steered by Mays's rich synthesizer voicings which, in combination with Vasconcelos's typically atmospheric vocal effects, immediately transport the listener

13 Podcast at http://www.patmetheny.com/news/full_display.cfm?id=81.
14 *Pat Metheny Song Book*, 440. The title 'The Bat' was derived from the surname of Metheny's then girlfriend, Shu Shubat, not the animal.
15 Podcast at http://www.patmetheny.com/news/full_display.cfm?id=81.
16 Viva, *Pat Metheny*, 120.

EX. 4.1a, 4.1b AND 4.1c 'Two Folk Songs': dyads, parallel thirds, and diatonic dissonances (AT). © 1980 Pat Meth Music Corp.

into the evocative soundworld of the Metheny-Mays album *As Falls Wichita, So Falls Wichita Falls* (also considered below). A comparison with the longer version on *80/81*—interpreted by two saxophones, guitar, bass, and drums, and including lyrical guitar, bass and saxophone solos absent from the later incarnation—fascinatingly demonstrates how the same basic musical material was susceptible to radically different textures and emotions in different arrangements: the only common element in

EX. 4.2 'The Bat': three-part voicing (ASB, 97). © 1980 Pat Meth Music Corp. All
rights reserved.

the two interpretations is the impressionistic use of cymbal washes in
the head. The enticing electronic timbres and eerie vocal effects of the
Offramp reworking sound as if they come from an altogether different
planet, but at the same time the full keyboard voicings demonstrate the
rich, resourceful, and strongly directional nature of the harmonies more
thinly voiced in the earlier recording.

'Turnaround', a Coleman composition from his 1959 quartet album
Tomorrow Is the Question, was included specifically in response to the
need for additional material once the decision had been taken to make
the release a double album. Coleman's tune elicits breezy blues playing
from Metheny recalling the manner of 'Broadway Blues' in *Bright Size
Life*, which had also been conceived with Coleman's example in mind.
Down Beat was pleased by this turn of events: 'Metheny proves he can
wring pure honest feeling out of the blues, thus dispelling the thought

in some circles that his playing lacks soul'.[17] The reviewer can have had little idea that Metheny was in fact playing the tune for the first time, and at very short notice. The shouted exclamation of praise for DeJohnette's drumming at the end, which was retained on the release track, came from Haden, not Metheny as is often thought.[18] Both saxes lay out on this track.

Several early reviewers of *80/81* were so startled by some of its boldest music that the words 'shock' and 'shocking' were used.[19] They principally had in mind the performance of 'Open', its title referring to the absence of any conventional formal structure, which lasts a little over 14 minutes and was one of the tracks omitted from the initial CD re-release. It begins with a lengthy free duet for guitar and drums, followed by a drum solo; the drums continue beneath interplay between Brecker and Haden's walking bass line; a bass and drum duet is then followed by a brief Redman solo before all the other participants creep eerily back into the swelling texture. The composition is credited in the sleeve notes to all five players, with only the concluding unison theme attributed to Metheny, and more than anywhere else on the album it demonstrates the deep (and unpredicted) empathy between the two saxophonists. Although exhilaratingly free for most of its course, the music's wild textures begin to cohere noticeably as the players variously adopt a descending pattern of slurred scale fragments after they are introduced by Metheny (Ex. 4.3) at around 11 minutes into the track, all participants layering them in free superimposition; the guitarist soon afterwards begins a purposeful ascent based on strong dyadic oscillations, as if literally leading his group out of the maelstrom.

The other temporarily omitted track, 'Pretty Scattered', incorporates open solos in time-no-changes, but features a strongly characterized head melody alternating chromatic and angular motifs in bebop style, which is performed with a great sense of swing—a rhythmic feature almost completely absent from the straight-eighths idiom of his regular band. This composition had originally been written for tenor saxophonist Bob Berg.[20] Again, the head is structured in an unorthodox manner while retaining the overall shape of a conventional AABA song form: all the A sections are 12 bars long, and metrically disrupted by

17 Hadley, review of *80/81*, 31.
18 Podcast at http://www.patmetheny.com/news/full_display.cfm?id=81.
19 See, for example, Hadley (review of *80/81*), and Cook and Morton, *Penguin Guide* (first edn.), 735.
20 *Pat Metheny Song Book*, 440.

shifts to 2/4 and 7/4, while the 8-bar bridge is half ad-libbed and also contains an unexpected bar of 5/4.

'Every Day (I Thank You)' was written by Metheny on tour with his quartet in Germany in 1979 and he described it as 'an even eighth-note groove sandwiched between rubato statements of a melody'; this was the tune that had suggested the idea of doing a record with Brecker in the first place.[21] It was ideally suited to the emotional weight of Brecker's playing and was structurally significant for developing the general notion of combining song form with improvised sections not necessarily based on the head, which became increasingly important in all of Metheny's repertoire. The opening section exemplifies the guitarist's characteristic rubato-shaped harmonic richness in ballad style, being replete with chromatic shifts and richly voiced seventh-based chords; the ensuing Brecker solo features a slower harmonic rhythm to begin with, but the changes are shaped to become more rapidly and strongly directional in the latter half, where the music is underpinned by a strong rhythmic riff. Metheny contributes an unaccompanied lyrical solo towards the closing restatement of the head; in this solo, and earlier in the track, there is a discreet use of swells from the guitar's volume pedal.

'Goin' Ahead' was originally planned as, and tried out as, a quintet number, but the results were not felt to be compelling, and the piece was adapted as a solo item with a view to placing it at the end of the double album when it became clear the latter was a viable proposition.[22] As well as providing a delicately lyrical coda to the project as a whole, the piece satisfyingly returns us to the luminous D major tonality and acoustic timbres of the opening 'Two Folk Songs', also echoing the melodic contours of the first theme in the latter: compare Example 4.4a ('Two Folk Songs') and Example 4.4b

21 *Ibid.*, 339–440.
22 *Ibid.*, 440.

('Goin' Ahead'). This track found Metheny unexpectedly using an acoustic guitar in the shape of a superannuated Ibanez instrument he found lying around in the studio; the on-the-spot performance was intended merely as a demo but was so warmly received by those present that it was enshrined on the album, with the addition of some overdubbing. A live performance is included in *Travels*, in the shape of a substantial improvised solo on the Gibson which leads without a break into 'As Falls Wichita, So Falls Wichita Falls' (see below). In spite of its almost accidental origin, 'Goin' Ahead' was the first recorded example of what Metheny termed 'a certain kind of vocabulary, or sound, or language' in his output, referring to the music's diatonic simplicity and directness, and this poignant idiom would reappear in *Beyond the Missouri Sky* and other later projects.[23] Both in this track and in the guitar solo on 'Every Day (I Thank You)', the gently lilting acoustic playing also looks ahead to Metheny's much later reflective solo albums for baritone guitar, *One Quiet Night* (2003) and *What's It All About* (2011). In his review of *80/81*, Hadley noted that both 'Goin' Ahead' and a shortened version of 'Every Day (I Thank You)' were currently enjoying extensive FM airplay and that these pieces suggested 'the guitarist's pop inclinations'.[24]

23 Podcast at http://www.patmetheny.com/news/full_display.cfm?id=81.
24 Hadley, review of *80/81*, 31.

NEW SOUNDS: POLYPHONIC SYNTHESIZERS AND BRAZILIAN INFLUENCES

80/81 was made during an eight-month break in Metheny's regular activities, owing to a considerable demand for live appearances by the *80/81* band. During the break, Mays collaborated with Swallow, providing a synthesizer backdrop to the bassist's album *Home*, recorded in September 1979 at Columbia Studios, New York. The brief hiatus had a most beneficial creative consequence, however, in the shape of *As Falls Wichita, So Falls Wichita Falls*, which allowed Metheny and Mays to push their musical activities in a fresh direction, as they had been planning to do for some time—and now with strikingly original results. On this occasion Metheny played bass himself (the trusty fretless Fender Precision), as he had previously done in *New Chautauqua*, in addition to nine other guitars; he took only a single solo in the entire album, a clear reflection of the project's firm emphasis on what he referred to as 'textural written material'.[25]

Made relatively soon after the introduction of polyphonic synthesizers, *As Falls Wichita* was (in Metheny's words) 'one of the first records to really take synthesizers seriously as an orchestrational device'.[26] Metheny's interest in the music of Weather Report—a band in which his old friend Pastorius played from 1976 until 1981—is attested by the quotation at the head of this chapter, and its influence on the debut Metheny Group album was discussed in Chapter 3. In both its rock-orientation and innovative timbres, Weather Report was an inspiring example of what could be achieved by a combination of stylistic flexibility and modern technology. The band's keyboard player and co-composer, Josef Zawinul, famously pioneered the Oberheim polyphonic synthesizer in their hit 'Birdland' on the best-selling album *Heavy Weather* (1977), a project in which he also played an ARP 2600 synthesizer and Rhodes electric piano. Zawinul felt that a major attraction in using synthesizers was that they permitted Weather Report's otherwise traditional quintet lineup to sound like a full orchestra, and Metheny's group increasingly came to transform its core quartet sound with electronics in a comparable way.[27] *As Falls Wichita* was a breakthrough venture for both Metheny and Mays, not only in its extensive use of synthesized sound but also in its creation of evocative soundscapes through overdubbing. Unusually for an ECM

---

25 Forte, 'Jazz Voice of the 80's', 114.
26 Carr, 'Bright Size Life', episode 3.
27 Coryell and Friedman, *Jazz-Rock Fusion*, 233; *Pat Metheny Song Book*, 440.

disc, the recording was made over three days (in September 1980), followed by two days of mixing; a foundation guitar track was laid down for most of the pieces, then gradually overdubbed, with percussionist Naná Vasconcelos finally adding his own spontaneous contribution.[28]

In spite of its use of studio production techniques, the album's music nevertheless preserved an important link with live performance. The extended title track—the two composers' longest recorded structure to date—began life as an experimental piece designed to commence offstage at the start of a live gig and gradually build up to a statement of the first tune of the evening's set. (Although not exploited fully at the time, this preludial concept was prophetic of the manner in which *First Circle* gigs in 1984-5 opened with the bizarrely theatrical 'Forward March' (see Chapter 6) and the expectantly atmospheric opening of live performances of *The Way Up* in 2005.) In the event, the 'Wichita' track was refashioned so as to use 'the studio itself as an instrument by utilizing overdubbing techniques'; the result was 'a piece that would essentially fill an entire side of an album'.[29] By this time, all of Metheny's live performances (including gigs with the *80/81* band and trios) made telling use of atmospheric lighting effects to enhance the spectators' experience during what could amount to up to three hours of music. This element of theatricality also accorded well with his regular band's evocative electronic soundscapes. For the first time in his output, Metheny likened the effect of the *Wichita* music to cinema, saying 'it almost creates a movie in your mind', and this parallel was also made by Mays.[30] (Years later, Metheny similarly described *Secret Story* as 'a very cinematic record. It seems to have a visual aspect to it'.)[31] The increasingly theatrical manner of live presentation came at a time when Metheny's ever-growing fan base meant that performances by all his ensembles were now given in much larger venues than had been the case on their earliest tours, but his commitment to memorable stage

---

28 Forte, 'Jazz Voice of the 80's', 114.

29 *Pat Metheny Song Book*, 440.

30 Forte, 'Jazz Voice of the 80's', 114; Viva, *Pat Metheny*, 104. In later years, ECM was to become closely associated with European cinema and film music, with Eicher enjoying a particularly fruitful creative relationship with French director Jean-Luc Godard: see Geoff Andrew, '*Leur musique*: Eicher/Godard—Sound/Image', in Müller, *Windfall Light*, 179-85, and Jürg Stenzl, 'Multitalents: Jean-Luc Godard and Manfred Eicher', in Enwezor and Müller, *ECM: A Cultural Archaeology*, 204-9. The ECM album *Nouvelle Vague* (1997) was a complete film soundtrack devoid of images, and with liner notes written by a blind commentator.

31 David Okamoto, 'Pat's Profile', *Jazziz* 9/5 (August/September 1992): 54.

presentation had in any case been strong since the very beginning of his bandleading days.

The electronic elements were consciously humanized by the addition of evocative vocals performed (in addition to his distinctive percussion contribution) by Vasconcelos, who at this time also recorded for ECM with Don Cherry's and Collin Walcott's free-jazz trio Codona (1978–82), an experimental acoustic group which used ethnic instruments and brought together repertoire as diverse as traditional world music, the music of Coleman, and songs by Stevie Wonder. Vasconcelos was a specialist on the berimbau, a single-string struck bow with a gourd resonator capable of subtle modifications to both its pitch and timbre, which is featured on *As Falls Wichita* as well as on the Codona albums. His role in Codona's soundscapes has been aptly described by Steve Lake: 'echoes of the rainforest are captured in the bush magic of Nana Vasconcelos's percussion, evoking animal cries and birdsong, scurryings in the undergrowth, cloudbursts, a sudden flapping of wings . . .'[32] In terms that might equally be applied to *As Falls Wichita*, Lake praised Codona's recordings for their 'expanding and contracting of the sounding-space, from track to track', which he felt to be 'quietly revolutionary': 'Overdubs do not draw attention to themselves, but are part of the organic flow.'[33]

Metheny described the addition of Vasconcelos's singing to his own group as 'a musical necessity' which supplied an 'earth factor' that would otherwise have been absent in a soundworld dominated by electronics and multiple guitar types.[34] As was shown by both Vasconcelos and his successors in the Metheny Group, untexted singing would remain what Metheny termed 'an effective tactic to get that vocal quality that I think everybody loves, but with still the possibility of keeping it vague in terms of actual textual meaning.'[35] Additionally employed by Metheny as an ancillary percussionist, Vasconcelos fulfilled a dual coloristic function that was to be maintained by a succession of versatile multi-instrumentalists and singers in later incarnations of his band; his Brazilian origins also helped develop a strong Latin flavour in some of their new repertoire, for example, in 'Estupenda Graça' (*As Falls*

---

32 Steve Lake, 'Codona: Sounds of the Earth and Air', booklet notes to *The Codona Trilogy* (ECM 2033-35, 2008), 5. For further on Codona, see Kodwo Eshun, 'Codona: Reorientation Point for New Planetary Values', in Enwezor and Müller, *ECM: A Cultural Archaeology*, 188–94.

33 Lake, 'Codona', 15.

34 Carr, 'Bright Size Life', episode 3.

35 Stuart, 'Jazz Guitar Greats'.

Wichita) and 'Más Allá (Beyond)' (sung by Vasconcelos's immediate successor, Pedro Aznar, on *First Circle*). Metheny, who was an admirer of bossa nova during his teens, later disagreed with what he felt was the overly simplistic view that his music had suddenly taken on a Brazilian flavour around 1980, commenting in an interview 10 years later:

> I'm writing the same kind of tunes that I've always written, and if you were to take Pedro or Nana or [Armando] Marçal into the studio, and overdub them on *Bright Size Life*, it would sound just like what I'm doing now ... A lot of people hear percussion and think 'It's Brazilian.' From a rhythmic standpoint, I suppose it's true, but in terms of the melodic stuff, and the kind of chords that I like, it's been the same for a long time.[36]

These remarks were made when the interviewer suggested that 'Phase Dance' (from the Metheny Group's debut 'white album') 'builds in a similar way to your new songs and arrangements, where you utilize a lot of percussion'.

ECM was certainly no stranger to Brazilian styles in this period: in addition to its Codona trilogy, the label issued recordings by Egberto Gismonti, and its eclectic guitarist Ralph Towner was also influenced by Brazilian music. Eicher had first introduced Metheny and Mays to both Vasconcelos and Gismonti, who had recently recorded *Dança Das Cabeças* for the label, in Oslo shortly before the recording of *Watercolors*. Charlie Haden and Jan Garbarek went on to record *Magico* with Gismonti in Oslo in June 1979. Mays later observed, referring to Gismonti's album *Fantasia* (1982), that the Brazilian musician's eclecticism had been inspirational on account of his willingness 'to use a child singing one minute and then have a chamber orchestra the next, then a whole bank of synthesizers'.[37] Coincidentally, the conjunction of children's voices and synthesized quasi-orchestral sound was to be a notable feature of the title track in *As Falls Wichita, So Falls Wichita Falls*.

---

36 Aledort, 'Pat Metheny: Straight Ahead', 62. Marçal performed with the Pat Metheny Group on their later albums *Still Life (Talking)* (1987), *Letter from Home* (1989), and *The Road to You* (1993), which Metheny saw as direct descendants from *First Circle*. Mays felt that Marçal's contribution was far more driven by rhythm ('Armando is almost like an entire samba school') than Vasconcelos, who was primarily concerned with 'sounds and textures': see Chris McGowan and Ricardo Pessanha, *The Brazilian Sound: Samba, Bossa Nova and the Popular Music of Brazil* (Philadelphia: Temple University Press, 1998), 175.

37 McGowan and Pessanha, *The Brazilian Sound*, 166.

Metheny was in Brazil during the break from his touring in the second half of 1980, following the band's appearance in Rio de Janeiro at the beginning of August. This was Egan's last concert with them, given before a crowd of 20,000 in a sports arena. Metheny immersed himself in Brazilian music during this trip: he had intended to stay for only three days, but the visit lasted three weeks.[38] He spent considerable time with the musicians who played in the band of Milton Nascimento, a leading exponent of MPB (*música popular brasileira*), a richly eclectic popular music which defies easy categorization. Like Metheny's, Nascimento's evocative music was rooted in the aura of his native region, in his case Minas Gerais. Metheny also worked with Nascimento's guitarist (and fellow Mineiro) Toninho Horta, whose playing—which had already been influenced by Metheny's own—he described as a more harmonically sophisticated version of João Gilberto's.[39] He later hailed Horta as 'one of the most harmonically sophisticated and melodically satisfying Brazilian composers of recent times' and 'the Herbie Hancock of Bossa-Nova guitarists'.[40] Metheny recorded with Horta on the tracks 'Prato Feito' and 'Manoel, O Audaz' for Horta's eponymous debut album while he was in Rio, and played on the title track of Célia Vaz's album *Mutação* at the invitation of her 12-string guitarist Ricardo Silveira.[41] (Both had been students of Metheny's at Berklee.) He also heard Vasconcelos in performance during this trip and had him (and all his instruments) flown over to Oslo to participate in the *As Falls Wichita* recording sessions, having previously encountered him again when his own band was performing in Tokyo in April 1980 and Vasconcelos and Gismonti were also appearing there.[42]

Interviewed in 1992, after having lived in the country himself for a number of years (from 1986 to 1990), Metheny summarized the importance of Brazil as 'the last place in the world where the pop music was really deeply involved in harmony ... Brazilian pop music is one of the great vestiges of chordal activity in the world.'[43] He was by no means alone in his high opinion of the country's music. Guitarist Charlie Byrd, who had

---

38 Schneckloth, 'A Step beyond Tradition', 16. In this source Metheny is quoted as saying the visit was in August 1981.

39 Forte, 'Jazz Voice of the 80's', 109.

40 Pat Metheny, liner notes to Toninho Horta, *Diamond Land* (Verve Forecast 835183, 1988). Metheny and Horta recorded a duet on acoustic guitars for Horta's later album *Moonstone* (Verve Forecast 839734, 1989), and Horta recorded with both Egan and Gottlieb after their departure from the Metheny Group.

41 See Viva, *Pat Metheny*, 99–101 for further details of Metheny's stay in Brazil.

42 *Ibid.*, 91.

43 Sonita Alleyne, 'Twentieth Century Nomad', *Straight No Chaser* 19 (Winter 1992): 39.

helped popularize bossa nova with Stan Getz on the best-selling album *Jazz Samba* in 1962, hailed Antonio Carlos Jobim as 'the most significant writer of popular music in the second half of the twentieth century' on account of his 'lyrical lines' and the way in which he 'rhythmically and harmonically constructed them like a fine watchmaker'.[44] Similarly, flutist Herbie Mann praised MPB singer-songwriter Ivan Lins—who appeared on Dave Grusin's and Lee Ritenour's album *Harlequin* (1985)—as 'a magician with harmony . . . His chords are complicated, but the melody is so strong.'[45]

The music of Nascimento and Horta belongs to a school which became known as *clube da esquina* ('corner club'), and both Metheny and Mays were deeply impressed by two double albums—*Clube da Esquina* and *Clube da Esquina 2*—which Nascimento and his associates recorded in 1972 and 1978. Mays, who had been introduced to the recordings by Metheny, recalled that they had both been thunderstruck by what the music represented:

> It was an amazing unpredictable combination of cultural influences of the Western classical harmonic sense and the African rhythmic sense, done in a completely different way from jazz . . . The *Clube da Esquina* records have things in common with the Beatles and Miles Davis, a combination of hipness, accessibility, and exoticness.[46]

Another recording that made a great impression on everyone in Metheny's band was *Native Dancer* (1975), Wayne Shorter's first Columbia album as leader, which featured Nascimento as a guest artist: Mays felt this landmark album was single-handedly responsible for introducing Nascimento's distinctive music-making to American jazz musicians. The Brazilian dimension of Chick Corea's *Light as a Feather* (1972), with its contributions from singer Flora Purim and drummer Airto Moreira, was another self-confessed influence. And Brazilian music's deep involvement with the nylon-stringed classical guitar inevitably invites comparison with Metheny's fondness for this particular instrument as a distinctive lyrical voice in jazz.

Echoing Metheny's view that his music had contained elements comparable to those of Brazilian music from the very outset, Mays drew a parallel between the Metheny Group's unwavering adherence in the ECM years to straight-eighth rhythms and the similarly (non-swung)

44 Quoted in McGowan and Pessanha, *The Brazilian Sound*, 66.
45 *Ibid.*, 93.
46 *Ibid.*, 111.

rhythmic foundation of Brazilian metres, citing 'San Lorenzo' and 'Phase Dance' (both on *Pat Metheny Group*) and, even more so, *Watercolors*: 'under the surface the actual rhythms had a whole lot to do with Brazilian music'.[47] He noted that this rhythmic trend was in any case much in the air at the time, and that Metheny had specifically inherited it from Burton's example. Metheny identified the general move from swung rhythm to straight rhythm in the early 1960s as a defining musical characteristic of the era, and suggested that this basic rhythmic shift across a wide range of genres was of more fundamental significance than the more readily acknowledged cultural contrasts between rock and jazz; he singled out Horace Silver's 'Song for My Father' (1965) as an example of the two rhythmic approaches being distinctively combined at this crucial time.[48] Mays was also fascinated by the combination of straight and swung rhythms in the music of Brazilian-influenced jazz performers since Getz's pioneering example, and by the use of sometimes complex harmonic extensions in Brazilian popular music—a richness that paralleled the harmonic idiom of Bill Evans, in whose music he was intensely interested at a formative time when rock seemed to be heading in an altogether simpler direction.[49]

METHENY AND MAYS

Interviewed just over a year after recording *As Falls Wichita*, Metheny paid tribute to his creative relationship with Mays.[50] Metheny told the BBC in 1998 that 85 percent of the time the initial musical ideas originated with him, and Mays took over in an editorial capacity.[51] The guitarist added, however, that even more important than their compositional collaboration was their instinctive rapport in performance. Mays echoed the view that each of them tended to serve as the other's editor:

> I think we have moved away from a real strict collaborative thing where Pat would write two bars and I would write two bars, 'cause that tends to make the music almost schizophrenic. Not that we ever did it, but it was more like that. Now [in 1985] it's more that one of us will write a section, have a concept for the whole tune, have a style

47 *Ibid.*, 175.
48 Stuart, 'Jazz Guitar Greats'.
49 Brodowski and Szprot, 'Lyle Mays', 41.
50 Forte, 'Jazz Voice of the 80's', 110.
51 Carr, 'Bright Size Life', episode 3.

in mind or rhythmic pulse, the basic melody. And the other one will maybe serve as the editor. It's more like one or the other of us will come up with the basic idea, and then the two of us will stand back like sort of impartial judges and say, 'This could be better and that's great.' It's pretty much at the stage now where one or the other of us comes up with a basic kernel of the main material.[52]

Mays revealed that charts or scores were rarely written out in full and that, although all the band members were fluent readers, a flexible combination of written materials and oral transmission was used in rehearsals.[53]

Metheny's music demonstrates an inextricable relationship between sonority, harmony, and tonal structure, as indeed does Mays's later music as an independent composer and bandleader.[54] Metheny finds that

> certain sounds suggest certain kinds of harmonies. That's true not only with synthesizer sounds, but also with the guitar experiments I've done. The sounds suggest the harmonies, and the harmonies suggest certain kinds of tunes. And occasionally, a tune will come along totally based on the *sound*. *Are You Going with Me* [from *Offramp*], for instance, came that way. It was all written on the Synclavier, and the sound seemed to suggest a certain kind of harmony and a certain kind of movement ... A tune like *San Lorenzo* [from *Pat Metheny Group*], which is based on a weird 12-string guitar tuning, came that way too ...
>
> On the other hand, if you write a melody that really has some detail and substance to it, it doesn't matter if you play it on a kazoo, a Synclavier, or an acoustic guitar. It's going to *sing*. And if you can combine *both*—a strong melody and a hip sound—then you're in business.[55]

52 Brodowski and Szprot, 'Lyle Mays', 40.
53 For further on the use of written parts in performance, see Jim Roberts, 'Pat Metheny: The Interview from Home', *Down Beat* 56/8 (August 1989): 17.
54 A comparison has sometimes been made between the collaborations of Metheny-Mays and Ellington-Strayhorn: see, for example, Wayne E. Goins, in *Emotional Response*, 78. In terms of their respective working methods, this is somewhat implausible; but the almost alchemical blending of sonority and structure in both musicians' music is at times conceptually similar to Ellington's thinking: see Mervyn Cooke, 'Jazz among the classics, and the case of Duke Ellington', in Cooke and David Horn (eds.), *The Cambridge Companion to Jazz* (Cambridge: Cambridge University Press, 2002), especially 159-62.
55 Schneckloth, 'A Step beyond Tradition', 15.

It is not surprising, therefore, that different pieces required different collaborative approaches, as Metheny and Mays explained in an article published in 1980.[56] The simplest starting point was the notion (as Mays put it) of 'playing over old ideas' which 'gives them new life', as seen in several of the tracks discussed in preceding chapters. Mays suggested that it was important to look at the material 'off the road', that is, to stand back from music that they might have been playing continuously on tour and consider it in a fresh, objective light. In the early years, exploratory play-throughs would take place on piano and guitar, but at around the time Metheny's interest in synthesizers developed he increasingly composed at the keyboard rather than at the guitar. On many occasions, Metheny commented that keyboard expertise was linked to harmonic sophistication, and that Mays's expert piano voicing had lent much to the music.[57] Mays recalled how their working methods remained fluid after the advent of more capable computer technology:

> the way we work together keeps evolving, keeps changing. It's hard to pin down. We've tried everything from sitting together to write together to going off into other rooms or each trying to come up with everything [*laughs*] and we've done a little bit of everything, I guess. What doesn't work is sitting down together and say, ok we're gonna write something together. What seems to have to happen is one or the other has to come up with a mood or a melody or some defining sort of ... musical nugget ... that is really the main element of the piece. And then we can each add details later, but that impulse for the piece, the sort of reason for being ... has to come from one or the other.
> ... [W]e both tend to make sequencer demos—real rough—of an idea. Usually not too complete ... so that they can be really finished later.[58]

Mays's distrust of setting out specifically to 'write something together' clearly echoes Metheny's disappointment with their method of

56 Forte, 'Garage Band'.
57 Martin Renzhofer, 'Pat & Howard—Eclectic Jazz vs. Pop; Metheny continues to push the envelope after 20 years', *Salt Lake Tribune*, July 17, 1998. On the benefits of composing at the piano, see also Metheny's comments in Douglas J. Noble, 'Metheny's Method', *Guitar Magazine* 2/5 (August 1992): 16.
58 Mike Brannon, interview with Lyle Mays (May 2001).

collaboration on 'The Epic' (*American Garage*), discussed in Chapter 3. Metheny commented in 1980:

> Generally, I'll have an A section and Lyle will write a bridge; or Lyle will have a whole tune and I'll try to build on it. I think most good ideas tend to come from individuals, as opposed to committee art, but we seem to have a way of enhancing each other's ideas. Even a couple of notes can make a difference.[59]

Although, as is implicit in this last quotation, their early compositions were still rooted in traditional jazz song forms, all this began to change markedly with *As Falls Wichita*. Metheny told *Down Beat* in 1982:

> we wanted to do a piece of music that was somehow *away* from the song form. So much of what we were doing were songs in which the improvisation was based on the harmonies in the song—in the jazz tradition.
>
> We wanted to try something where the improvisation happened not so much in a linear sense as in a *textural* sense.[60]

AS FALLS WICHITA, SO FALLS WICHITA FALLS

As noted above, the longest track on this album—occupying the entire A side of the original LP release—owed its genesis to a 15-minute piece designed to commence as the band walked on stage in a live gig and to build up to the performance of the opening tune in the set. The idea was not fully realised in practice before the album was recorded, and the preludial material instead became the second part of the definitive piece.[61] The orchestra-like nature of the synthesized parts was combined with the same 12-string tuning previously used in 'The Search' (*American Garage*), and the layered structure was enabled by extensive overdubbing. Something of the flavour of a live gig is nevertheless captured at the very beginning of the studio recording, where distant crowd noises are heard before the pulsating and highly expectant opening of the piece. (The musical effect here, both gesturally and harmonically, is momentarily not unlike the similarly expectant

59 Forte, 'Garage Band'.
60 Schneckloth, 'A Step beyond Tradition', 16.
61 *Pat Metheny Song Book*, 440.

opening cue in the later movie *Top Gun* (1986), with music by Harold Faltermeyer.) An early version of the material included a trumpet part for Mike Metheny.[62]

The working title for the piece was 'Apocalypse Later'—a humorous but revealing choice, given the parallels (discussed elsewhere) between film scoring and Metheny's music—and the definitive 'As Falls Wichita, So Falls Wichita Falls' wordplay was borrowed from an unperformed tune (with his permission) by Swallow.[63] Concerning the meaning of this designedly strange title, Metheny confessed that he liked the vagueness of it, and remarked: 'you wouldn't believe the letters we've gotten from people telling us what they think it's about. One guy thought it was about the takeover of the U.S. auto industry by Japan, and he had a four-page description of the events.'[64] Such an urban-centred reading is likely to have been inspired by the extensive use of electronics in the piece and would scarcely have been conceivable in the acoustic-rural soundworlds of some of Metheny's earlier music. Nevertheless, *Down Beat*'s reviewer—taking the flexible suggestiveness of the curious title to an interpretative extreme—described its suggestions in more pastoral terms as

a fascinating progression of moods: images of a stark plain capable of tornados, sudden afternoon storms, or a Saturday evening at that inevitable watery picnic spot just outside of town where Wichita Fallians must routinely go to communicate with nature and perform their Midwestern rituals. The war-like crowd noises that introduce the title cut could be imagined to be rural teens in their mating season, more extroverted the farther they get from pie-touting aunts and uncles. There's Eno and Faulkner in this music . . . a captivating atmospheric novella of sounds.[65]

62 Viva, *Pat Metheny*, 104.

63 Amusingly, Jan Garbarek's 1973 ECM album *Witchi-Tai-To*, with a title drawn from a tune by saxophonist Jim Pepper, has—since the success of the Metheny-Mays album—occasionally been garbled as *Wichita-Tai-To*: see, for example, Enwezor and Müller, *ECM: A Cultural Archaeology*, 221. Conversely, the location in the Metheny-Mays title is consistently mis-spelled as 'Witchita' in both Alexander, *Masters of Jazz Guitar*, chapter 14, and in the first two editions of Cook and Morton, *Penguin Guide to Jazz*.

64 Metheny, quoted in Schneckloth, 'A Step beyond Tradition', 16.

65 Robert Henschen, review of *As Falls Wichita, So Falls Wichita Falls*, *Down Beat* 47/9 (September 1980): 46-7.

The artwork on the front and rear of the album's sleeve seemingly reflects this co-existence of urban and pastoral readings of the music. The evocative photograph on the front of the sleeve (Fig. 4.2), which was not taken specifically for the disc, appropriately follows on from two types of image associated with *New Chautauqua*: a highway, and car headlights emerging from the distance (the latter an element in one of Metheny's own photographic choices for the earlier album which were not in the event used). Photographer Klaus Frahm had since 1976 been planning a series of conceptual images in which his hand would hold up objects to the horizon to see what relationships might thereby be evoked. The series became a reality when Frahm acquired a Nikon camera with a 24mm (wide-angle) lens, and he drove around in the

FIG. 4.2 *As Falls Wichita, So Falls Wichita Falls* sleeve art. Design by Barbara Wojirsch; photograph by Klaus Frahm. © ECM Records, 1981. Used by permission.

vicinity of Mainz scouting for photogenic skyscapes with a selection of everyday objects at the ready in the trunk of his car. The photograph on the sleeve of *As Falls Wichita* was the last in a series of three taken on infra-red film, with a telephone receiver held into the edge of the frame against a background of traditional wooden telegraph poles; the car appeared quite by chance after two shots had already been taken, and its illuminated headlights were unusual for that time of day. Frahm feels that the telephone in the hand suggests an 'imaginary dialogue' and is not untypical of 'Americana', though the highway in this instance is of course in Germany rather than America. The photographer contacted ECM's Barbara Wojirsch in 1978 about the possibility of his work being used in the company's sleeve designs; he began to attend gigs featuring ECM musicians at Onkel Pö's Carnegie Hall in Hamburg, and it was here that he presented Metheny with a signed print from the horizon series.[66]

The striking double portrait of Metheny and Mays on the album's rear cover (Fig. 4.3) more obviously suggests an urban ambience. The image was again the work of Rob Van Petten and was the first photo he took for Metheny, predating the vivid garage scene he photographed for the cover of *American Garage*. As with the garage picture, the *As Falls Wichita* monochrome image was hand-tinted with oil paints by Patti Roberts; in this case, however, the colorized image was reproduced faithfully on the album cover. The ghostly images of Metheny and Mays and other blurred, spectral figures are set against the evocative background of the Massachusetts Commonwealth Pier, a wharf building that had long been abandoned and which was secured for the shoot by Van Petten's assistant, Christopher Harting.[67] Both Frahm's and Van Petten's images, the one rural and the other quasi-industrial, perfectly complement the atmospheric suggestiveness of the album's title track.

The overall structure of 'As Falls Wichita, So Falls Wichita Falls' is outlined in Table 4.1. As noted above, the track commences with evocative crowd chatter, a ploy not unlike that which opens the title track of Weather Report's album *Black Market* (1976). Voice recordings also play a crucial role in creating a dreamlike atmosphere as the Metheny–Mays piece progresses. The section marked 'interlude' in the lead sheet

---

66 I am grateful to Klaus Frahm for supplying me with this information (personal communication via email, August 18, 2013). The full series of his horizon images from the late 1970s may be viewed at http://art.klaus-frahm.de (October 4, 2015).

67 Personal communication from Rob Van Petten.

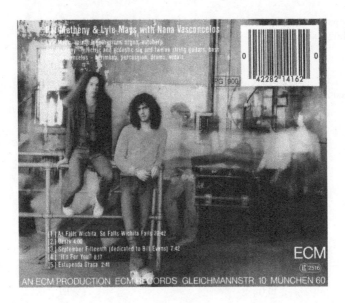

FIG. 4.3 *As Falls Wichita, So Falls Wichita Falls* rear of sleeve. Design by Barbara Wojirsch; photograph by Rob Van Petten. © ECM Records, 1981. Used by permission.

(F in Table 4.1) consists of gradually accumulated synthesizer chords, in free time, against which Metheny's voice reads out numbers from the relevant (random) point in the tape time-count: see Example 4.5. After the serenely pulsating parallel chords of the final section (G) have begun their steady journey through various tonal regions, indistinct children's voices join the mix and add considerably to the growing feeling of innocent euphoria in the closing stages of the piece, disappearing for a while when the texture becomes more contrapuntal (see below) but returning once more in the concluding bars. In between the two sections featuring the children, the solitary male voice—equally indistinct, but evidently speaking coherent text—re-enters, shortly after a particularly bright change of mode from C Dorian to E Mixolydian. These overdubbed voices may be related to the use of (wordless) singing in later Metheny compositions, where the impulse was specifically to humanize a soundscape in which electronic wizardry increasingly predominated.

TABLE 4.1 Structure of 'As Falls Wichita, So Falls Wichita Falls'
(studio version)*

Bars	Thematic/textural material	Harmony
[23 seconds]	Crowd chatter and distant percussion flourishes	–
'Intro'		
1–9	Synthesizer pedal point, pulsating quavers (chatter continues until 69)	G (no chords)
A		
10–69	Guitar and synthesizer chordal melody over short roving pedal points (the first three below immediately repeated as 26–39):	
	G (10–13)	Cmaj
	B♭ (14–15)	Fmaj
	F (16–25)	F Mixolydian
	D (40–41)	Dmi
	B♭ (42–4)	Dmi/B♭
	A (45–6)	A Phrygian
	F♯ (47–56)	–
	E (57–64)	E Aeolian/Locrian
	A (65–9)	A Phrygian
B		
70–181	Arpeggiated chordal ostinati beneath (from 100) lyrical sustained melody	A Aeolian
C ('perc. solo')		
182–[open]	Percussion solo (continues in background from 183 until 250)	–
D		
183–95	Sustained synthesizer chords, *senza misura*	Chromatic, ending on D7 with extensions
B'		
196–231	Modified recapitulation of lyrical synthesizer melody, over fifth-based riff	G Aeolian

(cont.)

TABLE 4.1   Continued

Bars	Thematic/textural material	Harmony
E ('free solo')		
232-[open]	Organ solo, *senza misura*	Roving: predominantly modal
233		Gsus4
B"		
234-49	Bass melody, forming transition to:	Chromatic
250-79	Climactic rhythmicized development of lyrical melody, culminating in	A Aeolian
280-88	*ff* cadences supported by return of percussion solo	
F ('interlude')		
289	Gradually accumulated synthesizer chords, *senza misura*, with voiced-over numerals read out from tape time counter (Ex. 4.5)	C Lydian Eb Lydian
G		
290-360	Syncopated parallel harmonies over simple V-I riff bass (Ex. 4.9), passing through unrelated keys:	
	290-303	Gb Lydian
	304-12	A Dorian
	313-32	C Dorian
	333-42	E Mixolydian
	343-50	Bb Mixolydian
	351-60	Cmaj (ending F/G)

Indistinct children's voices overdubbed at 307-22 and 347-60, and indistinct male voice at 335-43; three-note scalic motif layered above chordal texture throughout.

* This chart is based on the published lead sheet in *Pat Metheny Song Book*, 116-25, replacing rehearsal letters with letters denoting the components of the formal structure. Bar numbers reflect the actual lengths of sections notated using repeat marks in the score, apart from solos marked 'open', when the bar count is suspended. Section titles in inverted commas appear on the lead sheet.

EX. 4.5 'As Falls Wichita, So Falls Wichita Falls': time count (ASB, 122). © 1981 Pat Meth Music Corp. and Lyle Mays, Inc. All rights reserved.

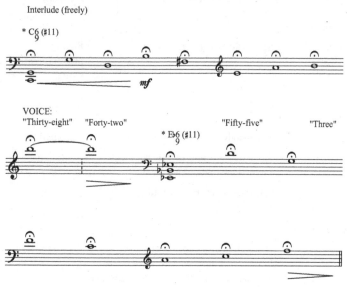

[* Build chords gradually, let ring]

The electronics in 'As Falls Wichita' are indeed spectacularly resourceful, and represent the absolute cutting edge of what was technologically possible at the time. The sound quality throughout the track is superb, and the quasi-orchestral timbres richly alluring. Keyboard instruments utilized as the textures become more elaborate are the Oberheim four-voice synthesizer, Prophet 5 synthesizer, Yamaha YC-20 electric organ, and Mays's acoustic Steinway series B. Mays confessed to admiring the simplicity of the Prophet 5 when he wanted to concentrate on the spirit of the moment and not 'get bogged down in technology'.[68] But to emphasize the remarkable creativity of the electronics should not be at the expense of Vasconcelos's equally arresting contribution to the music's haunting atmosphere, which includes his trademark vocal gargles and an idiosyncratic extended percussion solo (C) which recedes into the background as the music continues on its way.

68 Diliberto and Haas, 'Lyle Mays', 27.

The tonal language of 'As Falls Wichita' is relatively simple. After the opening use of throbbingly expectant pedal points, involving some piquant dissonances when the bass notes clash with the triad-based melodic line above, the vast majority of the piece is based on unadorned modes. A lengthy section (B), exclusively in Aeolian A, introduces a number of motivic patterns which will recur and be reworked in corresponding sections later in the piece (B' and B''). One of the most immediately recognizable, on account of both its pentatonic nature and strong rhythmic profile, is shown in Example 4.6 (bb. 115-20): this later forms the springboard for the most rhythmically active part of the composition (Ex. 4.7; bb. 250-54), following the bass solo that introduces B''. Also prominent in the long lyrical melody in the B section is the falling scalic pattern shown in Example 4.8a (bb. 148-50) which returns following the percussion solo in the form given in Example 4.8b (bb. 205-9).

While for the most part the track's vivid sonic engineering plays a considerable role in achieving atmospheric suggestiveness from fairly basic musical raw materials, it is notable that the final section (G) is assembled using more conventional compositional strategies to achieve a strongly directional approach towards the conclusion. While the seductively imaginative soundscape continues, thanks to the combination of synthesized timbres and the haunting overdubbed voices,

EX. 4.6 'As Falls Wichita, So Falls Wichita Falls': pentatonic motif (SB, 118). © 1981 Pat Meth Music Corp. and Lyle Mays, Inc.

EX. 4.7 'As Falls Wichita, So Falls Wichita Falls': pentatonic theme (SB, 118). © 1981 Pat Meth Music Corp. and Lyle Mays, Inc.

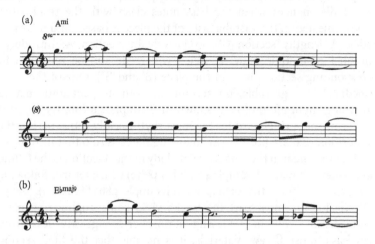

the syncopated parallel harmonies (all presented above highly stable V-I cadential patterns in the bass) move through contrasting tonal regions, and at the same time explore the different voicings shown in Examples 4.9a-e. Contrapuntal layering of a falling three-note scalic figure is gradually superimposed, as shown in its fullest form in Example 4.10 (bb. 325-32); and, for a short time, the voices disappear as the musical texture remains elaborate, before the final three key changes bring the piece to a close more simply. This is all achieved through what the lead sheet describes as a 'very gradual crescendo throughout', structurally significant dynamic gradations of this kind being something of a Metheny hallmark.

The live recording of 'As Falls Wichita' on *Travels* is noticeably shorter than the studio version, even when the time count includes the nearly four-minute introductory guitar solo loosely based on 'Goin' Ahead', which Luigi Viva praises for its telling use of open strings.[69] The 20-minute composition on the studio album is here truncated to just over 12 minutes, concluding with the climactic cadence at the end of B″ and omitting the following interlude (F) and closing section (G) in their entirety. The performance opens with far more nightmarish sound effects than the chatter in the studio version: Vasconcelos's gargles and cries are unsettling, even disturbing, and the synthesized throbbing noises suggest the threat of approaching helicopter rotor blades. Given

69 Viva, *Pat Metheny*, 130-31.

that the original working title for 'As Falls Wichita' was 'Apocalypse Later', the rotor effect comes across as an allusion to the Vietnam War movie *Apocalypse Now* (dir. Francis Ford Coppola, 1979), in which real and processed rotor noises are a highlight of the film's innovative and Oscar-winning sound design by Walter Murch. After the percussion solo (C), Mays performs a more elaborate and extended synthesizer-based solo passage than anything on the studio recording, followed by a solo on the Yamaha organ (as in the studio version), and in the lyrical melody-based sections the interplay between guitar and keyboards demonstrates a flexibility and freshness typical of Metheny's and Mays's spontaneous interactions in live performance.

If the title track of *As Falls Wichita* seemed to leave the whole notion of pastoral or rural jazz firmly aside, the first track on side B of the original album restored it with a vengeance. Entitled 'Ozark' after the highland region of Missouri, the piece bursts forth with a bubbling mix

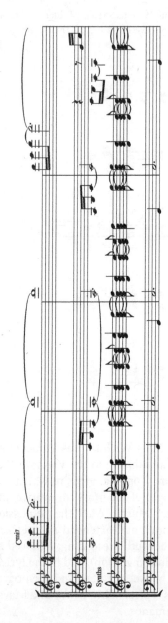
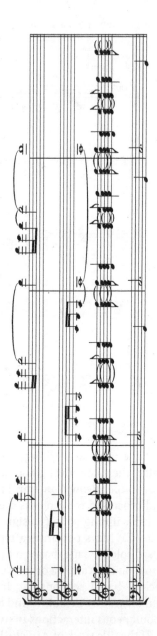

EX. 4.10 'As Falls Wichita, So Falls Wichita Falls': counterpoint (AT). © 1981 Pat Meth Music Corp. and Lyle Mays, Inc. All rights reserved.

of country-style diatonic melody and dynamic minimalism, with a firm emphasis on acoustic sonorities throughout: here Vasconcelos plays berimbau, while Metheny plays a prototype Ibanez instrument that would later bear the endorsement of his name.[70] This short piece sets out exclusively in the diatonic major (Ionian) mode on C, with the melody played on piano and answered by high acoustic bass, until Mays's highly rhythmic acoustic piano solo steers the music into alternative tonal regions; a simple recapitulation of the opening pandiatonic material then rounds off the basic ternary form. The interlocking keyboard figurations are an up-tempo equivalent to the 'groove vamp' textures identified by Peter Elsdon in his study of Jarrett's keyboard style. The following remark of Elsdon's, which is worth quoting at some length, would apply equally well to the effervescent playing on this track:

> There is an important tradition within jazz of the piano acting as the generator of groove in a solo context. In styles such as boogie-woogie, stride, and ragtime, the left hand functions both to generate rhythmic momentum through a repeated figure as well as to articulate harmony. This dual role is inherently virtuosic, in that particularly with accomplished practitioners it demonstrates independence of the two hands. Both seem to be doing completely different, but simultaneously related, things. The virtuosic effect comes from the juxtaposition of the two parts rather than the constitution of either one . . . [In Jarrett's case:] Rather than a clear demarcation between right and left hands, whereby one serves a melodic function and the other rhythmic/harmonic, in this case both hands work in much the same way. This interlocking is both literal and metaphoric. There is an effect whereby the rhythms in both hands create a resultant pattern when combined, . . . meaning that distinguishing between the two hands by ear is almost impossible.[71]

In live performances, for example a 1982 concert in Montreal which was televised in the UK by Channel 4, Vasconcelos improvised a lengthy berimbau introduction.

Metheny's and Mays's debt to pianist Bill Evans was noted in Chapter 2, and at around the time of *As Falls Wichita* Metheny reflected that his own group's manner of performing was a 'mutated' descendant of the close interaction between individual instruments in

70 *Ibid.*, 105.
71 Elsdon, *Keith Jarrett's The Köln Concert*, 106-7.

the piano trios led by Evans in the late 1950s and early 1960s.[72] Evans died on September 15, 1980, during the same month in which the album was recorded, and by way of tribute to him they combined two pre-existing pieces (written at different times) and included them on the album.[73] In sharp contrast to both the experimental title track and the infectiously bubbling intricacies of 'Ozark', the resulting duet for guitar and piano—'September Fifteenth (dedicated to Bill Evans)'—sounds like a spontaneous live performance with solely acoustic instruments, and brilliantly demonstrates the instinctive rapport between the two performers when playing with considerable rubato. This rapport is well demonstrated by a live video recording of the piece as it was performed by Metheny and Mays many years later, at Saratoga's Mountain Winery in July 1998, which culminated in a particularly rhapsodic and wide-ranging solo from Mays and a fresh, understated coda from the duo.[74]

Mays described the structure of 'September Fifteenth' as falling into three distinct parts: the first (written by him around 1977) inspired by Ravel and Debussy, both of whom had previously influenced Evans's harmonic language; the second written by Metheny (in 1974), during a Burton tour, for Towner and the group Oregon; and a concluding improvisation.[75] Viva notes that Metheny, unusually, plays his Guild nylon-string guitar with a pick, and that Mays's playing recalls the touch and melodic approach of Chopin—another composer by whom Evans was significantly influenced.[76]

The rich harmonies of the opening section, which sets out from diatonic G major but modulates to B major via D♭ (= C♯) major, are essentially a string of secondary-seventh-based chords interspersed with inversions and relatively consonant slash chords which create a strongly directional supporting bass line (often moving by step) beneath the poignant and lyrical melody. The second section moves into compound time for a lilting chromatic pattern anchored to a drone fifth, the guitar accompanying a synthesizer theme with a prominent major/minor inflection; this material is repeated sequentially in A major before both performers embark on their extended unison melodic flight, with considerable rubato, the music here moving swiftly through a variety of key centres. The concluding section is an elaborate and intensely

72 Forte, 'Jazz Voice of the 80's', 114.
73 *Pat Metheny Song Book*, 440.
74 Pat Metheny Group: *Imaginary Day Live* (DVD; Eagle Vision EREDV 265), 2001.
75 *Pat Metheny Song Book*, 440. Oregon did not in fact perform the Metheny tune.
76 Viva, *Pat Metheny*, 106.

expressive improvised piano solo, concluding with a brief reminiscence of the unison melody.

The last two tracks on the album are effectively contrasted. 'It's for You' originated in 1977 but was not completed until 1979, this being the first co-composition undertaken by Metheny and Mays (in a Florida practice room) when they were touring with Marlena Shaw and Metheny asked the pianist to join his new band—though it was not their first to be recorded.[77] (The title is an in-joke inspired by the telephone receiver being offered to the viewer of Frahm's photograph on the album cover.) The piece is the only track on the album to use the Gibson ES 175, and the introduction is played on an acoustic Guild DN40C and Guild F50R. The style of this introduction, which continues by way of accompaniment to the initial synthesizer melody, recalls the innovations of *New Chautauqua*, and the combination of electronics and acoustic (12-string) guitar strumming was unusual for its time. At the very opening, as footage of the more vigorous live performance in Montreal reveals, Mays (counterintuitively) plays the synthesizer melody with his left hand while the right hand supplies chordal support from a second keyboard; Steve Rodby's bass line is performed on a synthesizer rather than regular bass. After a shift from the opening E♭ major to B major (the dominant B♭ chord sliding up a semitone), the guitar continues a minimalist-like ostinato beneath slowly descending vocalese scalic figures from Vasconcelos and more rapidly rising statements of a three-note scalic motif on the synthesizer: see Example 4.11. The synthesizer material directly recalls the patterns in the textural climax of the album's title track (cf. Ex. 4.10). The remainder of the piece is a buoyant guitar solo on the Gibson, overdubbed onto the continuing strumming patterns and synthesizer motifs and ending in a gradual fade-out.

The final track, 'Estupenda Graça', was the first item ever to be sung as a conventional melody on a Metheny recording, and its accompaniment featured a new 12-string tuning. Metheny felt this arrangement of 'Amazing Grace' did not quite match up to the standards of the rest of the album,[78] but the interpretation is memorably atmospheric with its gently dissonant introduction and interlude, unexpected harmonisations, and evocative percussion effects which again recall aspects of the album's title track.

Mays, for whom *As Falls Wichita, So Falls Wichita Falls* was to remain a firm favourite amongst his Metheny projects, described the

---

77 *Pat Metheny Song Book*, 439.
78 *Pat Metheny Song Book*, 440; Viva, *Pat Metheny*, 106.

EX. 4.11 'It's For You': ascending three-note motif (AT). © 1981 Pat Meth Music Corp. and Lyle Mays, Inc. All rights reserved.

synthesizer-based experimental pieces on the album as very 'space age'.[79] Steve Lake also referred to what he called the project's 'sci-fi dimensions' and drew attention to the way in which the creative use of the studio made an 'intimate project ... sound immense'.[80] Although, as we saw above, Frahm's evocative photograph on the sleeve was not commissioned for the album, the feel of both the recording and its packaging was not far removed from comparable aspects of progressive rock and the contemporaneous ambient music which Thom Holmes explains as a 'by-product of the analog synthesizer sequencer' created by 'early adopters of modular synthesizers and technically savvy musicians'.[81] The title track was described in *Down Beat* as 'a stream-of-consciousness dreamscape.'[82] Resonating with the times in ways that fully accorded with Metheny's ongoing belief in the importance of a new paradigm in jazz that would be directly relevant to contemporary musical culture, the album reached the number one spot on the *Billboard* jazz chart, and received a (maximum) five-star review in *Down Beat* (quoted on p. 172). For all the project's technical wizardry and compositional experimentation, however, numbers such as 'September Fifteenth' continued to demonstrate a hauntingly memorable command of more traditional musical values and an undiminished appreciation of the power of simple, lyrical melody and the ability to communicate effectively through spontaneous performance on acoustic instruments.

79 Quoted in Viva, *Pat Metheny*, 103.
80 Enwezor and Müller, *ECM: A Cultural Archaeology*, 224.
81 Thom Holmes, *Electronic and Experimental Music: Technology, Music, and Culture* (New York: Routledge, 2012), 438.
82 Diliberto and Haas, 'Lyle Mays', 25.

CHAPTER 5

TURNING POINT

Before 1978, I was just a guitar player, you know, and
maybe I could play a little bit of piano, and I'd write
things on piano and give them to the cats in the band.
But since that time ... I really think of music
as this big thing now, of which the guitar is a
component and I really think a lot of that has to do
with what the Synclavier kind of forced me into
thinking about, you know, anything is possible.[1]

INTERVIEWED IN 1981, Metheny predicted that his next album
would make considerable use of guitar synthesizer, embody a 'new
group sound', and be a delayed opportunity to record pieces which
the band had been playing live for some time.[2] The new sound he had
in mind was the distinctive combination of acoustic bass and Naná
Vasconcelos's percussion and vocals.

After Mark Egan's departure in the summer of 1980 and the
recording of *As Falls Wichita, So Falls Wichita Falls* without an
independent bassist, the bass chair in the Metheny band became freshly
occupied (following auditions) by Steve Rodby. Classically trained

1 Mike Brannon, interview with Pat Metheny (June 2000), formerly available at http://www.
allaboutjazz.com.
2 Forte, 'Jazz Voice of the 80's', 114.

and well known to Metheny, Mays, and Gottlieb independently from jazz summer camps, Rodby quickly became not only a lynchpin of the Metheny Group as a performer—gaining in the process a reputation for meticulous attention to detail—but also as a valued co-producer. Rodby was proficient on electric bass, and indeed continued to play the same customized fretless Fender instrument that had been passed on from Jaco Pastorius to Egan.[3] But Rodby's importance arguably lay primarily in his expertise on acoustic bass, the potential of which as a member of the Metheny Group's lineup had been suggested to Metheny by his recent experiences of playing with Charlie Haden—and not least because the instrument allowed for the possibility of playing straight-ahead jazz for the first time in the context of his regular band's gigs, which had up until this point been anchored by electric bass.[4] Whereas Metheny felt Egan's conception of the bass's function had remained rooted in the example of Pastorius, he paid tribute to Rodby for 'dealing with the role of the bass in a very egoless way' and 'playing very simply yet still putting his own stamp on it'.[5]

Rodby's acoustic playing, which like Haden's was so instinctively supportive that it allowed for considerable flexibility in both harmonic and textural parameters, also meshed perfectly with Mays's continuing reliance on acoustic piano for his soloing, with the result that the new group format allowed for a full range of sonic possibilities: from a purely acoustic jazz quartet to complex quasi-orchestral electronic textures, and innovative blends of elements of both. Vasconcelos's coloristic yet natural percussion effects both complemented and reinforced Gottlieb's more conventional drumming, a new challenge that had not arisen in *As Falls Wichita*, on which the Brazilian was the sole percussionist. As Metheny put it:

There were times that Nana would lock into a groove with Danny, and suddenly we had a rhythmic power that we'd never had before. But he was as likely to be floating over the time and providing colors as he was to be functioning rhythmically with Danny.[6]

3 Schneckloth, 'A Step beyond Tradition', 16.
4 Forte, 'Jazz Voice of the 80's', 110. For Steve Swallow's insightful account of the essential differences between acoustic- and electric-bass playing in jazz, see Rosenbaum, 'Steve Swallow', 64.
5 Milkowski, 'Pat Metheny's Digital Manifesto', 61.
6 Mattingly, 'A Different View', 80.

The first album produced by the new lineup, *Offramp* (1982), embodied the group's most adventurous experiments to date, while at the same time including an easygoing tuneful piece ('James') of considerable popularity.[7] This kind of stark stylistic contrast may perhaps be compared with Weather Report's *Mr. Gone* (1978), which had also juxtaposed avant-garde experimentation with catchy hook-based numbers: Joe Zawinul aptly described their recording as 'our most complex album but also the most accessible'.[8] In a manner prophetic of the lambasting that Metheny's *American Garage* would soon receive from the same journal, however, the Weather Report album suffered a notorious mauling in the pages of *Down Beat*, which awarded it the minimum one star in a rampant overreaction both to its alleged commercial bias and lack of traditional improvisation; the music was summed up by the reviewer as displaying 'the sterility of a too completely pre-conceived project'. Zawinul, clearly hurt and perplexed by the reaction, responded to the tirade in the journal's pages during the following month, in an article during which his interviewer was careful to emphasize the positive, creative side of the band's distinctive idiom.[9]

The freedom of the avant-garde title track on *Offramp* in some respects looks ahead to Metheny's later work with Ornette Coleman (*Song X*, 1986) and contrasts markedly with both 'James' and the quasi-minimalist and pop influences evident in 'Eighteen'. In the case of the Metheny Group, the sharp idiomatic contrasts between pieces such as these were a direct reflection of their eclectic repertoire in live performances. In the analyses below, the album's performances will be compared with the live versions on the double album *Travels*, recorded at the group's gigs during a US tour undertaken between July and November 1982, which includes several compositions not represented on the studio recordings: among them are 'Song for Bilbao' and 'Farmer's Trust', which effectively juxtapose guitar-synthesizer timbres with the simplicity of nylon-stringed acoustic guitar played lyrically with a pick. *Offramp* also revisited 'The Bat', which had previously featured on the album *80/81* (discussed in Chapter 4).

---

7 For a jovial set of colour photographs of the Metheny Group at around the time of the *Offramp* release, see Enwezor and Müller, *ECM: A Cultural Archaeology*, 149.

8 Conrad Silvert, 'Joe Zawinul: Wayfaring Genius—Part II', *Down Beat* 45/6 (June 15, 1978): 58.

9 'Less', review of Weather Report, *Mr. Gone*, *Down Beat* 46/1 (January 11, 1979): 22. Zawinul's response appeared in Larry Birnbaum, 'Weather Report Answers Its Critics', *Down Beat* 46/1 (February 8, 1979): 14-16, 44-5.

The electronic soundscapes of *Offramp* were more complex than in Metheny's previous albums, the initiative driven both by his use of the Roland GR-300 guitar synthesizer, and by his commitment to the then-new Synclavier technology. The Synclavier nevertheless continued to demand traditional compositional skills, as editing material once it had been played into the computer was virtually impossible. Metheny noted that *Offramp* was the first recording to use guitar synthesizer as a front-line instrument, although it had previously been used as a background effect in music by King Crimson, Andy Summers, and Jimmy Page.[10] The instrument was also beginning to be used at this time by John McLaughlin and Adrian Belew.

SYNCLAVIER AND ROLAND GR-300/G-303

A major turning point in Metheny's compositional methods came with his adoption of the Synclavier, which he acquired in late 1979. After working on it for several months in Woodstock, a process which included tackling the challenge of synchronizing drum machines to the device, he felt there was considerable potential for its sequencing power to be deployed—for the first time in an improvisation-based ensemble—in the music of his own band when it performed live. The early fruits of this initiative were the compositions 'Barcarole' and 'Are You Going with Me?' (see below). Metheny explained that after this experience he had

> basically ... written everything on the Synclavier. At least on the keyboard, as opposed to writing on the guitar. I think that was a *real* big shift, and I think you hear a fairly substantial compositional change around that time ... It's keyboard oriented as opposed to guitar oriented.[11]

As already noted, jazz composers tend to find the keyboard indispensable for explorations of sophisticated harmony: Miles Davis was advised by Dizzy Gillespie to approach composition in this way, for example, and the view was echoed by Steve Swallow as well as

---

10 Kay, 'Pat Metheny', 56.
11 Aledort, 'Pat Metheny: Straight Ahead', 62. In spite of the new keyboard-driven impetus in his work with the Synclavier in the early 1980s, Metheny's own keyboard playing is not credited as such on the albums he released in this period.

by Metheny.[12] The latter commented that he found trying out ideas on a keyboard had a greater 'neutrality' than working on guitar—though alternating freely between guitar, keyboard, and computer according to the differing requirements of individual pieces was to remain his preferred, flexible working pattern. More fundamentally, the Synclavier's ability to help a composer 'form entire compositions with either simulated or real orchestrations in a very short time' now made the interrelationship between improvisation and composition far more immediate.[13]

The Synclavier was developed in 1974-5 at Dartmouth University, New Hampshire, and built and marketed in the late 1970s by the New England Digital Corporation at an initial retail cost in the stratospheric range of $50,000 to $300,000 per unit. (To set this in context, the average cost of a new house in the United States in 1975 was around $40,000.)[14] The machine, which was the first digital synthesizer to be made commercially available, utilized FM (frequency modulation) synthesis to modify the timbres of waveforms, and was performance-friendly in its ability to store prepared audio tracks that could be triggered by a live performer, who might use a keyboard, gestural controller (a principle used in the operation of the much earlier theremin), or—in a somewhat later development—a guitar-style controller. The Synclavier's 16-track recording capability in effect provided musicians with their own instant studio, and this meant that the device was potentially as useful as a compositional tool as it was as a generator of electronic timbres; at the same time, as the technology continued to develop, the machine's capability for reproducing and modifying sampled sounds across an entire keyboard range became truly formidable.[15] The Synclavier represented a quantum leap ahead from the Oberheim technology of the mid-1970s, which had multiplied a synthesizer expander module to permit polyphonic sonorities up to a maximum of eight sounding voices—and just four in the case of the particular machine used by Mays in previous

---

12 See Ian Carr, *Miles Davis: The Definitive Biography* (London: Harper Collins, 1998), 20-21. Gillespie specifically felt that using a keyboard would expand Davis's grasp of harmony: see Miles Davis with Quincy Troupe, *Miles: The Autobiography* (New York: Simon and Schuster, 1989), 48. Swallow's views are cited in Rosenbaum, 'Steve Swallow', 67.

13 Goldstein, *Jazz Composer's Companion*, 103.

14 'Median and Average Sales Prices of New Homes Sold in the United States'. www.census. gov/const/uspricemon.pdf (August 8, 2014).

15 Diliberto and Haas, 'Lyle Mays', 26-7.

repertoire. By contrast, the Synclavier models were capable of 64-voice (and, in later incarnations, 128-voice) polyphony. Made available in 1980, the Synclavier II (which quickly lost the 'II') was a more capable version which caught up with the digital-sampling and sequencing innovations of the Fairlight CMI (Computer Music Instrument) launched in Australia in the previous year; the new incarnation featured editing via video monitor, a potent sequencer, and the capability for re-synthesizing previously sampled sounds and drawing on a huge library of pre-set timbres. The new-generation Synclavier became the market leader in digital synthesizers before it was supplanted by burgeoning MIDI technology in the late 1980s.[16]

A particular breakthrough for Metheny was the discovery of a viable guitar synthesizer in the shape of the Roland GR-300, an analog device that could be played as convincingly as a real guitar (via the G-303 guitar controller) and whose potential he directly compared to the musical capabilities of his beloved Gibson 175. As he told Dan Forte, the Roland synthesizer

> sounds like me playing—my personality is still there. It's just that instead of sounding like a guitar, it sounds like a trumpet or a bass or an orchestra . . . My phrasing and everything just transfers over to this particular synthesizer totally intact. In other words, I can do all my sort of sliding kind of horn lines and they really come out intact. Plus, it allows me to play some real sort of angular stuff that I've been playing on the guitar all along, but on the synthesizer it has a certain rough edge to it that I've never felt comfortable getting on a regular guitar.[17]

Quizzed as to what he meant by 'angular', Metheny replied: 'Semi-atonal. But I've wanted to find something for a long time as a contrast

16 Holmes, *Electronic and Experimental Music*, 289–92. Holmes gives technical specifications for both incarnations of the Synclavier (488) and an overview of earlier jazz and rock musicians' experimentation with electronics, beginning with taped elements and then analog synthesizers played live in the late 1960s (400–11 and 442–53).

17 Forte, 'Jazz Voice of the 80's', 105. In the same issue of *Guitar Player* as Forte's article (December 1981), a Roland advertisement declares: 'Roland's Synthesizer units are designed to adapt to your playing style, rather than the other way around. Touch dynamics, string bending, slurring and other playing techniques are all tracked flawlessly. It is these dynamic qualities that allow the GR system to produce tonal textures and effects unlike any other instrument' (13).

to my regular sound, which is kind of dark, and this is like a real rough sound.' The new ideal was vividly achieved in the title track of *Offramp*.

As Roland expert Wayne Scott Joness notes, the GR-300's six-voice technology offers only limited timbral potential, and because Metheny became so inextricably associated with its sonority, it has remained a challenge for younger performers not to sound like his example. Joness draws a parallel between the Roland's basic sound and the trumpet, an instrument cited many times by Metheny when stressing the importance of breathing and horn-like phrasing in effective improvisations. As Metheny put it himself:

> The Roland has a high trumpet sound, which I particularly like and when I'm using it I tend to not think like a guitar player, but rather like a horn player and have always done so, even in my guitar playing, in the sense that I like to have natural 'breaths', which sound natural [as] if I were playing a wind instrument. All that was immediately translated, but there were even a lot of phrasing things which might sound all right on a guitar, but on a trumpet they would sound real stiff. You have to think in those terms.[18]

Another important breakthrough for the guitarist was the advent of a guitar-operated triggering system for the Synclavier, which was at first (in 1981) a stringless prototype made in Salt Lake City by Oncor.

Interviewed in 1984 with *Offramp* and *Travels* behind him, Metheny commented that an overly heavy reliance on synthesizers might easily lead to 'too many short cuts', especially in the case of untrained musicians who could combine a Synclavier and Linn drum machine and 'still be able to come up with some pretty hip stuff', and he stressed the importance of continuing to learn about three crucial, traditional parameters in order to create good music: rhythm, melody, and harmony.[19] Discussing in 2014 the far greater range of technological possibilities available to musicians today, he commented that the potential offered by music technology

> doesn't make writing music any easier—at all. It is just that there are tools available now that allow you to become deeply critical of things and to be able to render solutions with a kind of efficiency that

18 Nicholas Webb, 'Interview with Roland GR User Pat Metheny', *Guitarist* 1/12 (May 1986): 28–31.
19 Kay, 'Pat Metheny', 59.

before would have required a much higher percentage of time spent in the realm of erasers and busy work. It may be that something is lost by losing that busy work time and there is a kind of glibness that can enter into the composing process because of the obvious ease of getting to a few basic things. But the standards that make something great or not great are well in place by now, and the tools used are irrelevant to the result in music in a way that is unique to how music works.[20]

OFFRAMP

Offramp was recorded over three days, commencing on October 22, 1981, in the brand new Studio C at the Power Station, New York, which was henceforth to become one of Metheny's favourite recording venues. The occasion was recorded by photographer Deborah Feingold, whose on-the-spot portraits of the performers and a group shot in the studio were featured in the album: see, for an example, Figure 5.1.[21] In spite of the use of an American facility, the recording was on this occasion engineered by Kongshaug, and produced by Eicher. The album's cover (Fig. 5.2) featured a stark image by Gerd Winner which, as described by Thomas Steinfeld, 'shows a strip of asphalt with the inscription "Turn Left". But all you see is the street itself, and there is no indication as to where this direction leads'.[22] Along with water scenes, street or highway images were common in ECM's sleeve art at around this time, and we have already encountered two previous examples in Metheny's own output on the label (*New Chautauqua* and *As Falls Wichita, So Falls Wichita Falls*). But here the symbolism is more obvious: 'to take a left' in US slang means to do something new or to act out of character, an appropriate sentiment for an album which delighted in experimentation and startling stylistic juxtapositions. The sleeve was designed by Dieter Rehm (as was to be the case with *Travels*), whose 'deliberate slices of reality', according to Peter Kemper, were imbued with a 'new culture of the gaze' and 'an unmistakably cinematic quality'.[23] Then in his 20s, Rehm went on to become a master's student of Winner's at the

---

20 Metheny, interviewed in Goldstein, *Jazz Composer's Companion*, 103.
21 Lake and Griffiths, *Horizons Touched*, 327.
22 Steinfeld, 'When Twilight Comes', 39.
23 Peter Kemper, 'Along the Margins of Murmuring', in Müller, *ECM: Sleeves of Desire*, 11-12.

FIG. 5.1 *Offramp*: session photo (October 1981) by Deborah Feingold. *Left to right*: Nana Vasconcelos, Manfred Eicher, Pat Metheny, Jan Erik Kongshaug. © Deborah Feingold, 1981. Used by permission.

Academy of Fine Arts in Munich in the early 1980s, and at the time of writing he is the Academy's president.

The concept of a piece serving primarily as an introduction to another more substantial item had already arisen in live performances when the composition 'As Falls Wichita, So Falls Wichita Falls' was first planned (see Chapter 4), and *Offramp*'s three-minute opening track, 'Barcarole', served a similar function on a smaller scale. Created on the Synclavier and drum machine, it was written during an experimental session with Vasconcelos, who was loath even to touch the new technology, and the piece was designed as a prelude to 'Are You Going with Me?'[24] A sparse percussion introduction based on a pulse-like pattern continues to throb along underneath Metheny's expansive solo line and Mays's sustained chordal accompaniment on synthesizer (some of which had to be overdubbed owing to limitations of the two-track output), both of which are shaped by a relaxed rubato which contrasts markedly with the inexorable pulsations beneath. As we have already

24 *Pat Metheny Song Book*, 440.

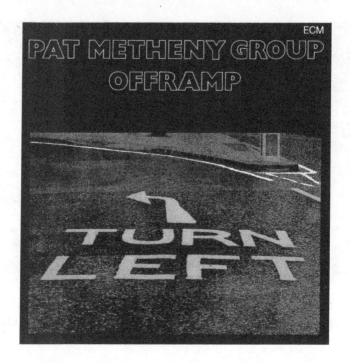

FIG. 5.2 *Offramp* sleeve art. Design by Dieter Rehm; photograph by Gerd Winner. © ECM Records, 1982. Used by permission.

seen, characteristic of this general period in Metheny's music is the effective juxtaposition of sections of relative harmonic stasis (based on pedal points) with more dynamic and rapid harmonic progressions: the piece commences in an evocative B♭ Lydian, the solo line emphasizing the raised fourth, then passes quickly through both sharp and flat regions of the circle of fifths with the aid of a strong bass line underpinning slash chords; the harmonic tension relaxes as the music shifts into E minor at roughly the mid-point, the F sharps then cancelled out as a long stretch of white-note pandiatonicism prevails before the return of the opening B♭ Lydian. The music fades away to nothing just after Metheny has embarked on an unexpectedly frenetic solo and Mays drops out.

The ensuing 'Are You Going with Me?' is, as noted above, the first composition Metheny wrote specifically for the Synclavier, the music having been played directly into the computer and orchestrated on the spot; he subsequently discovered how using the GR-300 over the top could create a new sound.[25] Mays's laid-back synthesizer pad over the introduction sets up a texture which immediately preserves a link with the preceding number in its superimposition of quiet, sustained harmonies over relentless repetitions of a simple dyadic riff, the latter syncopated in a Latin manner against a gently pulsating bass line moving in a slow harmonic rhythm. Above this, Mays doubles Metheny's modal melody in the prevailing C Aeolian, the harmonies alternating exclusively between Cmi7, A♭maj7, and A♭maj7/B♭ until a strong move into a functional C minor via a regular perfect cadence coincides with a descending line in parallel thirds and fourths. (In later live performances, these opening lyrical lines proved ideal for doubling by the wordless voices that were an increasingly prominent feature of the Metheny Group's soundscapes.) All this is by way of preamble to what Luigi Viva terms an 'extraordinary ride' from Metheny on the Roland machine, an extended solo which admirably demonstrates the trumpet-like way in which he played the new device.[26] After Mays performs a brief, harmonica-like synthesizer solo on his C minor melody, the key suddenly shifts up a semitone into C♯ minor, into which region the same chord changes are transposed, as Metheny embarks on his fluent and melodically memorable solo (transcribed in Ex. 5.1a, as far as the coda). A final ascending semitonal shift propels the harmonies yet further upwards, into D minor, at the conclusion of the solo. Joness describes the guitarist's habit of engaging 'the pitch offset to lift the end of his solos one octave up': 'Not only does this raise the pitch', he writes, 'but it also opens the [low-pass] filter up more, making for a brighter sound.'[27] Metheny demonstrated the effect to Richard Cook in the course of an interview in 1987 by playing an extract from this track, and saying: 'If I had to play that on a regular guitar I'd constantly be going *right up here*, to where there aren't any notes.'[28]

Owing to time constraints in the studio, no overdubbing was possible when laying down 'Are You Going with Me?': all instrumental lines had to be performed simultaneously. Three takes were recorded, but Metheny was dissatisfied with his solo as he ideally would have wished to spend more time honing it. The piece, the studio recording of which was issued on a 7-inch single with the same album's 'Au Lait' on

25 *Ibid.* See also Goldstein, *Jazz Composer's Companion*, 103.
26 Viva, *Pat Metheny*, 117.
27 Wayne Scott Joness, 'Roland GR-300 Analog Guitar Synthesizer', http://www.joness.com/gr300/GR-300.htm (August 5, 2013).
28 Richard Cook, 'Are You Going with Me?', *Wire* 43 (September 1987): 36.

the flip side, continued to evolve on the road. In due course, Metheny came to prefer the live solo preserved in the *Travels* release (Ex. 5.1b, placed under Ex. 5.1a to aid direct comparison), on which the piece is the opening track of the first disc; in this performance the GR-300's 'blue box' allowed him to jump up an octave halfway through, after the final change of key from C♯ minor to D minor.[29] Viva notes that the *Travels* version is even more overtly Brazilian in flavour than the studio recording, with the bossa/samba-like rhythm section featuring Vasconcelos's hypnotically pulsating tambourine and xequerê (gourd).[30] The opening statement of the accompanying riffs elicits a huge, expectant cheer from the enthusiastic crowd.

Both solos are impressive when taken on their own merits. Similarities between them include the emphatic elaboration of $\hat{2}$ in the opening 4 bars (in both cases followed by a melodic descent); leading into new phrases with strongly ascending figurations (bb. 16, 24, and 68-9); a rarer descending figuration occurring at the same juncture (b. 64); the culminating burst of energy in the most rapid rhythmic pattern (semiquaver triplets/sextuplets); and, most prominently and structurally important of all, the similar and powerful repeated-note climaxes as the key shifts up from C♯ minor to D minor (bb. 45-9). These climaxes are executed via different rhythmic patterns in each solo, and the live example is particularly exciting in its continuation of its hard-driving pattern into the first 2 bars of the D minor section, now extended by a quaver in order to create a thrilling rhythmic displacement, and its transformation in the third bar (51) into a turn figure embodying flat 5 before the final descent down the perfect fifth (52) when the blue note is cancelled. This accomplished moment perhaps suggests greater confidence with the instrument, and on the whole it is relatively easy to see why Metheny preferred the live take. The studio performance makes a more liberal use of rests in the first half, whereas the live solo constantly drives forward and, instead of rests, uses simply repeated or decorated target notes in order to keep up the tension at points where the melodic line is less agile: see, for example, Example 5.1b, bb. 53-5, 59, and 81-6. The studio solo is more reliant on the falling sixth patterns of the synthesizer theme from the opening section of the piece: see Example 5.1a, bb. 5, 13, 14, 27, and 28, and the transformation of this interval into a descending second-plus-fifth in bb. 18, and 20-23. As with the more plentiful rests, these readily comprehensible melodic ideas are concentrated in the first half of

29 Noble, 'Metheny's Method', 18.
30 Viva, *Pat Metheny*, 128.

EX. 5.1a AND 5.1b 'Are You Going with Me?': guitar synth solos (AT) in *Offramp*
(5.1a) and live on *Travels* (5.1b). © 1982 Pat Meth Music Corp. and Lyle Mays, Inc.
All rights reserved.

(cont.)

(cont.)

(cont.)

(cont.)

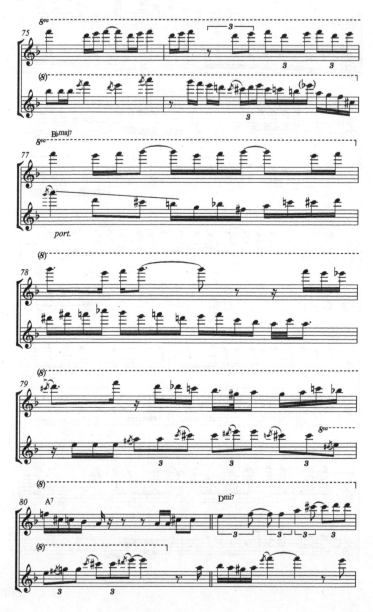

(cont.)

the solo; in the live performance, however, the idea appears in only one bar (Ex. 5.1b, b. 25). Metheny's melodic developments in his improvisations, as shown in both solos but particularly when playing to a live audience, are so intuitively shapely and finely balanced that an obvious reliance on recognizable motifs from a head melody (a potential strategy discussed in Chapter 1) is in fact entirely unnecessary and often does not occur.

In both these performances, sequential development of varying degrees of subtlety aids a feeling of organic growth: for examples, see Example 5.1a, bb. 22-3, 26-8, 56, 62-3, and 81-4, and Example 5.1b, bb. 33-6, 60-63, and 67-8. The relationship between melodic line and underlying harmony is also notably flexible, with the two solos rarely coinciding (except at the very start) in terms of the chord tones they stress, and sometimes showing quite different approaches to tonal questions: compare, for instance, the strong D minor feel with C♯ leading notes in Example 5.1a with the modal D minor again proceeding to include the flattened fifth in the corresponding passage of Example 5.1b (bb. 81-8). The live performance is notably angular in certain chromatic passages (Ex. 5.1b, bb. 64-5 and 76-8), a feature absent from the studio solo, and there is a gradual build-up of intensity from b. 81 onwards, to be released in a more virtuosic climax at the very end. The live performance also makes greater use of vibrato and portamento effects, whereas the studio version reveals just how considerable the digital delay effect is in the first half—a feature lost in the somewhat muggier mix in the live recording.

The first part of the third track on the studio album, 'Au Lait', was written by Mays following the experience of a bizarre dream in which a group of friends were seen emerging from a lunatic asylum, and he wanted to capture the spirit of innocent madness presented by the scene: the intention was irony, even if in the event the result sounded rather melancholic. Viva compares the first part of the piece to the music of Italian film composer Nino Rota,[31] and there is certainly an aura of surreal sad-clown circus music to the first section which makes such a comparison plausible. Gottlieb, too, remembers that some of the music on *Offramp* put him in mind of 'an old French movie with a kind of weird circus feeling.'[32] Mays's lilting melody, doubled by guitar and piano as it restlessly moves by step within a narrow intervallic range and roves through sequential harmonic cycles, is shaped by subtle metrical disruptions and floats above a strong and simple bass line articulating constant perfect cadences, everything gently urged on by quiet snare-drum rolls (see Ex. 5.2). Meanwhile, Vasconcelos sporadically supplies his trademark bird calls, and eerie drawn-out breath effects, gargles, and chattering. After the last of these, Mays's sparse and delicate acoustic-piano link leads into a guitar solo form created by Metheny and Mays together, and supported by a beautiful ongoing variation of the opening texture from accompanying piano and bass, the harmonic patterns rotating seamlessly as if they could last for ever. The music eventually remains firmly in G Aeolian as the bass continues to cycle through its fifth-based patterns, with B♭ major each time initiating a double ii-V-I movement back to G via a major dominant chord. Additional filigree melodic lines from Mays's piano and Vasconcelos's haunting vocalese now enhance the simple, lilting melody.

Something of a role reversal was responsible for producing the breezy number 'Eighteen', which was composed for the date by Metheny and then further fleshed out by Mays on guitar and Metheny on keyboard before they switched back to their more customary instrumental roles. Metheny noted the tune's

> kind of rock and roll, Beach Boys thing, something that was totally lost on the record producer at the time [Eicher] who insisted that we were attempting to rip off Steve Reich's Music for 18 Musicians, an

31 *Ibid.*, 118.
32 Personal communication from Danny Gottlieb via email, July 9, 2014.

idea so convoluted and bizarre that if it hadn't been so ridiculous would actually have been funny. But, that silliness eventually gave the song its title.[33]

Reich's work had been licensed and released by ECM in 1978, and Eicher had presumably noted similar harmonic and rhythmic gestures in both pieces, particularly Reich's penchant for pulsating cluster chords that broadly correspond in effect to the Csus2/G harmony animated in repeated quavers at the beginning of 'Eighteen', which are articulated in approximately the same pulse. In spite of what evidently became an over-stretched comparison, an engagement with quasi-minimalist textures was nonetheless undeniable, and this aspect of Metheny's music is considered in Chapter 6. In 'Eighteen', Metheny plays an Ibanez electric 12-string, the guitar's first melodic statement over the fifth-based ostinato bass making telling use of unison E effects, doubling the open E with a hammer-on on the string below. As with all good minimalism, the trick to maintaining interest is knowing when to time the harmonic shifts, and this is expertly done: the lengthy pandiatonic introduction in C, continued under the guitar melody, is followed by three 16-bar sections, each in a different tonal region (E♭, F, and G majors) and all based on an off-beat pattern which recalls the quasi-Weather Report ideas from 'San Lorenzo'; it also suggests the Reich mallet-instrument idiom which would later be encountered more frequently in the Metheny Group's work (for example, in 'Minuano (Six Eight)' from *Still Life (Talking)* in 1987): see Example 5.3. Metheny's concluding solo above the ongoing ostinato patterns is a good example of a high flight of lyricism based on almost exclusively diatonic materials. The simplicity and tunefulness of this refined modal improvising means that the sonic onslaught at the start of the next track is all the more startling when it comes.

This is not to imply that 'Offramp', in its own way, is not memorably 'tuneful'. Indeed, one of the features which distinguishes Metheny's near-atonal playing, as it had Coleman's before him, is his ability to shape phrases just as convincingly in melodic terms as he habitually does in more tonal contexts. The striking electronic timbres achieved in this track belie the piece's origins as a tune for Metheny's tour in 1980 which had promoted the earlier album *80/81*. In the touring band, the guitarist was joined by Dewey Redman and Charlie Haden (both of whom were

33 *Pat Metheny Song Book*, 440.

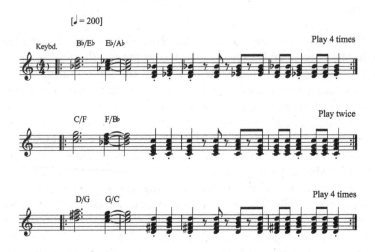

featured on the album), and drummer Paul Motian (who replaced Jack DeJohnette for the US portion of the tour), and it was Motian who came up with the title 'Offramp'. Metheny is reticent about the piece in his own explanatory notes to the published version, merely noting that it was 'designed to set up a particular kind of improvisation'.[34] On the tour, improvisatory freedom meant that the group would perform a small number of tunes, each at great length, but Metheny later recalled that he felt rather uncomfortable about giving instructions to such senior sidemen in a live situation ('I didn't feel like I was in a position to tell those cats when to start and stop') and preferred the album they cut because, in the studio, he could 'orchestrate' the material more.[35] Gottlieb recalls that Metheny did have a particular image in mind when he recorded it: 'I remember Pat saying that "Offramp" was supposed to sound like a painting collage where a bunch of different painters start at different ends of the canvas, and paint at their pace filling up the canvas, and criss-crossing each other'.[36]

As with 'The Calling' in the later trio album *Rejoicing* (see below), 'Offramp' consists of a short head melody, followed by open soloing of

34 *Pat Metheny Song Book*, 440.
35 Milkowski, 'Pat Metheny's Digital Manifesto', 19.
36 Personal communication from Danny Gottlieb via email, July 9, 2014.

indeterminate length, which in theory could be prolonged indefinitely. On the album, however, the track lasts only six minutes. The frenetic head melody, anchored over a succession of pedal points rather than chords, is given in Example 5.4. The astonishing speed with which this is performed on the album by Metheny's guitar synthesizer ($\rrcurrency$ = 268) makes it all the easier to comprehend the tune's essential nature as a highly chromatic elaboration of a C major triad, with the pedal dominant and tonic notes at the conclusion firmly clinching the tonal gesture. At the mid-point of the track, after the end of the guitar synthesizer solo, the focus shifts squarely to keyboards and bass, with Mays suddenly launching into a glittering explosion of shattered-glass timbres (harmonically recalling Messiaen) which subsides to showcase a bass solo supported by Vasconcelos's hand drums. The guitar synthesizer then re-enters insidiously, building the tension subtly until a sudden acceleration in Rodby's bass line propels the music back into the first recapitulation of the head melody, which is followed by a frantic double-time (no changes) jam session rounded off by a final explosive statement of the head.

Named after guitarist James Taylor, the catchy number 'James' which follows offers the greatest possible contrast in its easygoing tunefulness

EX. 5.4 'Offramp' (SB, 128). © 1982 Pat Meth Music Corp. and Lyle Mays, Inc. All rights reserved.

and sunny, almost pop-like nature. Cast in a conventional AABA song form, it was likened by Metheny to a Tin Pan Alley song, and he pointed out that its free-standing nature was very different from the tunes he composed specifically to fit his own manner of improvising or as a basis for experimentation.[37] Remarkably, the number was written for the same *80/81* tour as 'Offramp', which confirms that the astonishing stylistic diversity of the *Offramp* album as a whole was a direct reflection of the nature of Metheny's live gigs at this time; the amiable 'James' was typically played at the end of a gig. The guitar and piano solos on the studio recording are also breezy and popular-sounding in their melodic catchiness: Metheny's is deliciously laid back and economical, while Mays even adopts a popular locked-hand style at the beginning of his solo, and plays buoyantly off strong backbeats from Gottlieb's drums towards the conclusion.

Metheny quoted and elaborated the melody of 'James' in a solo guitar improvisation during a live gig with the Heath brothers at Cannes on January 28, 1983. This performance provides an excellent illustration of the fully harmonized textures in Metheny's unaccompanied playing, which are generally absent in his work with keyboard. The piece was also recorded on the second volume of Bob Curnow's big-band transcriptions of Metheny–Mays numbers, where the rich and strongly directional harmonies work particularly effectively when scored in close position for massed reeds, as is typical in this swing-band idiom. As often in Metheny's music, therefore, the same raw material works equally well in a variety of different contexts. The album concludes with 'The Bat, Part II' (discussed in Chapter 4), which further demonstrates this same quality of remarkable adaptability.

Offramp was released in April 1982 and won the band their first Grammy Award. Ironically, given Metheny's dislike of the catch-all term 'fusion', this and most of the group's later Grammys were to fall into the category of 'Best Jazz Fusion Performance, Vocal or Instrumental'. *Down Beat* commented on the group's combination of popularity and lack of predictability, identifying rock elements in 'Eighteen', the 'quintessential Metheny pop sound' in 'James' and the 'harried, hard-core soloing' of the title track.[38] As Stuart Nicholson put it, the album's 'diversity of material

---

37 Schneckloth, 'A Step beyond Tradition', 15.
38 Robert Henschen, review of *Offramp*, *Down Beat* 49/10 (October 1982): 33. This review gives us one of the most cringe-worthy puns in the history of jazz journalism when Henschen attributes the ongoing development of Metheny's music to 'a Mays & grace'.

satisfied [Metheny's] more temperate listeners, whilst the title track managed to rattle the bars of a few cages of those dismayed by his more commercial cadences.'[39]

TRAVELS

In the same month in which *Offramp* was released, Mays and Vasconcelos contributed their characteristic synthesizer, voice, and percussion sonorities to Bob Moses's album *When Elephants Dream of Music*, co-produced by Metheny at Vanguard Studios, New York, which deftly merged electronics with large-ensemble playing. The Metheny Group then toured the United States in the summer and autumn of 1982, playing a varied selection of numbers from their past and present recording projects. A double-album of live performances from this tour was subsequently released by ECM under the title *Travels*, which also won a Grammy, and featured recordings from gigs given in Dallas, Philadelphia, Sacramento, and Nacogdoches (Texas), all mixed in Oslo by Kongshaug.

Interviewed about life on the road many years later, Metheny admitted that 'Travel is a metaphor that often arises when describing our music . . . It's natural that that sense of motion and movement and travel finds its way into the music, because that is in fact the fabric of our lives.'[40] The travel metaphor also accords well with the concept of linear narrative in Metheny's music-making and had been explicitly suggested by the highway imagery of three of his previous album covers. *Travels* was regarded by Metheny as exemplifying the best of his work as it was customarily presented live, without any overdubbing.[41] It nonetheless received a lukewarm review in *Down Beat* for lacking 'edge' and was described in terms that suggested a general swipe at the ECM stable: 'Introspective journeys and intricate arrangements are fine, but they must engage the listener in their contemplation and transport them to those enraptured moments. The Metheny Group rarely does either, an exception being the live *As Falls Wichita, So Falls Wichita Falls* which does both.'[42]

---

39 Stuart Nicholson, *Jazz-Rock: A History* (Edinburgh: Canongate, 1998), 241.
40 Shore, 'Traveling Man'.
41 On the absence of overdubbing, see Ernie Santosuosso, 'Metheny Won't Stand Pat', *Boston Globe*, June 30, 1983.
42 John Diliberto, review of *Travels, Down Beat* 50/10 (October 1983): 33-4. As with the same journal's review of *American Garage* (see Chapter 4), only three stars were awarded to the double album.

Several tracks from *Travels*, including 'As Falls Wichita', have been examined in previous chapters in cases where they correspond to compositions on the studio recordings ('Are You Going with Me?', 'Phase Dance', 'Goin' Ahead', 'As Falls Wichita', and 'San Lorenzo'), and the remaining tracks are considered below. A particularly telling touch in the live package is the way in which the guitar solo 'Goin' Ahead' merges seamlessly into the opening of 'As Falls Wichita', as a result of which strategy the entire solo seems preludial in intent in the manner of other paired compositions in the Metheny repertoire.

'The Fields, the Sky' was written to feature Vasconcelos's trademark berimbau in live performance, Metheny commenting that this instrument 'functions well in a situation that has a harmonic pedal point'.[43] Unusually, the piece begins with an improvised solo, the berimbau bubbling along in the background as Metheny immediately sets a rustic tone on the Gibson: as the title of the piece suggests, this is wide-open rural music, tapping cultural resonances of the American Midwest rather than Brazil. Predominantly in diatonic G major, with localized inflections to Gmi9, the chord changes of the opening blowing section alternate between 16 bars on a pedal G and 16 bars with a bass line descending firmly by step from G to B♭, the latter region extended by way of coda with an appealing metric shift to duplets in rapid triple time (see Ex. 5.5). Both here and in the opening riffs (Ex. 5.6), which return to form the basis of a lengthy improvised duet for guitar and berimbau, including chordal strumming, the Mixolydian flat seventh carries folk-like connotations. The catchy syncopated interlude between the opening and closing solo sections, also beginning with the flat seventh (Ex. 5.7a) but then turning pentatonic (Ex. 5.7b), was pre-composed on the Synclavier; this material makes a reappearance to round off the piece.

The ballad 'Goodbye' was written to showcase Vasconcelos's vocal qualities, the voice doubled here by Mays on the Oberheim, and the piece was in later tours performed by Pedro Aznar following Vasconcelos's departure from the band. As with 'The Bat, Part II' (*Offramp*), Vasconcelos felt the piece was influenced by Nascimento.[44] The comparison is plausible not only in terms of vocal timbre but also harmonic idiom, especially the use of a descending chromatic bass in places. Vasconcelos's wordless rendering of the head is followed by a

43 *Pat Metheny Song Book*, 441.
44 Viva, *Pat Metheny*, 129.

EX. 5.5 'The Fields, the Sky': end of first section (SB, 143). © 1983 Pat Meth Music Corp. All rights reserved.

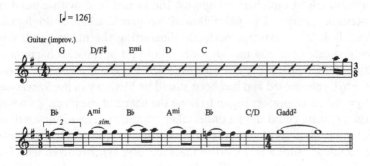

EX. 5.6 'The Fields, the Sky': opening riff (SB, 143). © 1983 Pat Meth Music Corp. All rights reserved.

EXX. 5.7a AND 5.7b 'The Fields, the Sky': two extracts from middle section (SB, 143-4). © 1983 Pat Meth Music Corp. All rights reserved.

two-chorus Metheny solo, after which the vocal head is repeated and the guitarist adds a simple, lyrical coda.

The exciting samba-feel 'Straight on Red' resulted from one of the first experiments Metheny undertook with the Synclavier, with Mays at first being 'infuriated' by 'its lack of features and poor user interface.'[45]

45 *Pat Metheny Song Book*, 441.

After an energizing percussion introduction, the opening melody (doubled by guitar and piano) commences as a set of pulsating repeated dyads, in triplet crotchets set against the samba beat, with a burst of pentatonic energy (Ex. 5.8) followed by manic tremolando figures which link into a passage perfectly illustrating the music's ability to combine catchy, strong melody with simple yet purposeful harmonies with popular appeal (Ex. 5.9). This hook section was the first part of the piece to be composed and had been stored by Metheny in the Synclavier before the collaborators began to hone the shape of the piece. As noted earlier, editing could not be undertaken on the pre-stored material, so additional ideas were composed conventionally and played back into the computer, with a DMX drum machine later synchronized with the band for live performances. This dynamic piece proved to be a brilliant showcase for Mays's virtuosic piano soloing, based on a substantial 72-bar chorus. These blowing changes start with the relatively simple and slow harmonic rhythm of the opening melody, but the more rapid changes from Example 5.9 duly return and are repeated four times at the end of the chorus. An equally substantial percussion solo follows, maintaining the Latin feel of doggedly repeating, highly danceable rhythms. The final restatements of the hook section feature a sudden modulation up a semitone for the last play-through of the tune.

Lee's Summit suggested the title of 'Farmer's Trust', a heading with a particularly endearing origin: it was the name of a local business which, as a child, Metheny thought 'had to do with where the farmers went to

EX. 5.8 'Straight on Red': pentatonicism (SB, 148-9). © 1983 Pat Meth Music Corp. and Lyle Mays, Inc. All rights reserved.

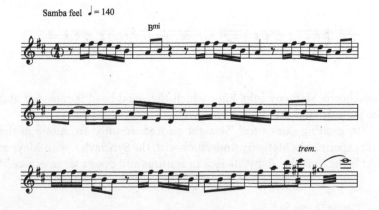

get their trust that the crops would grow'.[46] In fact, as he later discovered, it was merely the name of a savings bank. In the *Travels* performance of this slow waltz, he plays an Ovation nylon-stringed guitar with a pick, which he recalled was a new departure for him at the time in live gigs, and a manner of performance for which the piece was specifically conceived. After two statements of the head on guitar, accompanied by sustained synthesizer chords, Mays takes a single-chorus piano solo on the changes, as does Metheny in his turn. The final statement of the head melody is delicately doubled by glockenspiel, an instrument later to play a featured role on the album *First Circle* (see Chapter 6). 'Extradition' (its title conceived by Rodby on the basis of a then-current news story) was designed to show how the Roland GR-300 could function 'in a more "changes"-intensive environment'.[47] Another waltz-tempo piece, this composition has much more of a blues flavour owing to its inflections of the flattened fifth in the minor home key, and the prominent use of altered seventh chords (which include 'sharp 9', i.e. the blue flattened third superimposed on a regular dominant-seventh): see Example 5.10.

The double album's title track, 'Travels', was composed by Metheny on the Steinway at Oslo's Rainbow Studios during the mixing of *As Falls Wichita, So Falls Wichita Falls*, and then evolved considerably during

46 *Ibid.*, 440.
47 *Ibid.*, 440.

live performances.[48] Mays describes it—in terms that neatly fit Ake's concept of 'pastoral' jazz—as 'a country piece, very American, very simple, major chords, very close to the earth; this is not "city music".'[49] A straightforward 32-bar song form, the piece once again typifies the idiom's ability to capture both country and pop resonances without sacrificing harmonic and melodic originality; also typical of the band's musicianship is the sensitive, lyrical manner of performance which adds immeasurably to the emotional effect achieved. Arguably, performance at this exceptionally high level of subtlety could transform even the most banal material into a memorable listening experience. Years later, Metheny would record a more richly voiced guitar interpretation as the concluding track on the album *Trio 99→00* (2000).

The strident tone of the guitar synthesizer is blended with more traditional jazz timbres in the upbeat 'Song for Bilbao', the penultimate track on *Travels* (which concludes with 'San Lorenzo'). Inspired by pianist McCoy Tyner and conceived with the working title 'McCoy', it was recorded more than a decade later by Metheny with Tyner himself, on Michael Brecker's album *Tales from the Hudson* (1996). Another piece written on the Synclavier, the composition was eventually given

48 *Ibid.*, 440.
49 Viva, *Pat Metheny*, 131; quoted in Italian.

a title which was a grateful act of homage to the city of Bilbao, where the Metheny Group gave their first ever gig in Spain in 1983 and were especially moved by the warmth of the reception they were accorded by the local audience.[50] Impelled throughout by simple but infectiously pounding Latin rhythms from the percussion, the piece is a modified song form in which the bridge is contracted to just 4 bars of 3/4, providing a 28-bar format in the otherwise conventional AABA structure. The complete changes are voiced by way of introduction, with no melody—this is a fruitful way of foregrounding the underlying rhythmic patterns, and creating a sense of expectancy—before the guitar synthesizer enters to project the economical descending melody above a repeat of the chorus chords. The bridge disrupts the prevailing quadruple metre with its 4 bars of triple time and immediately recognizable whole-tone flavour in the chords of its second half. Example 5.11 gives the complete head melody, with the bass rhythm modified from the different syncopated pattern in the published score in order to correspond to the *Travels* performance; the whole-tone harmonies occur in bb. 10-12. The whole-tone passage relates satisfyingly to the prominent tritone leaps which characterize the changes in the A sections on either side.

REJOICING

Metheny's two final albums for ECM were destined to be *Rejoicing* (1983), for which he was reunited with Charlie Haden and also joined by drummer Billy Higgins, and the group project *First Circle* (1984), examined in Chapter 6. The alternation between straight-ahead jazz playing—in the case of *Rejoicing*, another trio album—and the contrastingly 'orchestrated' music of his group work was by this stage beginning to settle into a distinctive pattern, since *Offramp* had also been preceded by a keyboard-less project, *80/81*.

Rejoicing was the result of a North America tour undertaken by the new trio in July 1983, but this time Metheny's experiences in subsequently attempting to preserve his ensemble's music in the studio were far less congenial than had been the case with *80/81*. Indeed, the experience was sufficiently unrewarding to make him realise that it could now only be a matter of time before his departure from the ECM stable:

I did *Rejoicing*, which I really hated. That to me is one of the worst records I've ever made, if not the worst. That trio live had so much

---

50 *Pat Metheny Song Book*, 441.

EX. 5.11 'Song for Bilbao': head melody (ASB, 152). © 1983 Pat Meth Music Corp.

energy, had so much spirit. But, when we did the record, the vibe in the studio was *the worst vibe* I have ever had in a recording studio. That record is the reason that I left ECM. I could not take Manfred Eicher anymore. He made it really impossible to play on that date. What's on there is a struggle to try and get something over this dark blue barrier he had created between us and the tape. It was really bleak. There's a couple of things on there that are OK, like 'Lonely Woman.' The other thing is that the sound of that record is so weird. It's just so bad, muffled and reverby, and it doesn't have to be like that.[51]

This situation must have seemed particularly regrettable given the close relationships that already existed between the three performers, and their love for the repertoire they were recording, which revisited tunes by Coleman alongside compositions by Metheny and Haden, and a standard by Horace Silver ('Lonely Woman', singled out in the quotation above). Metheny had also continued to find Haden's instinctively logical bass-lines in a time-no-changes situation thoroughly inspirational.[52]

Many Metheny fans, including Luigi Viva, disagree with his harsh assessment of *Rejoicing*, which received a respectable enough review in *Down Beat* praising the 'scope and maturity' of his playing, and declaring it to be 'especially inspired' and swinging 'in ways that he rarely can with his own electrified group'.[53] For Richard Cook and Brian Morton, never lavish with their praise, this 'traditional' project was the best Metheny album so far: 'he finds a loneliness in Horace Silver's "Lonely Woman" and a happiness in Ornette Coleman's "Rejoicing" which more severe interpreters of those composers don't seem to have time or room for.'[54] And the guitarist himself was surprised to note

51 Aledort, 'Pat Metheny: Straight Ahead', 62.
52 Fordham, 'Rejoicing', 31.
53 Bill Milkowski, review of *Rejoicing*, *Down Beat* 51/7 (July 1984): 32.
54 Cook and Morton, *Penguin Guide to Jazz* (first edn., 1992), 735.

that, in spite of its sometimes challenging music, the album had by 1985 sold more than 100,000 units, which placed it on a level of popularity close to that of the ostensibly far more approachable *First Circle*.[55] If there were lingering questions about the recording quality, the album's packaging continued to be splendid, with a rust-hued, calligraphic sleeve designed by Barbara Wojirsch and an evocatively blurry monochrome photograph by Rob Van Petten showing the trio in relaxed conversation.

Recorded at the Power Station on November 29 and 30, 1983, in two six-hour sessions, *Rejoicing* built on its performers' deep involvement with the Coleman repertoire and the guitarist's new love for a custom-made instrument (the first manifestation of a commitment to innovation in instrument-making which would become a hugely important aspect of his later work), with prominence now accorded to a six-string acoustic guitar made by Linda Manzer. This distinctive six-string was to feature again in the instrumentation of *First Circle*, notably in that album's title track. *Rejoicing* also demonstrated Metheny's ongoing faith in the Synclavier and Roland GR-300 synthesizers, both used on the two tracks he composed for the project ('Story from a Stranger' and 'The Calling').

'Lonely Woman' was the first occasion on which Metheny played Manzer's steel-string acoustic instrument, possessed of a wonderfully limpid timbre, which he came to dub the 'Linda 6'.[56] In his review of the album, Bill Milkowski felt the 'gentle chording-the-melody work' in this track recalled the example of Montgomery, and certainly the playing here is another good illustration of the harmonic richness Metheny liked to explore on guitar in situations where there was no competing keyboard instrument. Furthermore, the soloing is characterized by a gently propulsive sense of swing which, as noted above, differed significantly from the rhythmic character of the almost exclusively straight-eighths Metheny Group performances at this time. Higgins's constant brush-work in the background, first on drums then cymbal, nicely offsets the clarity of the guitar and bass playing for the most part, though this strategy might at times be felt to contribute to the 'muffled' sound quality described above.

Even more infectiously swung rhythm characterizes the Coleman blues 'Tears Inside', into the melodic line of which Metheny injects characteristically incisive dyadic and chordal passages above Haden's

---

55 See Viva, *Pat Metheny*, 149, and Fordham, 'Rejoicing', 31.
56 Barth, *Voices in Jazz Guitar*, 346.

walking bass line. Certainly the sudden switch here from the bright clarity of the 'Linda 6' to the Gibson—with its very different, richly mellow timbre—might be felt to contribute somewhat to the impression of a far more 'muffled and reverby' overall effect than was the case in Metheny's other recorded performances on the same instrument. In spite of this almost 'bathroom' guitar effect, both bass and drums are recorded with seemingly close-miked clarity when they perform their central duet in the ensuing 'Humpty Dumpty', another tune by Coleman. This track follows strongly co-ordinated guitar and bass playing in the head, including some octave guitar passagework of the kind Metheny had avoided in his early years when trying not to sound like Montgomery, with freely exploratory improvised sections anchored by Haden's fluidly evolving walking-bass patterns; Haden and Higgins later take refined and economical solos. Haden's composition 'Blues for Pat' proved a suitable vehicle for Metheny's typically fluent (and here fairly understated) soloing, and side A of the original release was then rounded off with the brief title track, Coleman's 'Rejoicing', with its nervous opening repeated-note riffs quickly turning into rapid and exhilarating guitar passagework, crisply and slickly accompanied by the drums. The long echo after the final chord again clearly demonstrates how much the recording appears to have been reverbed.

Side B offered more startling music. Metheny's own compositions 'Story from a Stranger' and 'The Calling' allowed him to flex his analog muscles, still in good shape from the workout they had recently received in *Offramp*. 'Story from a Stranger' is a melancholic and harmonically rich triple-time ballad which commences lyrically on the 'Linda 6', overdubbed slightly out of exact synchronization to create appealingly expressive idiosyncrasies (including microtonal divergences in unison moments), and then moves into a substantial reflective solo on the GR-300, overdubbed onto Metheny's own strummed and arpeggiated acoustic-guitar textures, stiffened discreetly by background electronics at the climax. Not previously performed live, as had been the original intention when it was composed for a Santa Monica gig with the trio in 1983, it was nevertheless included on the album; but Metheny felt the arrangement was 'confused', presumably hinting at a dissatisfaction with the overdubbed textures rather than the typically well-judged harmonic and melodic trajectories of the piece.[57]

'The Calling' was the most experimental tune on the set, and in live performances on tour (in which Higgins played a sarod) its

57 Viva, *Pat Metheny*, 150.

open-ended structure might expand to any length up to 45 minutes; it would also be a feature of the later *Song X* tour, though it was not included on the related album.[58] Written for the GR-300, the 10-minute studio version was described in Milkowski's review as a 'triumphant freak-out session ... as daring and full of tension as anything [Metheny has] ever recorded', and the critic plausibly felt the piece was an obvious continuation of the experimentation on the title track of *Offramp*. The free-time head is an anthem-like, solidly diatonic conception, cast in an idiom which in some respects seems to look ahead to the manic 'Forward March' of *First Circle* (see Chapter 6). But the conventional nature of the theme is utterly belied by the cutting-edge sonic technology and completely free exploratory territory that follows. Metheny's playing, at times claustrophobically contrapuntal, ventures boldly into the 'semi-atonal' territory he mentioned in his discussion of the possibilities opened up by the sonic palette of the Roland guitar synthesizer—and, indeed, at times even into full atonality allied to violently distorted and nightmarishly expressionist timbres at the climax. Haden's extraordinarily intense bowed playing contributes towards the disturbing psychological terrain. By the time the opening melody returns, significantly modified as the process of development continues up until the very last moment, it carries a huge weight of emotional resonance after the monumental journey which has brought the listener to this point; in these closing moments, the three instrumentalists achieve the not inconsiderable feat of combining in a compellingly coherent climax while continuing to pursue quite independent lines (with Higgins's energetically militaristic snare-drum patterns intensifying the stirring effect). Finally, and in marked contrast, the haunting Metheny–Haden miniature 'Waiting for an Answer' picks up the low, growling pedal note from the end of the preceding track and might be thought to hark back to the atmospheric soundworld of *As Falls Wichita, So Falls Wichita Falls*, being likened by Viva to 'ambient music'.[59] Metheny recalled it as being 'just an improvised little piece that we made up in the studio—as was kind of [a] regular thing to do on most ECM records of that time.'[60]

Many years after *Rejoicing* was released, Metheny commented on how important trio playing remained to him, not least because it

58 *Pat Metheny Song Book*, 441.
59 Viva, *Pat Metheny*, 151.
60 http://www.patmetheny.com/qa/questionView.cfm?queID=616 (September 1, 2014).

offered a different creative environment from the greater degree of pre-composition that equally attracted him in other musical contexts:

> Writing music and playing music in a trio situation is so different than playing in the group. In the group you are kind of required to as the composer not only to write a great tune hopefully with a great melody and hip changes and all that stuff, but you sort of have to create an entire sonic environment for it to happen in. With trio it really is possible to just kind of write very almost sketchy material that then [is] going to get filled out with the talents of the people as improvisers. In fact it's kind of desirable to do that. I don't want to say that it's easier to write trio stuff, but it sort of is because there's less required in a way of the material. It's more like you are using the material as a starting place.[61]

Compared to *Bright Size Life*, however, *Rejoicing* shows just how far Metheny's musical conceptions had advanced in the intervening years, his trio work now embracing something of the memorable and occasionally nightmarish electronic soundscapes developed in his previous Group and *Wichita* recordings, and continuing to juxtapose effervescent straight-ahead jazz playing with sometimes exceptionally bold modernist improvisations and daring ensemble textures. Many listeners approaching 'The Calling', for example, might find it difficult to equate textures of such complexity and unpredictability with their expectations of what a 'trio' might reasonably achieve. In his final group project for ECM, *First Circle*, Metheny was to explore yet more varied sonic environments and bring his popular group's repertoire to a peak of technical sophistication and emotional resonance—a platform on which they would continue to build in subsequent years.

---

61 Charney, interview with Metheny, *Contemporary Jazz*.

CHAPTER 6

THE WAY UP

Having a killer presentation that's the equivalent of
going to see a great movie—something that really has
you nailed from the very beginning to the very end.
That's my goal in life: to play a set of music that
doesn't have any holes in it—that's just a solid work.
I haven't come close to it yet—but then I haven't
heard anybody who has, except maybe Miles.
But that's what I want to try to do.[1]

METHENY REGARDED *First Circle* (1984) as the finest recording
made for ECM by the Pat Metheny Group.[2] The project featured a new
drummer, Paul Wertico (replacing Gottlieb), and a fresh vocalist/multi-
instrumentalist, Pedro Aznar (replacing Vasconcelos). In its title track
in particular, *First Circle* demonstrated a technical sophistication and
ebullience in tackling a complex extended structure that surpassed
anything Metheny had recorded to date, and the album initiated a
trilogy of comparable recordings completed with two releases made
after his departure from ECM: *Still Life (Talking)* (1987) and *Letter*

---

1 Pat Metheny, quoted in Smith, 'Pat Metheny: Ready to Tackle Tomorrow', 53.
2 Metheny identified *First Circle* as 'the best group record' in Carr, 'Bright Size Life', episode
4. See also Viva, *Pat Metheny*, 153, where he is quoted as saying it was 10 times better
than any of the other group albums up to that point, having been recorded with 'the right
musicians, the right pieces, the right atmosphere and the right studio.'

from Home (1989), both issued on the Geffen label. In contrast to the trio album which directly preceded it, *First Circle* continued to explore the full timbral and structural potential of his band conception, and the timbral possibilities in particular were distinctively enhanced by the two new members of the lineup.

Metheny had tried unsuccessfully to hire Wertico in 1979, and it was not until December 1982 that the Chicago-based drummer was able to join him, in order to play at an audition for a potential second percussionist for the group (to replace Vasconcelos), Gottlieb having been unavailable for the session; on this occasion, Metheny and Wertico jammed for hours on tunes including 'Are You Going with Me?', and after a trio-format final audition with Steve Rodby in Chicago on New Year's Day 1983, Metheny hired Wertico for the Metheny Group's forthcoming tour of Europe.[3] The drummer's playing was equally suited both to the group's music, since he had been playing with the Simon & Bard Group (a fusion band formed in Chicago by Fred Simon and Michael Bard), and to Metheny's wish to use straight-ahead jazz elements now that he had Rodby on board as an acoustic bassist. As he had done with Gottlieb, Metheny continued to position the drum setup to face the guitars and keyboards rather than the audience in the interests of maximal rapport between the players. For a time, Wertico must have felt he was serving a demanding apprenticeship in which his leader frequently went into inordinate detail to secure the kind of sounds and effects he had in mind. Metheny explained:

> With the Group ... the way the music actually sounds is often equally important to the notes we write. I spend a lot of time with the drummers checking out cymbals and giving lots of direction about what types of sounds go with my guitar and the other elements of the Group. When Paul first joined the band, he was already a great drummer, but he needed to work on the details of his sound. For instance, it took us two tours to figure out exactly the right sticks for the dynamic range we were aiming for, the right kind of set for him to use, the right cymbals, the right this and that. To a lot of leaders, those things might seem superficial, but to me, they are essential parts of the whole sound. I can't see spending less energy thinking about that stuff than about which guitar to use for

3 Paul Wertico, interview with the author, July 19, 2014.

a particular piece. In a way, it's *more* important, because it's the thing all the rest of us are balancing to. The cymbals and guitar are setting the top level of the dynamic range, so I want those cymbals to sound *fan*-tastic. I physically set up so that my left ear is right next to the drummer's main ride cymbal so that I can really blend with that sound. I can also hear when a cymbal is starting to go, or when the stick isn't brand new. Those little details make a lot of difference to me.[4]

In some respects, this attention to detail—which Metheny himself admitted could drive his sidemen to distraction—recalls the way in which he had himself been trained when serving his apprenticeship in Burton's group, as recounted in Chapter 2. The difference lay in a shift of attitude once the new player had the music's rationale fully in his blood: as Metheny commented, during the first year with Wertico they might discuss every performance for several hours immediately afterwards, but by more than a decade together 'if I say five things to him during the course of a tour, that's a lot'.[5] Gottlieb felt that Wertico was a good choice for the more consistent (i.e., less spontaneously inflected) manner of drumming required by the 'ensemble oriented' compositions which would culminate in the title track of *First Circle*.[6]

The importance of the ride cymbal to the group's sound was discussed by Metheny in the context of a remark he once made to Gottlieb to the effect that their music should bring together aspects of jazz and rock without sounding like either. As early as their work together on Burton's *Passengers*, Metheny had been on hand to advise Gottlieb on the best choice of flat ride cymbals on a visit they made to the Zildjian factory, near Boston.[7] Since cymbal timbres were to become one of the defining features of his music, the leader's careful rationale for their use warrants quotation at some length:

At the time we started, letting the cymbal carry the groove and yet playing rock kind of beats was something you only found in certain jazz, like '60s Blue Note stuff with Tony Williams. He was an extremely important influence on virtually all the younger musicians

4 Mattingly, 'A Different View', 78.
5 Bonzai, 'Jazzing It Up', 87.
6 Personal communication from Danny Gottlieb via email, July 9, 2014.
7 *Ibid.*

I've played with in terms of that incredible articulation on the ride cymbal.

The sound of my Gibson 175 hollow-body guitar ... is kind of midrangey, which is in the same frequency range as toms. So if I'm playing with a drummer who's going totally crazy on the toms, I don't have a chance. Around the time I started my band in the late '70s, that was the peak of the heavy tom, Mahavishnu-style fusion. I was sort of reacting against that on an aesthetic level, but there was a practical thing, too. If I wanted to play my main guitar at the volume we were playing at, I had to clear up that upper mid-range area. The solution was to make the time come more from cymbals than from bass drum and a heavy backbeat.

There were a few drummers at that time—such as Jon Christensen, Barry Altschul, and, of course, Jack [DeJohnette]—who in a certain form of jazz were putting a lot of attention to detail on the cymbals, and Danny's thing was really an extension of that. Also, a big influence for me—and, I think, Danny too—was Airto [Moreira]'s playing on Chick Corea's *Light as a Feather* [1972], which was incredibly interesting patterns in duple-based music with the groove coming from the ride cymbal. Our basic thrust was to get away from the backbeat—have it sort of be implied, and have it loose the way Elvin Jones and Tony Williams are loose—while playing even 8th-note type music.[8]

Although Metheny elsewhere claimed that Wertico was less cymbal-oriented in his drumming than Gottlieb had been,[9] this comparison was made in 1983 and in later group performances the new drummer worked with a formidable array of varied cymbals, their timbres becoming an immediately recognizable feature of much of the music. ECM may perhaps take some of the credit for the initial development of this aspect of Metheny's soundworld, since Kongshaug's work at the studios in Oslo and Ludwigsburg was perfectly suited to 'a very clear sound, with some emphasis on cymbals and the high end of the kit'.[10] And Gottlieb had in any case already been singled out in a review of *Pat Metheny Group* for having 'brought the top cymbal into rock drumming', and delighted in the fact that Metheny liked to amplify the drum kit in stereo so that ride cymbals positioned on each side of the setup would literally envelop the

8 Mattingly, 'A Different View', 80.
9 Santosuosso, 'Metheny Won't Stand Pat'.
10 Bonzai, 'Jazzing It Up', 88.

listener antiphonally.[11] Wertico's own distinctive techniques included rapid alternations between two flat rides, giving the illusion of playing one cymbal at considerable speed; holding the sticks lightly without using all the fingers to grip them, which (in combination with a loose wrist) encouraged the sounding of higher partials; and using heavy sticks on the flat ride for added tone when playing in the large arenas for which the group was increasingly booked as their popularity soared.[12]

When Vasconcelos had joined Metheny and Mays for *As Falls Wichita, So Falls Wichita Falls*, a prime motivation for his inclusion was the perceived need to humanize the band's increasingly electronic soundscapes (see Chapter 4), although up until this point Mays had in any case always attempted to inject a vocal quality into his melodic work with synthesizers.[13] By the time Aznar replaced Vasconcelos, the group's enhanced jazz orientation meant that the vocal component could now also be considered as a front-line horn, providing an 'element of breath'. (Metheny once revealed that he had drawn a blank in his various searches for a horn player with the particular musical qualities he felt were essential for successful integration with the group.[14] The gap was eventually filled in 2001 with the arrival of the phenomenal trumpeter Cuong Vu.) Aznar, an Argentinean bass player and multi-instrumentalist with a singing voice influenced by Ivan Lins but also tapping associations with pop artists such as the Beatles and John Lennon, was the perfect solution to both these needs. Metheny had met him in Brazil in 1980 and was impressed by a demo tape which showed his equal competence on bass, guitar, piano, and voice. All that was lacking was percussion expertise, which Aznar gladly acquired in 1983 especially so he could join the Metheny Group; as part of his initiation into their soundworld, Vasconcelos also made a berimbau for him. Aznar's vocal dexterity was such that he could switch between tenor and falsetto registers with ease, and so convincingly that at times it sounded as if two entirely different voices were involved in the performance. Another advantage of hiring Aznar was that Metheny could at long last realise his dream of having a second guitar in the band, with all the textural and rhythmic

11 Stern, review of *Pat Metheny Group*, 30, and personal communication with the present author from Danny Gottlieb. For more on the creative use of overtones and discrete pitches in jazz cymbal playing, see the comments of Ralph Peterson Jr. and Michael Carvin in Monson, *Saying Something*, 61-2.

12 Paul Wertico, *Paul Wertico: Drum Philosophy* (Alfred DVD 31989), 2009 [1997].

13 Brodowski and Szprot, 'Lyle Mays', 41.

14 Bonzai, 'Jazzing It Up', 90.

possibilities that such an asset brought with it: these are fully exploited in the title track of *First Circle*, for example, in which Metheny plays a steel-string acoustic instrument and Aznar, on a nylon-string acoustic, joins him in a metrically intricate rhythmic-unison duet.

Metheny, Mays, and Gottlieb participated in Aznar's album *Contemplación* in December 1982 in Boston, which was the last occasion on which Gottlieb drummed alongside them. Aznar and Wertico both started their formal association with the group in January 1983 for a series of concerts in the United States and Europe.

FILM MUSIC

Metheny's work in the film studio during the period with which this study is concerned is important for two quite distinct reasons. In the first place, he on many occasions alluded to a cinematic quality in his music (see, for example, the heading quotation to this chapter), an extension of the storytelling quality of much of his most characteristic work. This dimension can only have been intensified by experience of the actual craft of producing film and television scores. The 'visual quality' of the group's music (as Metheny once called it) meant that they were often in demand for film projects but declined many of them on account of the poor quality of the scripts.[15] Secondly, it was Metheny's seminal encounter with film composer Jerry Goldsmith in 1983 which directly resulted in the composition of the rhythmically challenging title track on *First Circle*. Goldsmith cautioned Metheny to be vigilant about his 'tendency to write things that [he] could already play',[16] a common enough situation amongst composers who are proficient instrumentalists and find that certain note patterns fall instinctively and conveniently under the fingers.[17] Metheny accordingly set himself the challenge of tackling a novel 22-beat additive rhythm, with spectacular results.

Following the initial group tour with Aznar and Wertico, Metheny took receipt of his new Synclavier guitar controller, based on a Roland GR-303 specially adapted for him by Cal Gold of New England Digital, which he demonstrated during a promotional tour for the company

---

15 Santosuosso, 'Metheny Won't Stand Pat'.

16 *Pat Metheny Song Book*, 441.

17 For a close analysis of Metheny's fingerings, see James Dean, 'Pat Metheny's Finger Routes: The Role of Muscle Memory in Guitar Improvisation', *Jazz Perspectives* 8/1 (2014): 45–71.

in June.[18] Metheny put the device to creative use for the first time in his score for the Boston-set PBS television movie *The Little Sister*, also known as *The Tender Age* (dir. Jan Egleson).[19] Two Synclaviers were linked to a DBX two-track digital recorder with added reverb, and Metheny created the entire score in his bedroom.[20] His underscore included both conventional tension-building arpeggiated dissonances in slow harmonic rhythm, and a sombre main-title cue ending in quasi-minimalist hypnotic ostinati, pitting triplets against duplets. In May the same year he appeared as guitar soloist in the London recording of Goldsmith's score for the war-correspondent drama *Under Fire* (dir. Roger Spottiswoode), starring Nick Nolte as a photojournalist caught up in the Sandinista revolution in Nicaragua in 1979.[21] Metheny had initially been approached by the film's producer, who was an admirer of his music, with a view to his composing the score himself, but at this stage in his career he was somewhat daunted by the level of creativity and 'mathematical precision' involved in originating a major movie score, although at the producer's request he remained involved in the project as featured guitarist.[22] The solo parts in *Under Fire* were performed on an Ovation nylon-string guitar, Guild DN 40C, and Ibanez electric six-string 'mini-guitar'. Goldsmith's score was orchestrated by his long-time collaborator Arthur Morton, and conducted by the composer; it was significant in its time as a relatively early example of the successful combination of acoustic instruments and electronics (in this case, the Yamaha GS1 synthesizer favoured by Goldsmith) which was soon to become de rigueur in modern film scoring.

Goldsmith's music, and his practical advice, were inspirational and resulted in a 'blitz' of creative activity on Metheny's part. He suddenly wrote no fewer than 13 pieces as a direct result of 'hanging out with Jerry Goldsmith and reconsidering a lot of things from a compositional standpoint'.[23] The part of the *Under Fire* score which seems to have been most directly influential was a dynamic theme first heard in an action sequence more than three quarters of the way through the film, but placed

18 Viva, *Pat Metheny*, 142; the controller is illustrated on p. 143.
19 'American Playhouse', season 5, episode 9, aired on April 7, 1986. Two clips from the film are available at http://www.patmetheny.com/media2.cfm?categoryid=4 (August 8, 2013).
20 Quoted in Milkowski, 'Pat Metheny's Digital Manifesto', 17.
21 A photograph of the recording session is reproduced in Viva, *Pat Metheny*, 141. This source incorrectly gives the date of the revolution as 1977 (140).
22 Santosuosso, 'Metheny Won't Stand Pat'.
23 *Ibid.*

prominently at the head of the soundtrack album, where it is entitled 'Bajo Fuego' ('Under Fire'). The theme features catchy additive rhythms which lend a subtly modernist slant to traditional Latin American dance rhythms. The transcription of Goldsmith's theme in Example 6.1 is taken from a recapitulation of the theme in the album's track 'Sandino', which has added percussion rhythms. In both its additive rhythms and pulsating tambourine patterns the piece looks ahead to 'First Circle' (see below). Other features elsewhere which suggest general resonances with Metheny's style are the occasional use of Hispanic-sounding parallel thirds and prominent panpipe sonorities, as in the cue 'Sniper'.[24]

After the breakthrough of 'First Circle', complex additive rhythms became part and parcel of Metheny's technical arsenal. Amongst later examples which indicated metrical patterns by their titles are '45/8', composed in 1988, and '5-5-7' (both recorded on *Letter from Home*). Of '45/8', Metheny later said: 'That was written when I was heavily into my threes and twos thing. I don't think you can get away with more eighth notes in one bar.'[25] The full-length repeating pattern in '45/8' is in fact broken down in the published lead sheet into smaller bars of (6+6+6)+4+(6+6+6)+5 quavers. Metheny commented that the piece represented 'the rhythmic template idea taken to an extreme' and that Mays had contributed a contrasting 8-bar phrase 'that provided the antidote and some relief to all the counting'.[26] Metheny's jaunty quasi-Hispanic theme, which also incorporated the timbre of panpipes, included an entirely diatonic passage which is gradually layered by the inclusion of additional voices. The other piece, '5-5-7' (a title which lost its hyphens when published), is based on a simpler pattern comprising 2 bars of 5/4 followed by one of 7/4, though—characteristically—this scheme is abandoned in the solo in favour of a regular 6/4 metre.[27]

---

24 According to the substantial soundtrack-album review by Christian Clemmensen at http://www.filmtracks.com/titles/under_fire.html (August 24, 2013), the pipes involved were 'customized PVC pipes from a local store'. Clemmensen notes that panpipes had been used in the film's temp track for ethnic colour, but such instruments were in fact inappropriate to the film's specific geographical setting.

25 Mike Fish, 'Pat Metheny—Still Life with Guitar in 45/8', *Wire* 66 (August 1989): 22.

26 *Pat Metheny Song Book*, 442. The lead sheet is in the *Song Book*, 256-8. In fact, the 8-bar introduction (recapitulated as an outro) characteristically contradicts its regular 3/4 time signature by superimposing seven-beat stress patterns that cut across the bar lines.

27 The *Pat Metheny Song Book*, 442, notes that (for the first time) Rodby sat in on the collaborative writing session for this piece and gave valuable advice. However, Rodby was also responsible for originating what Mays described as '95 per cent' of his own bass parts in the Group's music: see Brodowski and Szprot, 'Lyle Mays', 40.

EX. 6.1 Jerry Goldsmith, 'Bajo Fuego', from *Under Fire* (AT).

Metheny's best-known film project was *The Falcon and the Snowman*, a true-life espionage drama directed by the critically acclaimed John Schlesinger, who invited Metheny to score the film in June 1983 at around the time the guitarist was touring with his Synclavier demo. Metheny visited the location shoot in Mexico City for inspiration and decided to compose music for both his regular band and orchestra (the latter conducted by Rodby), with the recording sessions taking place in London in September 1984.[28] Not surprisingly, given his current interest in the potential of the device, Metheny showcased the Synclavier throughout the film score, but he used the guitar interface in particular on the cue 'Daulton Lee'. In an interview two years later, however, he was rather dismissive about the result, which was a harmonica-like solo he described as 'a Toots Thielemans kind of thing' (of a kind to recur in several of the Metheny Group's later albums); he indicated that the Roland remained his preferred vehicle for synthesized soloing, while praising the Synclavier as primarily a compositional tool, especially its capacity to print out scores.[29] Mays regarded each of the cues for *The Falcon and the Snowman* as a microcosmic 'musical story' in addition to its specific function within the plot, thereby continuing the parallel with narrative structures that has frequently been noted elsewhere.[30] The score remains best known today in the shape of the its end-credit song 'This Is Not America', which Metheny co-wrote with David Bowie, and which is thematically related to the instrumental cue 'Chris'; the song begins against the final symbolic shots of a falcon in flight before its owner is incarcerated. A fine passage of unaccompanied choral music, the cue 'Psalm 121' is suggestive of the ecclesiastical background of the two amateur spies, who knew each other as altar boys; one of them, now adult, drops out of his seminary at the start of the film. On hearing this accomplished pastiche, the listener can only regret that Metheny was not able to devote more time to film work. Elsewhere the idiom of many of the cues will be familiar to Metheny Group connoisseurs: soft

28 For Metheny's own account of working with David Bowie and scoring *The Falcon and the Snowman* with the Metheny Group and members of the London Philharmonic, see Mengaziol, 'Classic to the Core', 29–30.
29 Brodowski and Szprot, 'Pat Metheny', 42.
30 Mays, interview with Mike Brannon (May 2001). Mays's own musico-dramatic instincts were later shown by his delightful scores to Meryl Streep's narration of tales by Beatrix Potter: see *The Tale of Peter Rabbit / The Tale of Mr. Jeremy Fisher* (Windham Hill WD 0708), 1988.

sustained chords and throbbing percussion rhythms in straight quavers beneath lyrical synthesizer melodies, for example. There are occasional nods to the formulaic conventions used in film scoring to build dramatic tension, and a nylon-string guitar solo for the story's incipient love interest, but for the most part the cues are brief and the music tends not to be foregrounded. (All the tracks issued on the soundtrack album—performed by a group including Aznar and Wertico, and therefore identical to the *First Circle* band—are more substantial and satisfying than the snippets from them which flit in and out of the film's soundtrack. This artistic strategy was something to which Metheny would remain true in his later soundtrack albums.) At the close, just before the Bowie song, there is an extract from 'The Bat' in its *Offramp* incarnation, included—as is so often the case in film scoring—because it had already featured in the film's temp track.

Earlier in 1984, two tracks from *As Falls Wichita, So Falls Wichita Falls* and one from *Travels* were used in the soundtrack to the road movie *Fandango* (dir. Kevin Reynolds), which began life as a student production but thanks to a major injection of funding from Steven Spielberg's Amblin Entertainment company hit the big screen and provided a first starring role for actor Kevin Costner. Set in Texas in 1971, the film is concerned with a madcap journey undertaken by a group of recently graduated young men before they are drafted into the army to fight in the Vietnam War. The eclectic soundtrack, with original music by Alan Silvestri, taps into the long-established association between hard-driving rock music and the road-movie genre, with the main titles energized by the accompaniment of Elton John's 1973 hit 'Saturday Night's Alright'. Later there is much play on an in-joke whereby one of the characters is reading Hermann Hesse's novel *Steppenwolf*: 'Born to be Wild', by the rock band Steppenwolf, famously accompanied the main-title sequence of the seminal biker movie *Easy Rider* (dir. Dennis Hopper) in 1969. Spanish music, whether in triple time or of any other kind, is scrupulously avoided since the title *Fandango* refers only to the slang definition of the word as foolish behaviour, and a parachuting crisis is instead played out to the hard-driving rhythms of Shostakovich's Eighth Symphony. The Metheny–Mays sequence plays without a break during the final 10 minutes of the film, beginning with the piano solo from 'September Fifteenth' and segueing abruptly into 'It's for You' (at which point diegetic sound is equally suddenly suppressed), and thence to Metheny's 'Farmer's Trust'; the music quickly lifts the film onto a notably more sensitive and bittersweet level for the wedding scene which brings the story to a close. Metheny's jaunty solo in 'It's for You', and its backing strumming, neatly coincide with Costner's call for an actual fandango to be danced at the party.

At around the same time, snippets from 'Yolanda, You Learn' (from *First Circle*) appeared as diegetic party music in the soundtrack to *Twice in a Lifetime* (dir. Bud Yorkin, 1985), alongside original music by Metheny. Recorded at Power Station, some of the music was orchestrated with string backing by Mike Gibbs. Based on a theatrical play, never the easiest of scoring assignments since such films tend to be dialogue-heavy and set-bound, the film's first significant original cue occurs well after an hour of the drama has taken place; like the main-title music, the idiom here involves heavy backbeats with string accompaniment, neither typical of Metheny's other music in this period. The most telling cue was an early version of what later became the poignant piece 'Letter from Home' (the title track of the group album from 1989), used as nondiegetic accompaniment to an intimate reconciliation scene between an unfaithful father and his daughter. The film concludes with an original title song commissioned from Paul McCartney, without Metheny's involvement—though he had been invited to work with the pop star, and to this day regrets that he was unable to do so.

Metheny's music continued to be heard in films during the following decade, both as re-uses of existing recordings (e.g., 'Goin' Ahead' in *Arachnophobia*, 1990) or in the shape of original scores. His original music for *A Map of the World* (dir. Scott Elliott, 1999) showcased his playing on acoustic guitar, an instrument suggested by the midwestern ambience of the film's Wisconsin setting; he also played keyboards and was joined by Rodby on acoustic bass, with an orchestral backing of Metheny's own arrangements orchestrated by Gil Goldstein. The soundtrack album was again more substantial than the music used in the film itself would suggest and included 'an additional 25 minutes or so of various expansions, improvisations and treatments based on either the actual thematic materials, or the implied sonic and harmonic language that was generated by the score'.[31]

Asked in 1998 to name his own favourite film score, Metheny replied without hesitation that it was Ennio Morricone's to *Cinema Paradiso* (dir. Giuseppe Tornatore, 1988).[32] This was a revealing answer, given that Morricone's music for the film had been characterized by a lyrical

31 Metheny's liner notes to *A Map of the World* (Warner Bros. 9362 47366), 1999.
32 Anon., JazzOnline Q&A with Pat Metheny, 1998. Formerly available at http://jazzonline. com.

simplicity to which several of Metheny's own ballad-type compositions aspired, including the nylon-string guitar theme in *The Falcon and the Snowman*; as we saw in Chapter 4, Metheny's first essay in this idiom had been 'Goin' Ahead' from *80/81*. In 1997, Metheny recorded an interpretation of both the love theme from *Cinema Paradiso* (composed by Morricone's son, Andrea) and Morricone's own principal theme to the film with Haden on *Beyond the Missouri Sky*—an album also notable, in addition to the rural elements discussed elsewhere, for its restrained and economical expressiveness. In keeping with the narrative metaphor so prevalent in Metheny's music, *Beyond the Missouri Sky* was subtitled 'short stories'.

MINIMALISM

As important as the new rhythmic complexity in 'First Circle' was a refreshing application of diatonic and pandiatonic harmony, in conjunction with propulsive ostinato-based textures which suggested an ongoing interest in minimalism. The metrical hand-clapping at the start of 'First Circle' inevitably suggests a general parallel with the work of Reich, whose *Clapping Music* (1972) consisted entirely of a repeated clapped rhythm performed by two musicians, at first presented in rhythmic unison and then systematically modified as one of the performers begins the pattern a quaver late, then two quavers late, and so on until both performers are eventually back in precise synchronization—a development of the composer's trademark 'phasing' technique. Reich's music was released on three ECM albums: *Music for 18 Musicians* (1978), *Octet/Music for Large Ensemble/Violin Phase* (1980), and *Tehillim* (1981). The first of these was a notable departure for the label's catalogue, as it was their first release to contain no improvisation whatsoever.[33] As we saw in the discussion of *Offramp* in Chapter 5, *Music for 18 Musicians* was felt by Eicher to have been a direct influence on 'Eighteen', though Metheny dismissed the idea that the whole piece had been inspired by the Reich work as ridiculous. Stuart Greenbaum suggested that Metheny and Mays may well have been aware of *Tehillim*, which explores additive rhythms based on cells involving two or three quavers and in some respects may be related to 'First Circle', and wondered (in 1992) whether, 'in time, perhaps both pieces may be seen

---

33 Enwezor and Müller, *ECM: A Cultural Archaeology*, 223. The same source reproduces several photographs from Reich's ECM sessions for the later *Octet* album (166-71).

as clear examples of 1980's post-minimalism'.[34] Metheny was indeed aware of *Tehillim* at around this time, and at one point contemplated performing a version of it with his band; but Goldsmith was the specific inspiration behind 'First Circle'.

In 1987, Reich himself seemed to acknowledge a potential parallel between his own work and some of Metheny's techniques when he asked him to perform and record *Electric Counterpoint*. In this work, commissioned by the Brooklyn Academy of Music's Next Wave Festival with Metheny specifically in mind, the guitarist lays down 10 guitar tracks and two electric-bass tracks and then performs live over the recordings. Both men learnt considerably from the experience of working together on the piece: Reich knew little about guitar technique and relied on the guitarist to demonstrate things to him, while Metheny found it inspiring to be working with a composer who (like Goldsmith) did not come from the background in improvisation shared by all his other collaborators. Metheny found the need for precise synchronization challenging, since it was quite different from anything he had done previously and his innate tendency towards rhythmic flexibility in phrasing made the process of overdubbing more difficult than it would have been had his instincts been strictly metronomic. As it turned out, however, Reich came to like this approach, which he felt was not how a classical guitarist would have played the piece.[35]

Following Metheny's rewarding experience of working closely with Reich on *Electric Counterpoint*, minimalist tendencies in Metheny's own music became more widespread, though—as in the albums considered here—they tended to be reserved for short numbers or distinctive passages in longer, sectionalized pieces. Another related development was the 'ambient vibe' with which Metheny came to start his concerts, placing multiple boomboxes around the venue as the audience arrived, these devices issuing slightly offset pulses and harmonic changes. In longer pieces, the static nature of Reichian ostinati-based passages, which often remained rooted in pentatonic or diatonic scales for very long periods, could be effectively offset by contrasting moments of dynamic harmonic progression completely alien to the Reich style. An excellent example occurs in the piece 'Minuano (Six-Eight)' on *Still Life (Talking)*, in which a substantial syncopated interlude for marimba

---

34 Stuart Greenbaum, 'Pat Metheny and Lyle Mays *The First Circle*: Transcription and Analysis' (MMus dissertation, University of Melbourne, 1992), 31-3; quotation from 33.
35 Fish, 'Pat Metheny—Still Life with Guitar', 22. See also Mead, 'Open Secret', 49-50.

(an instrument favoured by Reich) throbs along for many bars in minimalist style, sticking to limited modal regions based on A and seemingly poised either to go on forever or fade out without resolution; but neither of these outcomes is allowed to happen, because a sudden and spectacularly chromatic harmonic surge for synthesizers breaks the hypnotic spell abruptly and steers the music inexorably back into an exuberant recapitulation of the main theme. Moments of compositional control such as these, in which the timing of events is crucial to their effectiveness, are typical of the experience gained by both Metheny and Mays in their work on *First Circle*, and (as we saw at the start of the present chapter) both these albums and the later *Letter from Home* were considered by their originators as a trilogy united by common technical and aesthetic aims.

FIRST CIRCLE

First Circle was recorded at Power Station, New York, between February 15 and 19, 1984, after the group had first tried out some of the album's music at the University of Arizona during the previous month. In contrast to the *Rejoicing* sessions, this was an entirely pleasurable recording experience, with the musicians working at their own pace, and finding an excellent assistant engineer in the person of Rob Eaton, who would become Metheny's first choice of engineer after he left ECM.

The release was packaged in a simple and elegant sleeve design which seemed to hark back to the whiteness of the *Pat Metheny Group* sleeve from six years before: indeed, the same designer—Barbara Wojirsch—worked on both releases. As we saw in Chapter 3, Wojirsch expressed her fundamental aesthetic philosophy as 'wanting to remove as much as possible from my designs until only something essential, only a thought or gesture, remains.'[36] She had already furthered this aim with her characteristically handwritten sleeve design for *80/81*, which could well have been dubbed the 'purple album'. In the case of *First Circle*, the title is handwritten in pastel, rainbow-like shades on the white background of the sleeve front, with a highly atmospheric photograph of a real rainbow on the reverse. This evocative image, monochrome apart from similar pastel tints in the bands of the rainbow itself (rendered with photo oils), is a brooding cloudscape captured in Waldo, New Mexico, by photographer William Clift in 1978—coincidentally the

36 Müller, *ECM: Sleeves of Desire*, 9-10.

same year in which *Pat Metheny Group* had been released. Clift had a strong attraction towards the landscape in the region of La Bajada Mesa, around 20 miles south of Santa Fe, and the image of the rainbow on this occasion seemed to him to be 'reaching up towards something higher than just this earth'.[37] Both front and rear covers are far too subtle in their colour gradations to be reproduced effectively here in monochrome and were particularly striking in the original LP-sized artwork.

The album opened with the short but memorably eccentric number 'Forward March'. Both the title and the suggestion that the piece should begin the album came from Wertico.[38] The number is an exuberant parody of the American high-school marching band, an amateur performing experience well known to the members of the group, and one which they recalled from childhood days with mixed emotions. Asked about this unique piece in the year after the album's release, when interviewer Bill Milkowski described the overall musical effect as akin to that of an imaginary band from 'Ornette Coleman High', Metheny replied that it was in essence 'a message from our collective unconsciousness'; all members of the band, except Aznar, had 'spent our Friday nights out on the football field marching around with instruments.'[39] Metheny had played French horn during half time in a desperate attempt to notch up the credits necessary in order to graduate, and he would then 'race into Kansas City to make my gig, still in my marching band uniform, switch clothes, and go and play in this organ trio.' The delayed result was a cathartic composition which permitted him 'to somehow channel every little bit of residual high school angst and marching band frustration into a short, but very effective live piece.'[40] The key to the number's success is its enhanced sense of liveness, even in the studio recording: it was used as a theatrical and enticing opener to live gigs, but Metheny later wondered if it had been an entirely successful idea to put it at the head of the album.

As a piece of surreal Americana, 'Forward March' continued to sound a distinctly un-European tone in the ECM catalogue. Its head-on take on the marching-band idiom and its cultural resonances may be compared to Bill Frisell's later album *Have a Little Faith* (1992), which included an

37 Personal communication from William Clift via email, May 31, 2014.
38 Interview with Paul Wertico, July 19, 2014.
39 Milkowski, 'Pat Metheny's Digital Manifesto', 18.
40 *Pat Metheny Song Book*, 441.

ebullient interpretation of John Philip Sousa's *Washington Post March* alongside tributes to well-known pieces of American classical, popular, and folk music. In his tribute to Sousa, Frisell adds some electric-guitar distortion to his otherwise acoustic sonic mix, which includes accordion and clarinet, but went to nothing like the extremes in which Metheny and his band revelled in order to capture their 'residual high school angst'. For a start, Metheny's performers are all playing the 'wrong' instruments and have no qualms about making mistakes: Mays appears on trumpet (which he had played in his own high school band) and Rodby on bass drum, with Aznar taking the glockenspiel, and Wertico a field drum and cymbal. The whole bizarre, out-of-tune soundscape is driven by the brass-like sounds of the new Synclavier guitar, exploiting a special octave ratio which changed the normal correlation between pitches and frets: this technique extended the guitar's range enormously at both ends by stepping the frets at intervals of just over a minor third rather than the customary semitone. Some listeners were misled into thinking the piece was a parody of free jazz, an idea that could hardly have been further from the players' minds.[41] Nevertheless, the dimension of humour in free and experimental jazz is often overlooked in commentators' attempts to plumb its serious depths, and Steve Swallow reminds us that, for example, Charles Mingus 'was a deeply funny composer whose humor could coexist with rage—an underdog humor that goes way back in jazz and blues in the black community. Humor, especially ironic humor, helps us survive the vicissitudes of life.'[42]

The wit in 'Forward March' also comes almost entirely from its liveness, and the sense of inept amateurishness cannot be reproduced or even suggested in notated form. For this reason, the short score published in the *Pat Metheny Song Book* gives little impression of the music's effect: on paper, it seems a harmless, designedly naïve imitation of the idiom, stuck in a rut of basic tonic, dominant, and subdominant harmonies in the inevitable marching key of B♭ major. Only in three places are mild jokes written into the music: a dissonant corruption of V of V at two cadential points (C major substituted by F♯7♭5); a sequential call-and-response pattern in which the increasing tessitura of the calls

---

41 Brodowski and Szprot, 'Pat Metheny', 42.
42 Rosenbaum, 'Steve Swallow', 67. For more on the neglected topic of humour in jazz, see Charles Hiroshi Garrett, 'The Humor of Jazz', in David Ake, Garrett, and Daniel Goldmark (eds.), *Jazz / Not Jazz: The Music and Its Boundaries* (Berkeley: University of California Press, 2012), 49–69.

on each repetition takes the music higher than the comfortable range of the instruments (at which point the performance on the album nearly collapses, though this is not evident from the score itself); and a gentle tripping-up of the duple metre by the insertion of occasional 3/8 bars during the glockenspiel and trumpet solos (neither of which melodic lines are indicated in the score). Also missing from the score is the bizarre introduction, with Metheny improvising crazily in the manner of 'Offramp' as the percussion tries to remain stable: this wild section varied from gig to gig, though the general pattern was that Metheny was onstage improvising on the Synclavier guitar while his sidemen marched in from the back of the hall playing their acoustic instruments. A shrill drum major's whistle cuts this energetic musical mêlée off abruptly, and standard military-style drum rudiments then launch us into the idiosyncratic march.

The deliciously haphazard nature of the opening track makes the powerful rock-style drum introduction to the next one, 'Yolanda, You Learn', all the more exciting and dynamic in context. The piece is credited primarily to Mays, with Metheny listed on the album as co-composer.[43] Both in its pounding introduction and in later passages involving strong drum fills and bold, simple keyboard gestures, the track partially transports the listener back to the quasi-rock atmosphere of the title track in *American Garage*. Structurally, the piece is relatively simple. The 8-bar drum introduction is followed by an 8-bar vamp from the rhythm section, the bass and piano alternating between chords a tone apart (G major and A minor), leading directly into the 16-bar main theme, announced by synthesizer over a continuation of the vamp, with the bass pattern transposed up a perfect fourth at the beginning of the second set of 8 bars: the effect is of a 32-bar song form compressed into half the length, including the briefest of bridges for harmonic contrast. The theme is then repeated with the more nasal timbre of Metheny's Coral electric sitar guitar doubling the synthesizer line. (On this track, Mays plays a Prophet 5 and Rhodes Chroma.) An interlude is heralded by snappy syncopations from the bass set against a starkly simply drum beat, followed by a new 8-bar theme on the sitar guitar. The first 6 bars are repeated, but the theme is interrupted by 4 bars of rock drumming followed by a repeat of the new theme with added glockenspiel decoration

43 Viva, *Pat Metheny*, 155. On the question of Mays's input into this track, see Metheny's interview with Arne Schumacher, 'Pat Metheny (Talking)', *Jazzthetik* 2/3 (March 1988): 26–31.

before an 8-bar build up over a pedal A returns us to the opening G/A vamp. The glockenspiel, already prominent in 'Forward March', will remain a featured sonority in the album, and even small dashes of its distinctive colour aid the sonic coherence of the project as a whole. The remainder of the track consists of fresh melodic strands superimposed above the ongoing vamp: a rising synthesizer countermelody in stately minims (a Mays hallmark), vocalese from Aznar, and statements of the main theme by sitar guitar and voice in unison. The melody continues as Metheny starts to improvise a guitar-synthesizer solo against it; the theme then drops out so the solo can develop above the relentless vamp beneath, the track ending in a fade-out.

In many ways, the most notable feature of 'Yolanda' is Rodby's bubbling electric-bass playing, which propels the music forwards with infectious energy and is another reason why the music is more redolent of the Egan era than many other tracks from this later period. In live performances, such as one given in Tokyo in 1985, Rodby sometimes presented the number's main theme as a lyrical solo set against a wash of synthesized sonorities as an alternative to the simple pounding introduction by the drums in the album version; he would also take a more virtuosic bass solo in the course of the piece. The album version of 'Yolanda' was selected as the basis for a promotional music video for *First Circle* released by ECM and their US distributors, Warner, which features colourful psychedelic animations, plentiful freeway imagery and, towards the close, stills of a live gig with Mays playing trumpet (presumably in 'Forward March', though this is not heard on the soundtrack). The music fades out early, before Metheny's concluding solo has had the chance to get properly under way.

The album's title track, as already recounted, was inspired by Metheny's creative encounter with Jerry Goldsmith: the latter warned him about writing things he could already play 'rather than the more composerly thing of writing things beyond one's playing ability with the faith that somehow it will eventually be performed.'[44] The guitarist recalled the circumstances:

> I was talking a lot with Jerry at that time about writing, 'cause he'd write this complicated stuff. I said, 'How do you do that? Do you play it on the piano?' He said, 'No, no, no. See, that's the trouble with you guys who are players. You don't write anything that you can't

44 *Pat Metheny Song Book*, 441.

play.' And it dawned on me that he was 100% right, that everything I wrote, I would learn to play it before I wrote it. It was like, 'Oh, yeah, that's true!' So I said, 'OK, this time I'm gonna write something and *then* learn how to play it,' and that's what 'First Circle' was.[45]

The piece that resulted from this epiphany was a model of the mutually beneficial collaboration between Metheny and Mays. Metheny established the 22-beat metrical pattern (which he notated 'literally on an envelope, while walking around with my girlfriend'),[46] and then composed the bulk of the piece with the introduction, the main theme, and its bridge, as well as laying down the general structural outline and the basis for the piano solo. Mays then developed the opening vocalese and an interlude section to come after the conclusion of the solo. Both worked together on the ending, with Mays 'writing the great counterpart line to the final statement of the melody.'[47] Metheny subsequently realised that not only was the album as a whole 'a real breakthrough for me': the magnificent title track, he felt, 'was easily the best thing I had written for the Group. That's a serious tune.'[48] In addition to its compositional substance and originality, the piece also showed how Aznar's wordless vocals had by this stage become a vital and integral part of the underlying conception of the music. In spite of its complexity, the piece was recorded in the same 'live' manner as much of the group's earlier work, with the challenging rhythmic material laid down in a single take.[49]

The composition's overall structure is summarized in Table 6.1. Following the introduction, which is a stark exposition of the metrical patterns conditioning much of the pre-composed material in the piece, the music falls into a broad arch form comprising an extended exposition of the principal melodic and harmonic material (B, bb. 6-105), a substantial piano solo (C, bb. 106-226), and a combined recapitulation and coda in which the process of ongoing development continues to the very end of the work (D, bb. 227-68). The second half of the exposition (B, bb. 40-105) is shaped by a familiar AABA song-form pattern, with the bridge based on a strong ascending scale. As suggested above, such scales are a Metheny-Mays signature, and they return as part of

45 Aledort, 'Pat Metheny Straight Ahead', 63.
46 *Ibid.*
47 *Pat Metheny Song Book*, 441.
48 Aledort, 'Pat Metheny Straight Ahead', 63.
49 Interview with Paul Wertico, July 19, 2014.

TABLE 6.1   Structure of 'First Circle"

Bars	Thematic/textural material	Harmony
A ('intro')		
1–5	Hand claps and syncopated monotone in 22/8. Continues under →	–
B ('melody')		
6–17	Guitar and vocalese in unison	C Mixolydian
18–39	Guitar *moto perpetuo* (18–27), repeated with descant from second guitar and glockenspiel countermelody (28–39)	C Ionian
40–105	Development of A and B (40–45), tambourine ostinato added	Cmaj/Emi/A♭mi7/ F♯mi7/Amaj7/ Emaj7/DslashE
	Cadential theme in 6/8 (46–54) Repeat of 40–54 (55–70)	Cmaj Lydian/Gmaj Cmaj/Emi/A♭mi7/ F♯mi7/Amaj7/ Emaj7/DslashE Cmaj Lydian/Gmaj
	Closing theme: ascending scale, alternating phrases in 4/4 and 6/8 (71–90)	Emi
	Repeat of 40–54 (91–105)	Cmaj/Emi/A♭mi7/ F♯mi7/Amaj7/ Emaj7/DslashE Cmaj Lydian/Gmaj
C (piano solo)†		
106–226	Two choruses predominantly in 6/8, on 33-bar changes adapted from 40–54 (106–71)	Cmaj/Emi/A♭mi7/ F♯mi7/Amaj7/ Emaj7/DslashE Cmaj Lydian/Gmaj
	Modulating transition (163–72)	Cmaj → Emi

(cont.)

TABLE 6.1   Continued

Bars	Thematic/textural material	Harmony
	One chorus on changes from 71–90 (173–84)	Emi
	Closing section on fresh harmonies (185–226)	Roving from and to Cmaj; interrupted cadence links to →
B' (recap/coda)		
227–68	Recapitulation of A, in 22/8, combined with rising synthesizer scale (227–35)	Roving from and to E♭maj
	Recapitulation of closing theme from 71–90 (236–55)	Emi
	Recapitulation and further development of 40–46, with modified harmony and fresh countermelody (256–64)	Roving from Cmaj to Gmaj via A♭maj
	Coda: three statements of rhythm from A, with new, rapid chromatic harmonies; clapping from opening returns on third and final statement (265–8)	Gmaj (with chromatic decoration)

* This chart is based on the published lead sheet in *Pat Metheny Song Book*, 160–66, replacing rehearsal letters with letters denoting the components of the formal structure. Bar numbers reflect the actual lengths of sections notated using repeat marks in the score. Section titles in inverted commas appear on the lead sheet. Detail in the solo sections is based on the studio recording released on *First Circle*.

† The second half of the piece is labelled 'coda' on the lead sheet, but this is solely on account of the *dal segno* convention used to notate the preceding repeated sections.

the process of ongoing development in the final part of the piece: the device is a good example of the unpretentious kind of clear structural signposting which helps music of this complexity appeal to both trained and untrained listeners. The improvised piano solo commences approximately halfway through the piece and is at first based on blowing changes adapted from the second half of the exposition, where they underpinned the vocalese melody; but it later switches to a single chorus based on the changes of a quasi-bridge section of the exposition (signalled, as in the corresponding place earlier, by a prominent metrical shift to 4/4 and therefore following the form of the principal theme) before finally moving into a fresh harmonic plan designed to steer the music towards the recapitulation, which coincides with the added excitement of a dynamic tom-tom solo. In addition to the latter, the recapitulation of the opening rhythmic idea here is immediately enriched by a fresh harmonisation and the addition of a new synthesizer countermelody, creating a strong feeling of ongoing momentum in spite of the general familiarity of the recapitulated material. The organic process of reworking—in which the texture becomes wonderfully rich as contrapuntal ideas are superimposed over the heady rhythmic patterns from the beginning and the harmonic changes become yet more elaborate—continues in a similar way until the conclusion. The broadly cumulative strategy in operation here is, in principle, not unlike that which had shaped the concluding section of 'As Falls Wichita, So Falls Wichita Falls', which also reserved contrapuntal intricacy for its closing stages (see Chapter 4), but now it conditions a lengthy passage of culminating development in which the energy and excitement generated thereby are truly exceptional. Particularly noteworthy in this concluding section is the paradoxical sense of finality achieved by what is in effect a long-term modulation to the dominant (G major), the piece having set out from, and repeatedly tended back towards, C major.

In 1992, almost two decades before the publication of the *Pat Metheny Song Book*, the Australian composer Stuart Greenbaum made a detailed aural transcription of 'First Circle' in its entirety. His accurate rendering of the clapped additive rhythms at the opening of the work had to be arrived at after careful examination of the various possibilities for metrical subdivision, which shows (as might also be argued in the case of a composition such as 'Sueño con Mexico' from *New Chautauqua*) that the position of the downbeats only becomes clear some way into the passage.[50] Because the clapping pattern begins with a quaver rest, the moment where everything falls into place is the first downbeat supplied by the entry of the steel-string guitar after three full statements of the clapped rhythm; from this point on, as

---

50 Greenbaum, 'The First Circle', 3-5.

Greenbaum notes, the guitar 'simply substitutes notes for the rests in the clapping part'.[51] This process is clarified in Example 6.2. Greenbaum provides a detailed analysis of how various rhythmic cells operate throughout the piece and makes the important general observation that, in the piece as a whole, the 'pitch element . . . is grafted on the rhythmic cell structure and adheres to it closely in all sections except the Piano Solo'.[52] In all, the opening 22-beat metrical pattern, falling naturally into a 12/8 bar followed by a 10/8 bar, is repeated 25 times, occasionally enlivened by semiquaver decorations on tambourine and simplified when the percussion drops out as Aznar's nylon-string guitar enters to double Metheny's line. Two emphatic bars of 12/8 articulating an Fmaj7 chord mark the end of the first statement of this guitar duet, which is then repeated with the nylon-string instrument now doubling the melodic line at the third above. The entire guitar duet is white-note pandiatonic, remaining strictly in C Ionian and delighting in unpredictable cross-accentuations within the prevailing metrical scheme.

Greenbaum discusses the music's tendency to superimpose different metrical patterns as it progresses, most strikingly when the piano and glockenspiel are added to the guitar duet on the repeat. Example 6.3 reproduces Greenbaum's alternative barring of the countermelody, which may be compared with Example 6.4 from the published lead sheet.[53] (Mays's classical keyboard technique is reflected in the highly legato manner in which these octaves are performed, with the right hand's little finger silently swapped with the fourth finger before the little finger moves onto the next octave in the sequence.)[54] As Greenbaum notes, the two lines interact with complementary stress patterns, combining to produce a more elaborate hocket effect of the kind first suggested by the simple interlocking of the clapping with the repeated guitar Cs at the opening. In the piano solo, Greenbaum identifies an accompanying rhythm performed by a cabasa-like instrument (akin to Vasconcelos's xequerê)—actually laid down on the Oberheim DMX drum machine, on which Mays worked

51 *Ibid.*, 5. Elsewhere, when comparing the music of 'First Circle' with techniques characteristic of minimalism, Greenbaum notes that Reich referred to 'substitution of beats for rests . . . in many of his writings' (*ibid.*, 33).

52 *Ibid.*, 15.

53 *Ibid.*, ex. 10, 8; *Pat Metheny Song Book*, 161.

54 This is evident from close-up video footage taken during a live performance on *We Live Here: Live in Japan 1995*.

EX. 6.2 'First Circle': opening (AT). © 1984 Pat Meth Music Corp. and Lyle Mays, Inc.

EX. 6.3 'First Circle': polymetric glockenspiel line, as notated by Stuart Greenbaum in 'Pat Metheny and Lyle Mays *The First Circle*: transcription and analysis,' MMus dissertation, University of Melbourne, 1992, ex. 10. Reproduced by permission.

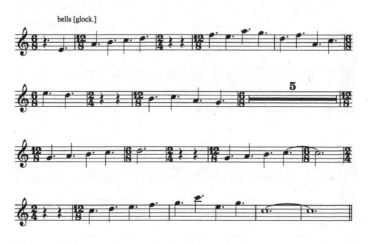

EX. 6.4 'First Circle': ex. 6.3 as notated in *Pat Metheny Song Book* (161-2). © 1984 Pat Meth Music Corp. and Lyle Mays, Inc. All rights reserved.

extensively for this track—that is independent from the underlying pulses of the piano part and follows a regular pattern of its own in spite of the apparent complexity caused by its dislocations when transcribed: see Example 6.5 (C, bb. 111-32).[55] Greenbaum's rendering of the regular pattern in re-barred form is shown in Example 6.6,[56] and (apart from some minor local deviations) this is maintained for some considerable time.

Mays's piano solo in 'First Circle' is one of his most substantial, and is persuasively shaped throughout in its exploration of three basic melodic patterns. The most pervasive of these is the descending profile in lilting compound rhythm seen in the last 3 bars of Example 6.5, which is derived from the cadential phrase in the exposition shown in Example 6.7a (bb. 46-54) and recurs in modified form several times, often across harmonic shifts from Cmaj7 to either E minor or G major: see, for instance, Examples 6.7b (bb. 141-5) and 6.7c (bb. 163-7). This pattern is also intensified by doubling at the sixth in the right hand, in conjunction with quasi-hemiola syncopations, which takes place at the more significant harmonic shifts, generally as part of a crescendo: see Examples 6.7d (bb. 176-7) and 6.7e (bb. 193-5). At the conclusion of the solo, the right-hand dyadic patterns take over and completely dominate the texture, with the upper voice articulating a series of consecutive inverted pedal notes above the final melodic phrases in the lower voice, at the top of the loudest crescendo of all (Ex. 6.8; bb. 209-25). The second basic idea that serves a structural function involves simple elaborations of an ascending scale in E minor, which occurs at those moments in the bridge where the vocalese had sung such a scale in plain semibreves: see Example 6.9 (bb. 181-5). Alternating with the descending figures in compound time just examined, these quadruple-metre ascents provide an effective sense of ebb and flow. Lastly, and less immediately recognizable, the remaining portions of the improvisation tap the unpredictably lilting manner of the guitar material presented in the first (diatonic) part of

---

55 Greenbaum, 'First Circle', score transcription, bb. 144-64. The bar numbering in Greenbaum's transcription differs from that in Table 6.1 owing to the latter's adoption of the complete 22/8-bar units in the lead sheet, in contrast to Greenbaum's earlier use of alternating 12/8 and 10/8 metres, which doubles the bar count in the passages based on this pattern. The passage shown in Example 6.5 does not retain Greenbaum's change of metre to 12/8 three bars from the end which, although musically logical, is not to be found in the lead sheet.

56 Greenbaum, 'First Circle', ex. 11.

EX. 6.5 'First Circle': beginning of piano solo (after Greenbaum, full-score transcription, bb. 144-64). © 1984 Pat Meth Music Corp. and Lyle Mays, Inc. All rights reserved.

EX. 6.6   'First Circle': Oberheim DMX rhythm (after Greenbaum, ex. 11).

the melody (bb. 6–39). Compare, for example, the guitar contours at b. 18 (Ex. 6.10a) with the intervallic patterns in the piano solo shown in Examples 6.11a (bb. 137–9) and 6.11b (bb. 144–53), emphasizing sevenths and ninths, and—in the case of the piano solo—enlivening them with a type of syncopation suggested by the implied upper-register voice in Example 6.10a. Video footage of a live performance given on a tour of Italy and France in 1992 reveals that the piano plays this upper-register voice discreetly throughout the entire passage as a sustained melodic line (Ex. 6.10b), though this is not so clearly audible in the studio recording.[57] The same film reveals that the synthesizer melody in the second half of section B is performed with the left hand, freeing up the right to supply the plentiful off-beat accompanying chords which constantly animate the texture. Both live piano solos available at the time of writing repeat none of the motivic strategies from the studio recording examined here, though all three culminate (at the end of the final crescendo) with emphatic homophonic passages in duplets which signify the imminent arrival of the recapitulation.

The heartfelt simplicity and expressiveness of the ballad 'If I Could', which follows the intricately conceived 'First Circle' on the album by way of marked contrast, were a conscious and deeply felt tribute to the artistry of Montgomery, whom Metheny described as 'the greatest guitarist in history' and whose performance when he met him briefly in 1968 (when Metheny was 13) 'directly affected the course of virtually every waking minute of my life since.'[58] The title was a recognition of the sad fact that Metheny could not personally thank Montgomery, who died soon after they met, for the tremendous impact Montgomery's musicianship and personality had exerted on his artistic development. The track was recorded in a single take on the plectrum-played Ovation nylon-string guitar, its timbre inevitably conjuring up the delicate aura of the earlier 'Farmer's Trust'. Metheny recalled that this was

the first time I've ever had the experience of playing something in the studio, and after finishing playing it, being glad that the tape was running because I'll never ever be able to do it again; like one of those special moments that happen, not every night, but almost every night. Usually when you see that red light go on, you know it's going to be transcribed in a guitar magazine or something, and you start thinking all the wrong things like 'what if I make a mistake!' But that whole day it was just loose and we were having a blast; the stuff was sounding good and we were having fun.[59]

---

57 See the VHS release *More Travels* (1992), a performance also issued on the live album *The Road to You* (1993). This video and another live performance filmed in Japan three years later (*We Live Here: Live in Japan 1995*) show the audience's delight at joining in with the opening hand-clapping, evidently appreciated by the performers in spite of the inevitably erratic results.

58 *Pat Metheny Song Book*, 441.

59 Nicholas Webb, 'Interview with Roland GR User Pat Metheny', *Guitarist* 1/12 (May 1986): 28–31.

EXX. 6.7a, 6.7b, 6.7c, 6.7d AND 6.7e 'First Circle': motivic patterns in piano solo (after Greenbaum, full-score transcription). © 1984 Pat Meth Music Corp. and Lyle Mays, Inc. All rights reserved.

The ballad is a straightforward 64-bar song form in the conventional AABA format. At first, Mays alone accompanies the guitar melody with gentle, sustained chords on the Oberheim; cymbal washes and acoustic bass are then added on the repeat of the A section. The changes form the basis for a delicate and economical guitar solo, ending with a brief but poignant coda.

EX. 6.8 'First Circle': conclusion of piano solo (after Greenbaum, full-score transcription). © 1984 Pat Meth Music Corp. and Lyle Mays, Inc. All rights reserved.

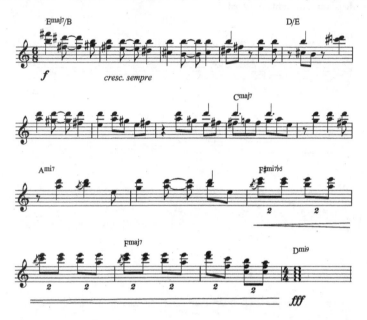

EX. 6.9 'First Circle': E minor scale elaboration (after Greenbaum, full-score transcription). © 1984 Pat Meth Music Corp. and Lyle Mays, Inc. All rights reserved.

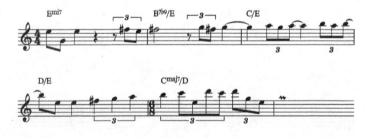

'Tell It All' was regarded by Metheny as particularly significant, because it represented the achievement of a distinctive sonic landscape which embraced the specific talents of new group members Aznar and Wertico. The starting point was a jam session in which Metheny and Wertico played a groove together 'for about an hour',[60] and the

60 *Pat Metheny Song Book*, 441.

EX. 6.10 'First Circle': guitar and piano contours (adapted from Greenbaum, ex. 29).

EX. 6.11a AND 6.11b 'First Circle': motivic development in piano solo (after Greenbaum, full-score transcription).

type of rhythm they explored was reflected in the track's opening groove. The latter again demonstrates the influence of minimalism, with its pentatonic motif displaced to disrupt the regular metre: see Example 6.12. Other fresh features were the unison combination of bowed acoustic bass and vocalese at the conclusion, Mays's doubling of acoustic piano with metallic-sounding go-go bells when playing the displaced riff, and Metheny's exploration of the Roland's potential for acting like an orthodox guitar (albeit with a grittier sonority). Careful attention was also paid to the interaction between guitar and keyboards as a defining characteristic of the group's sound. Nevertheless, Peter Mengaziol noted that the improvisations in this piece still reflected a general aesthetic which he termed 'straight-ahead bebop on a happy

EX. 6.12 'Tell It All': opening (SB, 180). © 1984 Pat Meth Music Corp. and Lyle Mays, Inc. All rights reserved.

EX. 6.13a AND 6.13b 'Tell It All': hooks in interlude (SB, 181-2). © 1984 Pat Meth Music Corp. and Lyle Mays, Inc. All rights reserved.

groove thing', and felt that the music had a 'real "jazz" flavor'. That it was necessary to state this serves as a reminder that some commentators considered Metheny's group to have strayed rather far from orthodox jazz territory, with the result that an occasional critical corrective was required in order to emphasize their music's ongoing debt to self-evident jazz roots. Mengaziol felt that on 'Tell It All', Metheny's solo 'pays homage to straight-ahead jazz guitar playing, right out of the Benson/Martino/Farlow school of improvisation', and added that such 'jazz harmonicism' was 'sorely missing from a lot of the fusion players'.[61] Metheny and Mays each take a substantial solo in turn, their efforts separated and then followed by complete statements of a catchy tutti interlude which is typical of the group's most memorable tunes in its use of pop-style parallel chords (Ex. 6.13a) and a riff-based hook over dynamic harmonies (Ex. 6.13b).

Metheny compared 'End of the Game' to 'Are You Going with Me?' (from *Offramp*), since both were written on the Synclavier, but he also recalled that the new piece was seldom performed live owing to difficulties in executing 'the "drumming" stuff' which Wertico and Aznar play together throughout the number'.[62] This is another piece featuring an occasional dash of glockenspiel timbre as an ongoing sonic feature of the project as a whole. After the guitar solo gradually fades away, a lyrical coda, composed and performed by Mays on acoustic piano—against a quasi-orchestral wash of synthesized harmonies in his richest vein—reaches a tom-tom-dominated climax before the appearance of a tutti closing melody over the slowly moving changes previously used as the basis for the guitar solo. Wertico's pounding toms round the piece off with a return of their earlier suggestion of threat.

In the early 1980s, Metheny was interested in the possibility of including texted songs in his group's repertoire. 'Más Allá (Beyond)' was one of the results. Originally conceived for Vasconcelos as a vocalese, the song features lyrics subsequently written, in Spanish, by Aznar.[63] This was the first conventional song in Metheny's recorded output—though it is hardly conventional in the extreme demands of accurate chromatic pitching it requires of the vocalist—and, given its quasi-Brazilian flavour, it comes as little surprise to find Metheny later

---

61 Mengaziol, 'Pat Metheny: Classic to the Core', 30.

62 *Pat Metheny Song Book*, 441.

63 *Ibid.*, 441. The tune is presented as an instrumental in this source, with the lyrics and an English translation given in an appendix (437).

saying he would have loved to hear Nascimento sing it.[64] Impressionistic and elusive, as are Mays's rhapsodic introduction on piano and Metheny's delicate improvised countermelody (performed on the Gibson) during the repeat, Aznar's text recounts feelings of loneliness in a setting where 'time has vanished' and (ironically) there are 'no songs to be heard': a journey in the afternoon erases painful memories of the preceding morning, but strong images of the sea, clouds, and wind combine to make the meaning ambiguous and potentially metaphorical. Since the lyrics were not included in the album's packaging, any listeners not versed in Spanish might produce any number of emotional responses to this haunting song.

The album's concluding track is unashamedly outgoing and popular in mood. 'Praise' was written in response to the possibilities offered by a new acoustic 12-string guitar made for Metheny by Linda Manzer. To the body of Metheny's tune an introduction and bridge were added by Mays, and they created the 'Beatle-esque middle section' together.[65] Once more, the pop resonances here are partly created by parallel chord voicings. Alongside the strummed acoustic timbres of the Manzer instrument, a further technological innovation was made: the sound of Aznar's pan flute had been sampled by the Synclavier so it could be played back by Metheny's guitar controller. Neatly summing up the album as a whole, reviewer Jim Roberts commented that it 'begins with a march and ends with a hymn, choices that reflect the group's firm roots in the American heartland.'[66]

END OF AN ERA

First Circle was released globally in September 1984 and won the Metheny Group their third Grammy. A five-star review in *Down Beat* declared the album to be both a summation of their previous work and also 'a stepping-off point for the future'; particular praise was given to the balancing of acoustic and electronic elements, and the 'new maturity to the compositions'.[67] This warmly received project proved to be Metheny's final album for ECM. As explained in Chapter 5, Metheny had already become disillusioned during the recording sessions for *Rejoicing*, which he felt were uncongenial to the point of being detrimental to the success

---

64 Viva, *Pat Metheny*, 158.
65 *Pat Metheny Song Book*, 441.
66 Jim Roberts, review of *First Circle*, *Down Beat* 52/1 (January 1985): 29.
67 *Ibid.*

of the disc. The parting of the ways came at a time when ECM's fortunes were otherwise flourishing: 1984 saw the launch of their New Series, which in time would significantly expand their catalogue of recordings of contemporary classical music, film soundtracks, early music, and creative projects uniting music and literature. But, on top of the *Rejoicing* experience, Metheny may also have been disheartened that Eicher did not discuss his work in an interview about the company's progress published in an international issue of the Polish journal *Jazz Forum* (January 1984), and he felt this indicated that the producer did not personally value his music.[68] The interview, by Pawel Brodowski, was entitled 'ECM: "Music with Integrity"', and coincided with both the impending 15th anniversary of the company's founding and its first releases on the new medium of compact disc. (ECM's first CD was a re-release of Jarrett's *Köln Concert*, which continued to be a bestseller in the new format.) In his preamble, Brodowski noted that from its inception the label had 'pursued a very distinct artistic policy, reflecting its producer's personal tastes rather than trying to document whatever is going on in contemporary music'.[69] Eicher mentioned Metheny's name in passing when he expressed regret that listeners tended to typecast the ECM idiom rather rigidly, in spite of the high degree of stylistic diversity represented by its releases, but he ignored his work altogether when listing some of the albums which he rated highly (including examples by Burton, Corea, Garbarek, Gismonti, Jarrett, Rypdal, Towner, Weber, and Wheeler) and those artists he felt ECM had been directly responsible for nurturing. The interview concluded with a pessimistic view of the contemporaneous American record market, Brodowski quoting the opinion of ECM's stateside representative (Bob Hurwitz) that the US market was 'oversaturated'. In response, Eicher readily agreed that 1983 had not been a good year for the industry, and stated that he would 'really like to slow down the production'.[70] For Metheny, however, by far the most important reasons for his decision to leave ECM were his specific dissatisfaction about the handling of *Rejoicing* and a general desire for greater creative freedom.

The Metheny Group undertook a major tour of European cities from February to May 1985, which began and ended in the United Kingdom

---

68 Viva, *Pat Metheny*, 152.

69 Pawel Brodowski, 'ECM: "Music of Integrity"', *Jazz Forum* 86 (January 1984): 47. Elsewhere, the same issue featured detailed appreciations of the music of Garbarek and Vasconcelos.

70 *Ibid.*, 50. Hurwitz left ECM to run Nonesuch Records at around the time Metheny moved from ECM to Geffen: see Niles, *Pat Metheny Interviews*, 65.

and in between took in Scandinavia, Germany, France, Belgium, Poland, Hungary, and Austria. Subsequent solo Metheny performances in the Americas included a gig with Carlos Santana in Philadelphia for Live Aid (July) and his first ever recording with Nascimento, in Rio (August); the Metheny Group then resumed touring in the autumn, giving concerts in Japan, Australia, and Hawaii. Metheny formally parted company from ECM when he signed a contract with Geffen to distribute his landmark experimental album *Song X*, featuring Ornette Coleman, who had greatly admired Metheny's trio with Haden and Higgins when it appeared at the Village Vanguard. For the duration of his time with Geffen, the guitarist was the sole jazz artist circulated by a label which otherwise specialized in pop and rock. Geffen was distributed and supported by Warner Bros. Records, who had already distributed ECM's releases in the United States, but Metheny's own new company (Metheny Group Productions) would retain the rights in their work from here on and license their recordings to Geffen—and, in later years, to Warner and Nonesuch. Before opting for Geffen, he had been headhunted by several other companies, and later commented:

> When I decided to leave ECM, it was kind of funny. Like Duran Duran or something. All these labels were sending me fruit and stuff! I got it down to three or four labels I thought would be possible, and I met David Geffen and he said, we want you to do what you're doing, not a collaboration with Wang Chung [Geffen's commercially successful new-wave band] or something.[71]

Song X was recorded at the Power Station in December 1985 and engineered by Kongshaug, who was joined in the mixing process by Eaton. Coleman's and Metheny's group on this momentous occasion also included Haden, DeJohnette, and Coleman's son Denardo (on additional percussion). It must have seemed like a cathartic liberation from the expectations of ECM where, as Metheny put it, there was always 'a certain amount of pressure to do a certain thing'.[72] Even so—as he revealed in a liner note for the album's 20th-anniversary re-release, with additional tracks, in 2005—the disc still had to be recorded and produced fairly rapidly, with consequences for both the selection of material and its sonic characteristics, though on another occasion he commented that the budget had been large and there was a palpable

71 Cook, 'Are You Going with Me?', 37.
72 Charney, Metheny interview, *Contemporary Jazz*.

sense of freedom engendered by the relatively generous number of recording and mixing sessions.[73] In spite of its boldly experimental nature, this unique album—in which Geffen had placed their complete faith—quickly sold around 200,000 copies.[74]

Although the free improvisations of Song X, which continued to showcase Metheny's often hard-hitting Roland/Synclavier combination, seemed to indicate that he may have (at least temporarily) turned his back on his regular group's distinctive blend of intricate pre-composition and harmonious blowing changes, the pattern of his later career has indicated that he has no problem in moving sometimes quite rapidly between highly contrasting musical mindsets and performative contexts. In a 1986 interview, he reflected that some of his experiences on the Coleman project felt rather similar to his group work, and he again cited the fundamental need of all his playing 'to tell a story'; but he also commented that the challenging nature of the album's harmonic idiom meant that audiences might find it harder to grasp what he regarded as its still essentially melodic nature.[75] In spite of his astonishing facility as a straight-ahead improviser (which tends to be the aspect of his output most warmly admired by jazz connoisseurs), he maintained that the Metheny Group was in fact the arena in which his most characteristic musical ventures were staged.[76] He told Ian Carr in 1998 that the group 'is the place where I can play more of the music I like the most' and that it was also 'the place to experiment'; he disliked its being labelled mainstream because he regarded it as an experimental forum, which not only included new instruments but also explored the 'traditional problem in jazz' of combining written material with improvisation in a balance designed to stimulate players to give of their best. As noted in the general discussion of Metheny's aesthetics in Chapter 1, in his work with the group his priority was 'constructing environments for improvisation

73 Carr, 'Bright Size Life', episode 4.
74 Cook, 'Are You Going with Me?', 36. For a discussion of Song X and its personal significance for Metheny and Coleman, see their substantial interview with Art Lange ('Songs of Innocence and Experience') in Down Beat 53/6 (June 1986): 16-19, 53.
75 J. C. Costa, 'Pat Metheny: Learning, Teaching & Expanding the Art of Improvisation', College Musician 1/1 (Fall 1986): 32-6.
76 A striking example of resistance on the part of certain commentators to Metheny's output with his regular band is provided by the British publication The Penguin Guide to Jazz (ed. Richard Cook and Brian Morton), which reviewed several Metheny Group albums in its first two editions (1992 and 1994), in fairly lukewarm terms, but by the time of the 2010 edition had jettisoned all its reviews of Metheny's albums apart from Bright Size Life and Song X.

that are malleable yet at the same time in many cases ... searching for a certain kind of drama in the music that is dangerous territory'.[77]

The ongoing significance of the achievements represented by *First Circle* was revealed soon after the break with ECM, when the Metheny Group reconvened for the Geffen-released albums *Still Life (Talking)*, recorded in the spring of 1987, and *Letter from Home*, recorded in the spring of 1989. (Both projects were engineered by Eaton at the Power Station.) As already mentioned, these three records together were felt by Metheny to constitute a logical trilogy in stylistic terms, and they also did exceptionally well in sales figures: *Still Life (Talking)* went gold in the United States in 1992, for example, by which time it had sold around 1 million copies worldwide.[78] Mays had also released his first album as a leader in his own right: *Lyle Mays* (on which Frisell was the guitarist) appeared on the Geffen label in 1986, also under the aegis of Metheny Group Productions, and its finely crafted idiom, keen sense of drama and atmosphere, and exquisitely moulded solo passages were all a natural development of Mays's earlier work with Metheny. In an interview for the album's promotional disc, Mays mentioned that he had at first tried to break away from the Metheny Group sound in planning his debut album but then realised that the attempt was futile since so much of his own musical character had evolved during Metheny's long-term development of the group's idiom.[79]

The examination of Metheny's ECM albums in the preceding chapters has demonstrated a fascinating balance between composition and improvisation in the context of a fresh and distinctive style with a contemporary relevance, at times embracing elements of rock, pop, folk, and ethnic music as part of the overall aim to achieve a 'new paradigm', yet also tapping the structural sophistication and tonal adventurousness of modern classical music. 'Right from the start', Metheny commented in 2005, 'one of the major tenets of the group was that we wanted to go beyond song form type material whenever we could.'[80] This is most obviously demonstrated by the fact that only three of the Pat Metheny Group tracks discussed in this book ('James', 'Travels', and 'Song for Bilbao') adopt the standard jazz formula of an AABA head melody followed by improvisations on the same harmonies as the head, and two of those tunes defeat the expectation of regularity in the classic 32-bar

77 Carr, 'Bright Size Life', episode 3.
78 Milward, 'Wandering Minstrel'.
79 Both Metheny and Mays discussed their first Geffen releases on promotional discs made for the Warner Bros. Music Show: *Song X* (GHS 24096) and *Lyle Mays* (GHS 24097).
80 Anon., 'A Fireside Chat with Pat Metheny' (February 2005).

pattern ('James' having 10-bar A sections and an 8-bar bridge, and 'Song for Bilbao' having a 4-bar bridge in a different metre from the rest of the melody; similarly modified and sometimes irregular song forms are also encountered in the non-group albums, as we have seen). Five of the other Metheny Group pieces have free-form heads followed by improvisations on the same changes ('Phase Dance', 'April Wind', 'April Joy', 'The Search', and 'Are You Going with Me?'), but many more introduce fresh harmonic changes for their solos in spite of the memorability of the head (as laid out on 'Midwestern Nights Dream', 'Watercolors' and 'Lakes' from the early albums). As mentioned earlier, this is one strategy by which Metheny maintained a sense of linear narrative in the music rather than getting stuck in the potentially endless cycle of chorus-based solos which strictly follow the same harmonic pattern as the initial melody. Of the later group album *Speaking of Now* (2002), he explained the initiative in these terms:

> We do spend a lot of time writing solo form, which often is quite different than what the original tune suggests. On this record, there are tunes where the form that we solo doesn't happen anyplace else, other than the solo. Or, we'll build modulations into the solo form to give it a dramatic structure, as opposed to just playing the same 32 bars over and over again.[81]

Throughout the group's ECM albums, there is a steady increase in the number of pieces which embody a significant quantity of pre-composition, these works also demonstrating how a flexible approach to the harmonies underpinning improvised sections helps to integrate the solos seamlessly into the piece as a whole—again as part of a strong feeling of purposeful linearity—so that, at no point, does the listener feel there is an abrupt shift from composed to improvised modes of expression. This achievement is a clear reflection, too, of Metheny's belief that improvisation and composition are similar activities that simply take place at 'different temperatures'. Elsewhere, Metheny said of his work after *Still Life (Talking)*, in terms that could be applied equally well to his earlier projects:

> I've tried to make records that have a certain kind of detail and the capacity to be listened to over and over again, finding new things

---

81 Fred Gerantab, 'An Interview with Pat Metheny: Speaking of Now' (February 15, 2002). Formerly available at http://www.jazzreview.com.

each time ... It's kind of natural in that certainly one of the things that the group has increasingly got involved in over the years has been the sense of ensemble. Lyle and I have been concerned with the eternal quest of reconciling our improvisational interest with our compositional and arranging interests.[82]

Improvised solos nevertheless remained the essential core of the musical aesthetic, Metheny commenting elsewhere that

> we're still a jazz group in the sense that the songs are always vehicles for playing ... Even though we might have very elaborate arrangements, it still, 90 percent of the time, revolves around somebody playing a solo. The success or failure of the tune is the solo.[83]

In the more straight-ahead keyboardless albums, improvisation— often headily spontaneous, and sometimes experimental—was brought firmly to the forefront, though structural adventurousness and surprises remained in evidence. In all Metheny's music, the concept of memorability in the musical raw material was crucial, whether this be melodic, rhythmic, or harmonic. In this regard, Metheny likened the idea of a pop or jazz 'hook' to the compositional techniques of Stravinsky and Bach, as well as to popular styles, and identified the same quality of 'memorable moments' in Coleman's playing. Of his own music, Metheny noted:

> Those moments can happen in a variety of ways. It can be a melodic thing, it can be the way certain chords move from one to the next, it can be a sound thing, it can be the way the music changes or breaks or shifts from one meter to the next ... I try to include as many of those things as possibly reoccurring or developing devices as I can.[84]

Such constant memorability not only lent coherence to the music: it undoubtedly helped Metheny's music net a huge popular following with an audience that cut across any perceived boundaries between jazz, rock, pop, and the classics.

One consequence of Metheny's creative ambitions was the writing of self-contained pieces of up to 10 or more minutes' duration. This

82 Bonzai, 'Jazzing It Up', 87–8.
83 Okamoto, 'Pat's Profile', 54.
84 Charney, Metheny interview, *Contemporary Jazz*.

meant that some of his music did not fit well into commercial airplay schedules, although in the early years the Metheny Group did find a significant niche even in traditional jazz stations such as New York's WRVR (later known as WLTW);[85] this was, however, of relatively little practical consequence since they had built up the strong core of their fan base primarily from live gigs and the sale of recordings. The culmination of Metheny's and Mays's efforts as co-composers on a large-scale compositional canvas was *The Way Up* (2005), a remarkable and continuous *c*.76-minute work (split into tracks on the album solely for the listener's navigational convenience) that finally realised the ambition expressed by Metheny in the quotation at the head of this chapter, which had been made in the year of his first group album for ECM (1978): he aimed towards 'something that really has you nailed from the very beginning to the very end. That's my goal in life: to play a set of music that doesn't have any holes in it—that's just a solid work.' In several interviews, he noted that albums such as *As Falls Wichita, So Falls Wichita Falls* (see Chapter 4), *Secret Story* (1992), and *Imaginary Day* (1997) had been important intermediate steps along this route, and once *Speaking of Now* (2002) had introduced several new members and allowed them to find their stylistic feet, the way was finally paved for the most ambitious structure of all. Other releases in the interim had explored fresh territory: *We Live Here* (1995), for example, featured loops based on samples from then-current pop grooves and was driven primarily by rhythmic material: this was the first Metheny recording conceived in the studio rather than being previously honed in live performances, but it was quickly followed by the all-acoustic *Quartet* (1996), which restored the format of his group to its very origins. Aspects from both these projects then fed into the more synthetic *Imaginary Day*. Metheny viewed his album *Secret Story*, a disc intimately connected with his personal experiences of Brazil, as the natural descendant of the title track of *As Falls Wichita* in terms of its underlying and unusually substantial compositional plan,[86] and in this respect both albums (which he also linked on account of their quasi-cinematic natures) anticipated *The Way Up*.

In an interview he gave shortly before *The Way Up* was released, Metheny noted that structurally the piece was closer to classical music than anything else; it had taken Mays and him six weeks to compose but

---

85 Personal communication from Danny Gottlieb via email, July 9, 2014.
86 Noble, 'Metheny's Method', 15. For more on *Secret Story*, see Goins's monograph on the album (*Emotional Response*).

had required seven prior years of conceptual development in order for it to have become a reality. Once more, he commented that

> it's sort of a zone that I think we've been leading to all along. We've always been interested in pushing form and trying to expand what the core meaning of the group could be in terms of the structures that we play. This is sort of where it had been heading for a while ...
>
> And in many ways this is a protest record for us. It's a protest against a world where fear of creativity has become the norm, where people are more interested in reducing things down to their minimum rather than expanding things to their maximum. And it's a culture that seems to be celebrating the kind of achievements that take very little in terms of wisdom and insight, depth, development and nuance and are much more about 'let's get the most obvious thing that we can possibly come up with and then just repeat it over and over and over again.'[87]

Perhaps the most extraordinary quality of Metheny's gradual expansion of the 'core meaning' of all his music is the stylistic integrity which makes it instantly recognizable in spite of the strikingly eclectic musical explorations and influences which lie behind it. As we have seen, the range of musics from which he drew his inspiration was enormously varied, embracing jazz of all kinds, rock, pop, country, minimalism, film music, classical music, and the avant-garde. The paradoxical sense of coherence arising from the satisfying melding of disparate elements such as these meant that his newest music was, in Metheny's own phrase, always '100% backwards compatible' with his earlier output, resulting in a massive accumulated repertoire of original compositions which could be drawn upon in live appearances without the slightest sense of stylistic incongruity.[88] When *The Way Up* was performed in Oslo on May 15, 2005, for example, Metheny was not content merely to perform the new 76-minute work: without any interval, he immediately followed this with a substantial selection from the band's earlier repertoire, the whole evening amounting to more than three hours of uninterrupted music-making of the highest standard conceivable. In the ongoing commitment and professionalism demonstrated by occasions such as this, a vivid glimpse was afforded of the punishingly hard work which

---

87 Nathan Rodriguez, 'Reflections from Metheny' (January 26, 2005). http://www.jambase. com/Articles/5933/REFLECTIONS-FROM-METHENY (May 3, 2014).
88 Barth, *Voices in Jazz Guitar*, 329.

had established their word-of-mouth fan base in the early touring years, when (as Wertico recalls) they would strive to meet exactly the same high standards no matter whether their audiences were large or small.[89] Metheny's goal, as expressed at the head of this chapter, may have been to achieve 'a killer presentation that's the equivalent of going to see a great movie—something that really has you nailed from the very beginning to the very end', but the apparent effortlessness and infectious sense of enjoyment which characterized his performances with all his various ensembles belied the extraordinary, sustained effort which had made such widely admired music possible in the first place. With the *Orchestrion* project in 2010, hiding the mechanics behind the artistic experience now became part of the intention: in this case, the 'killer presentation' created a sense of mystery almost like a magic show.[90]

The development of Metheny's unique musical voice had been, in a very literal sense, a balancing act. As he put it to Moira Stuart in a BBC interview in 2013, this had involved 'trying to find exactly the right mix of the spiritual and the "mathematical" ... to try to find the right amount of loud notes versus soft notes, between lots of chords and simple chords, between free and structured'.[91] Ultimately, however, this balancing act constantly aspired to promote the overriding ideal of the new paradigm which lay behind all Metheny's music: the passionate commitment to find ways in which a jazz-based idiom might communicate meaningfully to a contemporary audience versed in contemporary musical styles.

89 Interview with Paul Wertico, July 19, 2014.
90 Stuart, 'Jazz Guitar Greats'.
91 *Ibid.*

BIBLIOGRAPHY

Ake, David. *Jazz Matters: Sound, Place, and Time since Bebop.* Berkeley: University of California Press, 2010.

Ake, David, Charles Hiroshi Garrett, and Daniel Goldmark, eds. *Jazz/Not Jazz: The Music and Its Boundaries.* Berkeley: University of California Press, 2012.

Aledort, Andy. 'Pat Metheny: Straight Ahead.' *Guitar Extra!* 1/1 (Spring 1990): 56-75.

Alexander, Charles, ed. *Masters of Jazz Guitar: The Story of the Players and Their Music.* London: Balafon Books, 1999.

Alleyne, Sonita. 'Twentieth Century Nomad.' *Straight No Chaser* 19 (Winter 1992): 36-7, 39.

Andrew, Geoff. '*Leur musique*: Eicher/Godard—Sound/Image.' In *Windfall Light: The Visual Language of ECM*, ed. Lars Müller, 179-85. Baden: Lars Müller Publishers, 2010.

Anon. JazzOnline Q&A with Pat Metheny, 1998. Formerly available at http://jazzonline.com.

Anon. 'A Fireside Chat with Pat Metheny' (October 29, 2003). http://www.allaboutjazz.com/php/article.php?id=727 (August 11, 2013).

Anon. 'A Fireside Chat with Pat Metheny' (February 24, 2005). http://www.allaboutjazz.com/php/article.php?id=16664&page=1 (August 11, 2013).

Barth, Joe. *Voices in Jazz Guitar: Great Performers Talk about Their Approach to Playing.* Pacific, MO: Mel Bay, 2006.

Berliner, Paul F. *Thinking in Jazz: The Infinite Art of Improvisation.* Chicago: University of Chicago Press, 1994.

Birnbaum, Larry. 'Weather Report Answers Its Critics'. *Down Beat* 46/2 (February 8, 1979): 14-16, 44-5.

Birnbaum, Larry. Review of Pat Metheny, *New Chautauqua. Down Beat* 46/9 (September 6, 1979): 36.

Bjerstedt, Sven. 'The Jazz Storyteller: Improvisers' Perspectives on Music and Narrative', *Jazz Research Journal* 9/1 (2015): 37-61.

Blumenthal, Bob. Liner notes to *Gary Burton: Artist's Choice*, RCA Bluebird ND 86280, 1987, n.p.

Blumenthal, Bob. Liner notes to Bob Curnow's L.A. Big Band, *The Music of Pat Metheny & Lyle Mays*, MAMA 1009, 1994, 1-5.

Bonzai, Mr. 'Pat Metheny: Jazzing It Up.' *Mix* 19/3 (March 1995): 83-90.

Brannon, Mike. Interview with Pat Metheny (June 2000). Formerly available at http://www.allaboutjazz.com.

Brannon, Mike. Interview with Lyle Mays (May 2001). Formerly available at http://www.allaboutjazz.com, and http://www.jazzreview.com/articledetails.cfm?ID=657.

Brannon, Mike. 'Pat Metheny: Speaks of Now' (March 2002). Formerly available at http://www.allaboutjazz.com.

Brodowski, Pawel. 'ECM: "Music of Integrity"' [interview with Manfred Eicher]. *Jazz Forum* 86 (January 1984): 46-50.

Brodowski, Pawel, and Janusz Szprot. 'Pat Metheny.' *Jazz Forum* 97/6 (June 1985): 34-5, 38-9, 42-3. http://www.polishjazzarch.com/en (August 31, 2013).

Brodowski, Pawel, and Janusz Szprot. 'Lyle Mays.' *Jazz Forum* 97/6 (June 1985): 36-7, 40-41, 44-5. http://www.polishjazzarch.com/en (August 31, 2013).

Burton, Gary. *Learning to Listen: The Jazz Journey of Gary Burton*, ed. Neil Tesser. Boston, MA: Berklee Press, 2013.

Butterfield, Matthew M. 'Music Analysis and the Social Life of Jazz Recordings.' *Current Musicology* [commemorative Festschrift in honour of Mark Tucker], 71-3 (2001/2): 324-52.

Carr, Ian. 'Bright Size Life.' Pat Metheny interviewed by Ian Carr, broadcast in four episodes: BBC Radio 3, June 27 to July 25, 1998.

Carr, Ian. *Miles Davis: The Definitive Biography*. London: Harper Collins, 1998.

Charney, Jeff. Interview with Pat Metheny for *Contemporary Jazz* (February 15, 2002). http://www.contemporaryjazz.com/interviews/pat-metheny-2002 (July 18, 2014).

Clemmensen, Christian. Review of soundtrack album of Jerry Goldsmith's score to *Under Fire*. http://www.filmtracks.com/titles/under_fire.html (August 24, 2013).

Clift, William. Personal communication with the author via email, May 31, 2014.

Cohen, Aaron. 'Still Smoldering: Guitarists Marvel at Wes Montgomery's *Smokin'* at the Half Note 40 Years after Its Recording.' *Down Beat* 72/7 (July 2005): 47-51.

Cook, Richard. 'Pat Metheny: Are You Going with Me?', *Wire* 43 (September 1987): 35-7.

Cook, Richard, and Brian Morton. *The Penguin Guide to Jazz on CD, LP and Cassette*. London: Penguin Books, 1992; second edition, 1994.

Cook, Richard, and Brian Morton. *The Penguin Jazz Guide: The History of the Music in the 1001 Best Albums*. London: Penguin Books, 2010.

Cooke, Mervyn. 'Jazz among the Classics, and the Case of Duke Ellington.' In *The Cambridge Companion to Jazz*, ed. Mervyn Cooke and David Horn, 153-73. Cambridge: Cambridge University Press, 2002.

Cooke, Mervyn, and David Horn, eds. *The Cambridge Companion to Jazz*. Cambridge: Cambridge University Press, 2002.

Coryell, Julie, and Laura Friedman. *Jazz-Rock Fusion: The People, the Music*. Milwaukee, WI: Hal Leonard, revised edition, 2000 [1978].

Costa, J. C. 'Pat Metheny: Learning, Teaching & Expanding the Art of Improvisation.' *College Musician* 1/1 (Fall 1986): 32–6.

Davis, Miles, with Quincy Troupe. *Miles: The Autobiography*. New York: Simon and Schuster, 1989.

Dean, James. 'Pat Metheny's Finger Routes: The Role of Muscle Memory in Guitar Improvisation.' *Jazz Perspectives* 8/1 (2014): 45–71.

Diliberto, John. Review of Pat Metheny Group, *Travels. Down Beat* 50/10 (October 1983): 33–4.

Diliberto, John, and Kimberly Haas. 'Lyle Mays: Straight Talk on Synths.' *Down Beat* 50/7 (July 1983): 25–7.

Egan, Mark. Personal communication with the author via email, July 11 and 14, 2014.

Elsdon, Peter. 'Style and the Improvised in Keith Jarrett's Solo Concerts.' *Jazz Perspectives* 2/1 (2008): 51–67.

Elsdon, Peter. *Keith Jarrett's The Köln Concert*. New York: Oxford University Press, 2013.

Enwezor, Okwui, and Markus Müller, eds. *ECM: A Cultural Archaeology*. Munich: Prestel Verlag, 2012.

Eshun, Kodwo. 'Codona: Reorientation Point for New Planetary Values.' In *ECM: A Cultural Archaeology*, ed. Enwezor and Müller, 188–94. Munich: Prestel Verlag, 2012.

Feather, Leonard. 'Blindfold Test: Pat Metheny.' *Down Beat* 48/2 (February 1981): 47.

Ferguson, Jim. 'Portrait of Wes.' *JazzTimes* (July/August 1995): 30–38, 93–6.

Fish, Mike. 'Pat Metheny—Still Life with Guitar in 45/8.' *Wire* 66 (August 1989): 22–4.

Fonseca-Wollheim, Corinna da. 'A Jazz Night to Remember.' *Wall Street Journal* (October 11, 2008). http://online.wsj.com/article/SB122367103134923957.html (July 18, 2012).

Fordham, John. 'Rejoicing.' *Wire* 15 (May 1985): 28–32.

Fordham, John. 'ECM and European Jazz.' In *Horizons Touched: The Music of ECM*, ed. Steve Lake and Paul Griffiths, 13–20. London: Granta, 2007.

Forte, Dan. 'The Pat Metheny Group—Jazz's Foremost Garage Band.' *Musicians' Industry* 2/2 (March 15, 1980): 32–41.

Forte, Dan. 'Pat Metheny: Jazz Voice of the 80's.' *Guitar Player* 15/12 (December 1981): 90–94, 96, 98, 100, 102, 105–10, 113, 114, 117.

Frahm, Klaus. Personal communication with the author via email, August 18, 2013.

Garelick, Jon. 'Pat Metheny: Making Melodies with Jazz's Favorite Guitar Wizard.' *Boston Phoenix*, March 2–9, 2000. http://www.bostonphoenix.com/archive/music/00/03/02/pat_metheny.html (June 25, 2014).

Garrett, Charles Hiroshi. 'The Humor of Jazz.' In *Jazz/Not Jazz: The Music and Its Boundaries*, ed. David Ake, Charles Hiroshi Garrett, and Daniel Goldmark, 49–69. Berkeley: University of California Press, 2012.

Gerantab, Fred. 'An Interview with Pat Metheny: Speaking of Now' (February 15, 2002). Formerly available at http://www.jazzreview.com.

Gilmore, Mikal. Review of Pat Metheny, *Bright Size Life. Down Beat* 43/12 (December 2, 1976): 22, 24.

Givan, Benjamin. 'Gunther Schuller and the Challenge of Sonny Rollins: Stylistic Context, Intentionality, and Jazz Analysis'. *Journal of the American Musicological Society* 67/1 (Spring 2014): 167–237.

Goins, Wayne E. *Emotional Response to Music: Pat Metheny's Secret Story*. Lewiston, NY: Edwin Mellen Press, 2001.

Goldstein, Gil. *Jazz Composer's Companion*. Mainz: Advance Music GmbH: third edition, 2014.

Gottlieb, Danny. Personal communication with the author via email, July 9, 2014.

Greenbaum, Stuart. 'Pat Metheny and Lyle Mays *The First Circle*: Transcription and Analysis.' MMus dissertation, University of Melbourne, 1992. http://www.stuartgreenbaum.com/downloads/index.html (May 2, 2014).

Guregian, Elaine. Review of Pat Metheny Group, *American Garage*. Down Beat 47/4 (April 1980): 42.

Haden, Charlie. Liner notes to *Beyond the Missouri Sky*, Verve 537 130, 1997, 4-7.

Hadley, Frank-John. Review of Pat Metheny, *80/81*. Down Beat 48/1 (January 1981): 31-2.

Hamlin, Jesse. 'Pop Quiz: Q & A with Pat Metheny.' *San Francisco Chronicle*, February 19, 1995.

Harker, Brian. *Louis Armstrong's Hot Five and Hot Seven Recordings*. New York: Oxford University Press, 2011.

Henschen, Robert. Review of Pat Metheny and Lyle Mays, *As Falls Wichita, So Falls Wichita Falls*. Down Beat 47/9 (September 1980): 46-7.

Henschen, Robert. Review of Pat Metheny Group, *Offramp*. Down Beat 49/10 (October 1982): 33.

Himes, Geoffrey. 'Hybrid Harmony: Bill Frisell Pitches His Tent at the Intersection of Country and Jazz.' *Chicago Tribune*, April 20, 2001.

Holmes, Thom. *Electronic and Computer Music: Technology, Music, and Culture*. New York: Routledge, fourth edition 2012.

Ingram, Adrian. *The Gibson ES175: Its History and Players*. Foreword by Pat Metheny. Ely: Music Maker Books, 1994.

Joness, Wayne Scott. 'Roland GR-300 Analog Guitar Synthesizer.' http://www.joness.com/gr300/GR-300.htm (August 5, 2013).

Kay, M. 'Pat Metheny.' *Music U.K.* 25 (January 1984): 56-9.

Kemper, Peter. 'Along the Margins of Murmuring.' In *ECM: Sleeves of Desire*, ed. Lars Müller, 7–14. Baden: Lars Müller Publishers, 1996.

Lake, Steve. 'Looking at the Cover.' In *ECM: Sleeves of Desire*, ed. Lars Müller, 253–63. Baden: Lars Müller Publishers, 1996.

Lake, Steve. 'The Free Matrix: An Interview with Manfred Eicher.' In *Horizons Touched: The Music of ECM*, ed. Steve Lake and Paul Griffiths, 217–30. London: Granta, 2007.

Lake, Steve. 'Codona: Sounds of the Earth and Air.' Booklet notes to Don Cherry et al., *The Codona Trilogy*, ECM 2033-35, 2008, 5-17.

Lake, Steve, and Paul Griffiths, eds. *Horizons Touched: The Music of ECM*. London: Granta, 2007.

Lange, Art. 'Ornette Coleman and Pat Metheny: Songs of Innocence and Experience.' *Down Beat* 53/6 (June 1986): 16-19, 53.

'Less'. Review of Weather Report, *Mr. Gone*. Down Beat 46/1 (January 11, 1979): 22.

Mattingly, Rick. 'A Different View: Pat Metheny.' *Modern Drummer* (December 1991): 78-84.

Mays, Lyle. Radio broadcasters' interview with music from *Lyle Mays*. Warner Bros. Music Show promotional disc, GHS 24097, 1986.

McGowan, Chris, and Ricardo Pessanha. *The Brazilian Sound: Samba, Bossa Nova and the Popular Music of Brazil*. Philadelphia: Temple University Press, new edition 1998 [1991].

Mead, David. 'Open Secret: Pat Metheny.' *Guitarist* 9/4 (September 1992): 44-52.

'Median and Average Sales Prices of New Homes Sold in the United States'. www. census.gov/const/uspricemon.pdf (August 8, 2014).

Mengaziol, Peter. 'Pat Metheny: Classic to the Core.' *Guitar World* 6/3 (May 1985): 26-33.

Metheny, Mike. 'Q&A with . . . Pat Metheny.' *Jam* [*Jazz Ambassadors Magazine*], August/ September 1995. http://www.kcjazzambassadors.com/issues/1995-08/q&ametheny. html (May 10, 2014).

Metheny, Pat. Radio broadcasters' interview with music from *Song X*. Warner Bros. Music Show promotional disc, GHS 24096, 1986.

Metheny, Pat. Liner notes to Toninho Horta, *Diamond Land*, Verve Forecast 835 183, 1988, n.p.

Metheny, Pat. Liner notes to *Beyond the Missouri Sky*, Verve 537 130, 1997, 8-9.

Metheny, Pat. Liner notes to *A Map of the World*, Warner Bros. 9362 47366, 1999, n. p.

Metheny, Pat. *Pat Metheny Songbook: The Complete Collection—167 Compositions*. Milwaukee, WI: Hal Leonard, 2000.

Metheny, Pat. Keynote address for conference of International Association of Jazz Educators, New York City, January 2001, printed in Lloyd Peterson, *Music and the Creative Spirit: Innovators in Jazz, Improvisation, and the Avant-Garde*, 317-23. Lanham, MD: Scarecrow, 2006.

Metheny, Pat. Transcript (courtesy of Ed Hazell) of workshop given at Berklee College of Music on January 23, 2003, formerly available in edited form as 'Improvisational Theater: Making Up Melodies with Guitar Great Pat Metheny', http://www.berklee. edu.

Metheny, Pat. 'The Stories behind *80/81*: A Collection of Commentaries and Interviews' (November 1, 2013). http://www.patmetheny.com/news/full_display.cfm?id=81 (August 31, 2014).

Metheny, Pat. Interactive web pages at http://interact.patmetheny.com/qa (April 1, 2013).

Metheny, Pat. Personal communication with the author via emails, August 2014, April 2015, and September 2015.

Metheny, Pat, with Greg Federico. *Orchestrion: The Complete Score*. Milwaukee, WI: Hal Leonard, 2010.

Metheny, Pat, and Lyle Mays. *The Way Up: The Complete Score*, ed. Steve Rodby. Milwaukee, WI: Hal Leonard, 2005.

Micallef, Ken. 'Study Hall: Pat Metheny Analyzes the Hall Phenomenon.' In 'Jim Hall and Pat Metheny: Mutual Admiration Society' (1998). http://www.guitar.com/ articles/jim-hall-and-pat-metheny-mutual-admiration-society (August 15, 2012).

Milkowski, Bill. Review of Pat Metheny, *Rejoicing*. *Down Beat* 51/7 (July 1984): 32.

Milkowski, Bill. 'Pat Metheny's Digital Manifesto'. *Down Beat* 52/1 (January 1985): 16-19, 61.

Milkowski, Bill. *Jaco: The Extraordinary and Tragic Life of Jaco Pastorius*. Milwaukee, WI: Backbeat Books, 2005.

Milward, John. 'Wandering Minstrel.' *Boston Globe Magazine*, August 23, 1992.

Monson, Ingrid. *Saying Something: Jazz Improvisation and Interaction*. Chicago: University of Chicago Press, 1996.

Moon, Tom. 'Pat Metheny Gets Serious.' *Jazz Times* 23/6 (July/August 1993): 24-7, 97.

Müller, Lars, ed. *ECM: Sleeves of Desire*. Baden: Lars Müller Publishers, 1996.

Müller, Lars, ed. *Windfall Light: The Visual Language of ECM*. Baden: Lars Müller Publishers, 2010.

Müller, Markus. 'ECM in Context: Independent Record Companies and the Self-Determination of Musicians in the 1950s, '60s, and '70s.' In *ECM: A Cultural Archaeology*, ed. Okwui Enwezor and Markus Müller, 54-62. Munich: Prestel Verlag, 2012.

Nettl, Bruno. 'Thoughts on Improvisation: A Comparative Approach.' *Musical Quarterly* 61/1 (1974): 1-19.

Nicholson, Stuart. *Jazz: The 1980s Resurgence*. New York: Da Capo Press, 1995.

Nicholson, Stuart. *Jazz-Rock: A History*. Edinburgh: Canongate, 1998.

Nicholson, Stuart. *Is Jazz Dead? (Or Has It Moved to a New Address)*. New York: Routledge, 2005.

Niles, Richard. *The Pat Metheny Interviews*, ed. Ronny S. Schiff. Milwaukee, WI: Hal Leonard, 2009.

Niles, Richard. 'Working on *American Garage* with the Pat Metheny Group (1979).' http://richardniles.com (July 30, 2014).

Noble, Douglas J. 'Metheny's Method.' *Guitar Magazine* 2/5 (August 1992): 14-16, 18.

Noble, Douglas J. 'Pat Metheny: Guitar Techniques.' *Guitar Magazine* 2/5 (August 1992): 78-82.

Okamoto, David. 'Pat's Profile.' *Jazziz* 9/5 (August/September 1992): 52-4, 56, 68.

Panisset, Jacques, and Claude Moulin. *Pat Metheny: Improvisations. Concepts et techniques*. Paris: HL Music/Editions Henry Lemoine, 1993.

Peterson, Lloyd. *Music and the Creative Spirit: Innovators in Jazz, Improvisation, and the Avant-Garde*. Lanham, MD: Scarecrow, 2006.

Petten, Rob Van. Personal communication with the author via email, September 3, 5 and 7, 2013.

Piper, Julian. 'Time to Re-group' [interview with Pat Metheny]. *Guitarist* (May 2002): 126-8.

Porter, Eric. 'Incorporation and Distinction in Jazz History and Jazz Historiography.' In *Jazz/Not Jazz: The Music and Its Boundaries*, ed. David Ake, Charles Hiroshi Garrett, and Daniel Goldmark, 13-30. Berkeley: University of California Press, 2012.

Porter, Lewis. 'John Coltrane's *A Love Supreme*: Jazz Improvisation as Composition.' *Journal of the American Musicological Society* 38 (1985): 593-621.

Potter, Gary. 'Analyzing Improvised Jazz.' *College Music Symposium* 30 (1990): 64-74.

Pryor, Sam. 'An Interview with Pat Metheny.' http://www.enjoythemusic.com/magazine/music/0402/methenyinterview.htm (May 7, 2014).

Renzhofer, Martin. 'Pat & Howard—Eclectic Jazz vs. Pop; Metheny Continues to Push the Envelope after 20 Years.' *Salt Lake Tribune*, July 17, 1998.

Roberts, Jim. Review of Pat Metheny Group, *First Circle*. *Down Beat* 52/1 (January 1985): 29.

Roberts, Jim. 'Pat Metheny: The Interview from Home.' *Down Beat*, 56/8 (August 1989): 17-19.

Rodriguez, Nathan. 'Reflections from Metheny' (January 26, 2005). http://www.jambase.com/Articles/5933/REFLECTIONS-FROM-METHENY (May 3, 2014).

Rosenbaum, Joshua. 'Steve Swallow: Renegade Jazz Bassist.' *Guitar Player* (December 1981): 60-1, 64, 67-8, 70, 72.

Santosuosso, Ernie. 'Metheny Won't Stand Pat.' *Boston Globe*, June 20, 1983.

Schneckloth, Tim. 'Pat Metheny: A Step beyond Tradition.' *Down Beat* 49/11 (November 1982): 14-16, 66.

Schuller, Gunther. 'Sonny Rollins and the Challenge of Thematic Improvisation.' *Jazz Review* 1 (November 1958): 6-11, 21. Reprinted in Gunther Schuller, *Musings: The Musical Worlds of Gunther Schuller*, 86-97. New York: Da Capo Press, 1999.

Schuller, Gunther. *Musings: The Musical Worlds of Gunther Schuller*. New York: Da Capo Press, 1999.

Schumacher, Arne. 'Pat Metheny (Talking).' *Jazzthetik* 2/3 (March 1988): 26-31.

Shipton, Alyn. *A New History of Jazz*. New York: Continuum, revised and updated edition, 2007.

Shore, John. 'Traveling Man: Jazz Guitarist Pat Metheny Discusses His New Album and Life on the Road'. *SLAMM Magazine*, undated transcript, 1998.

Silvert, Conrad. 'Joe Zawinul: Wayfaring Genius.' *Down Beat* 45/6 (June 1978): June 1, 13-15; June 15, 21-2, 58.

Small, Mark. 'Pat Metheny: No Boundaries.' First published in *Berklee Today* (2004). http://www.thescreamonline.com/music/music4-3/metheny/metheny.html (July 17, 2012).

Small, Mark L. ' Pat Metheny: Solo on "Phase Dance" ' [transcription]. *Guitar Player* (December 1981): 92-3.

Smith, John Alan. 'Pat Metheny: Ready to Tackle Tomorrow.' *Down Beat* 45/13 (July 13, 1978): 23-4, 53.

Solis, Gabriel. *Thelonious Monk Quartet with John Coltrane at Carnegie Hall*. New York: Oxford University Press, 2014.

Steinfeld, Thomas. 'When Twilight Comes.' In *Windfall Light: The Visual Language of ECM*, ed. Lars Müller, 35-41. Baden: Lars Müller Publishers, 2010.

Stenzl, Jürg. 'Multitalents: Jean-Luc Godard and Manfred Eicher.' In *ECM: A Cultural Archaeology*, ed. Okwui Enwezor and Markus Müller, 204-9. Munich: Prestel Verlag, 2012.

Stern, Chip. Review of *Pat Metheny Group*. *Down Beat* 45/12 (December 21, 1978): 30.

Stuart, Moira. Interview with Pat Metheny. 'Jazz Guitar Greats', BBC Radio 2, September 3, 2013.

Tesser, Neil. Review of Pat Metheny, *Watercolors*. *Down Beat* 45/1 (12 January 1978): 24.

Tesser, Neil. Liner notes to Gary Burton, *Reunion*, GRP 9598-2, 1990, 3–6.

Tesser, Neil, and Fred Bourque. 'Pat Metheny: Musings on Neo-Fusion' [analysis by Tesser and interview by Bourque]. *Down Beat* 46/6 (22 March 1979): 12-13, 15, 43.

Trachtenberg, Jay. 'Pat Metheny Trio Blows into Austin.' *Austin Chronicle*, October 6, 2000. http://www.austinchronicle.com/music/2000-10-06/78850 (September 1, 2013).

Trethewey, Ken. *Pat Metheny: The Way Up Is White*. Torpoint: Jazz-Fusion Books, 2008.

Tucker, Michael. 'Northbound: ECM and "The Idea of North".' In *Horizons Touched: The Music of ECM*, ed. Steve Lake and Paul Griffiths, 29–34. London: Granta, 2007.

Tucker, Michael. 'Hearing Colours.' Booklet notes to Eberhard Weber, *Colours*, ECM 2133-35, 2009, 8-26.

Vandercook, Chris. Liner notes to Kenny Burrell, *Blues—The Common Ground* [1965], Verve CD 589 101-2, 2001, n.p.

Viva, Luigi. *Pat Metheny: Una chitarra oltre il cielo*. Rome: Editori Reuniti, 2003.

Webb, Nicholas. 'Interview with Roland GR User Pat Metheny.' *Guitarist* 1/12 (May 1986): 28-31. http://www.joness.com/gr300/metheny.htm (August 5, 2013).

Wertico, Paul. Interview with the author via Skype, July 19, 2014.

DISCOGRAPHY
AND FILMOGRAPHY

[*Note:* Dates are those of the albums' and films' first release.]

AUDIO

Aznar, Pedro. *Contemplación* (EMI-Odeon Argentina 797756/Interdisc-Slin 3580), 1984.

Nik Bärtsch's Ronin. *Llyrìa* (ECM 2178), 2010.

The Beatles. *Sgt. Pepper's Lonely Hearts Club Band* (Parlophone PMC 7027), 1967.

The Beatles, featuring Billy Preston. *Get Back/Don't Let Me Down* (Apple 2490), 1969.

Bley, Paul. *Open, to Love* (ECM 1023), 1973.

Bley, Paul. *Pastorius/Metheny/Ditmas/Bley* [reissued as *Jaco*] (IAI 373 846), 1976.

Brecker, Michael. *Tales from the Hudson* (Impulse! IMPD 191), 1996.

Brüninghaus, Rainer. *Freigeweht* (ECM 1187), 1981.

Burrell, Kenny. *Blues—The Common Ground* (Verve V6-8746), 1968; CD reissue (Verve 589 101-2), 2001.

Burton, Gary. *Tennessee Firebird* (RCA LSP-3719), 1966.

Burton, Gary. *The Time Machine* (RCA LSP-3642), 1966.

Burton, Gary. *Gary Burton: Artist's Choice* (RCA Bluebird ND 86280), 1987.

Burton, Gary. *Reunion* (GRP 9598-2), 1990.

Burton, Gary. *Like Minds* (Concord CCD 4803-2), 1998.

Gary Burton Quartet. *Lofty Fake Anagram* (RCA LSP-3901), 1967.

Gary Burton Quartet. *Country Roads & Other Places* (RCA LSP-4098), 1968.

Gary Burton Quartet with Eberhard Weber. *Passengers* (ECM 1092), 1977.

Gary Burton Quintet. *Dreams So Real: Music of Carla Bley* (ECM 1072) 1976.

Gary Burton Quintet with Eberhard Weber. *Ring* (ECM 1051), 1974.

Burton, Gary, and Keith Jarrett. *Gary Burton and Keith Jarrett* (Atlantic SD 1577), 1971.

Burton, Gary, and Steve Swallow. *Hotel Hello* (ECM 1055), 1975.

Cherry, Don, Naná Vasconcelos, and Collin Walcott. *Codona* (ECM 1132), 1978.

Cherry, Don, Naná Vasconcelos, and Collin Walcott. *Codona 2* (ECM 1177), 1980.

Cherry, Don, Naná Vasconcelos, and Collin Walcott. *Codona 3* (ECM 1243), 1982.

Cherry, Don, Naná Vasconcelos, and Collin Walcott. *The Codona Trilogy* (ECM 2033-35; boxed re-issue of 1132, 1177 and 1243), 2008.

Coleman, Ornette. *Tomorrow Is the Question* (Contemporary Records M 3569), 1959.

Corea, Chick, and Gary Burton. *Crystal Silence* (ECM 1024), 1973.

Corea, Chick, and Return to Forever. *Light as a Feather* (Polydor 5525), 1972; two-CD reissue with additional tracks (Verve 557 115), 1998.

Bob Curnow's L.A. Big Band. *The Music of Pat Metheny & Lyle Mays* (MAMA 1009), 1994.

Bob Curnow Big Band. *The Music of Pat Metheny & Lyle Mays*, volume 2 (Sierra 22011), 2011.

Davis, Miles. *'Four' and More* (Columbia CL 2453), 1966.

Friedman, David [with Hubert Laws and others], *Winter Love, April Joy* (Inner City IC 6005), 1978 [1975].

Frisell, Bill. *Have a Little Faith* (Elektra Nonesuch 9 79301), 1993.

Frisell, Bill. *Nashville* (Nonesuch 79415), 1997.

Garbarek, Jan. *Witchi-Tai-To* (ECM 1041), 1973.

Jan Garbarek Quartet. *Afric Pepperbird* (ECM 1007), 1970.

Getz, Stan, and Charlie Byrd. *Jazz Samba* (Verve 521 413), 1962.

Gismonti, Egberto. *Dança das Cabeças* (ECM 1089), 1977.

Gismonti, Egberto. *Fantasia* (EMI Odeon 31C 064 422915), 1982.

Godard, Jean-Luc. *Nouvelle Vague* (ECM New Series 1600/01), 1997.

Goldsmith, Jerry. *Under Fire*, original motion picture soundtrack (Warner 923 965-1), 1983.

Grusin, Dave, and Lee Ritenour, with Ivan Lins. *Harlequin* (GRP D-9522), 1985.

Haden, Charlie. *Quartet West* (Verve 831 673), 1987.

Haden, Charlie, Jan Garbarek, and Egberto Gismonti. *Magico* (ECM 1151), 1980.

Haden, Charlie, and Pat Metheny. *Beyond the Missouri Sky* (Verve 537 130), 1997.

Hall, Jim, and Pat Metheny. *Jim Hall & Pat Metheny* (Telarc CD-83442), 1998.

Horta, Toninho. *Toninho Horta* (EMI-Odeon 064422881), 1981.

Horta, Toninho. *Diamond Land* (Verve Forecast 835183), 1988

Horta, Toninho. *Moonstone* (Verve Forecast 839 734), 1989.

Jarrett, Keith. *The Köln Concert* (ECM 1064/65), 1975.

Jarrett, Keith, with Dewey Redman, Charlie Haden, and Paul Motian. *Eyes of the Heart* (ECM 1150), 1979.

Lloyd, Charles. *The Water Is Wide* (ECM 1734), 2000.

Mays, Lyle. *Lyle Mays* (Geffen 924 097), 1986.

Mays, Lyle. Radio broadcasters' interview with music from *Lyle Mays* (Warner Bros. Music Show promotional disc, GHS 24097), 1986.

Mays, Lyle. *Street Dreams* (Geffen 924 204), 1988.

Mays, Lyle. *The Tale of Peter Rabbit/The Tale of Mr. Jeremy Fisher*, narration by Meryl Streep (Windham Hill WD 0708), 1988.

Metheny, Pat. *Bright Size Life* (ECM 1073), 1976.

Metheny, Pat. *Watercolors* (ECM 1097), 1977.

Metheny, Pat. *New Chautauqua* (ECM 1131), 1979.

Metheny, Pat. *An Hour with Pat Metheny: A Radio Special*, promotional disc (ECM PRO-A-810), 1979.

Metheny, Pat. *80/81* (ECM 1180/81), 1980; single-CD reissue, omitting two tracks (815 579), n.d.; double-CD reissue, complete (843 169), n.d.

Metheny, Pat. *Rejoicing* (ECM 1271), 1984.

Metheny, Pat. Radio broadcasters' interview with music from *Song X* (Warner Bros. Music Show promotional disc, GHS 24096), 1986.

Metheny, Pat. *Secret Story* (Geffen GED 24468), 1992.

Metheny, Pat. *Zero Tolerance for Silence* (Geffen GED 24626), 1994.

Metheny, Pat. *A Map of the World*, original motion picture soundtrack (Warner Bros. 9362 47366), 1999.

Metheny, Pat. *Trio 99→00* (Warner Bros. 9362 47632), 2000.

Metheny, Pat. *One Quiet Night* (Warner Bros. 9362 48473), 2003.

Metheny, Pat. *What's It All About* (Nonesuch 7559 79647), 2011.

Pat Metheny Group. *Pat Metheny Group* (ECM 1114), 1978.

Pat Metheny Group. *American Garage* (ECM 1155), 1979.

Pat Metheny Group. *Offramp* (ECM 1216), 1982.

Pat Metheny Group *Travels* (ECM 1252/53), 1983.

Pat Metheny Group. *First Circle* (ECM 1278), 1984.

Pat Metheny Group. *The Falcon and the Snowman*, original motion picture soundtrack (EMI-Manhattan CDP748411), 1985.

Pat Metheny Group. *Still Life (Talking)* (Geffen 24145), 1987.

Pat Metheny Group. *Letter from Home* (Geffen 24245), 1989.

Pat Metheny Group. *The Road to You* (Geffen 24601), 1993.

Pat Metheny Group. *We Live Here* (Geffen 24729), 1995.

Pat Metheny Group. *Quartet* (Geffen 24978), 1996.

Pat Metheny Group. *Imaginary Day* (Warner 9362-46791), 1997.

Pat Metheny Group. *Speaking of Now* (Warner 9362-48205), 2002.

Pat Metheny Group. *The Way Up* (Nonesuch 7559-79876), 2005.

Metheny, Pat, and Ornette Coleman. *Song X* (Geffen 924 096), 1986.

Metheny, Pat, and Ornette Coleman. *Song X: Twentieth Anniversary* (Nonesuch 7559 79918), 2005.

Metheny, Pat, and Lyle Mays. *As Falls Wichita, So Falls Wichita Falls* (ECM 1190), 1981.

Metheny, Pat, and Lyle Mays. Promotional interviews for Warner Bros. Music Show (Geffen WBMS 137), 1986.

Mitchell, Joni. *Hejira* (Asylum 7E-1087), 1976.

Mitchell, Joni. *Don Juan's Reckless Daughter* (Asylum BB-701), 1977.

Mitchell, Joni. *Mingus* (Asylum 5E-505), 1979.

Mitchell, Joni. *Shadows and Light* (Asylum 704), 1979.

Montgomery, Wes. *Smokin' at the Half Note* (Verve V6-8633), 1965.

Montgomery, Wes. *A Day in the Life* (A&M SP-3001), 1967.

Montgomery, Wes. *Down Here on the Ground* (A&M SP-3006), 1968.

Moses, Bob. *When Elephants Dream of Music* (Gramavision R2 79491), 1982.

Muldaur, Maria. *Midnight at the Oasis/Any Old Time* (Reprise K14331), 1973.

Nascimento, Milton. *Clube da Esquina* 2 (BR/EMI 164 422831 32), 1978.

Nascimento, Milton, and Lô Borges. *Clube da Esquina* (BR/EMI MOAB 6005-6), 1972.
North Texas State University Lab Band. *Lab 75!* (A&R 57X06), 1975.
Pastorius, Jaco. *Jaco Pastorius* (Epic 33949), 1976.
Reich, Steve. *Music for 18 Musicians* (ECM 1129), 1978.
Reich, Steve. *Octet/Music for Large Ensemble/Violin Phase* (ECM 1168), 1980.
Reich, Steve. *Tehillim* (ECM 1215), 1982.
Reich, Steve. *Different Trains and Electric Counterpoint* (Nonesuch 7559-79176-2), 1989.
Rollins, Sonny. *Saxophone Colossus* (Prestige LP 7079), 1956.
Rypdal, Terje. *Waves* (ECM 1110), 1977.
Shorter, Wayne. *Native Dancer* (Columbia PC 33418), 1975.
Silver, Horace. *Song for My Father* (Blue Note, BST 84185), 1965.
Stone Free: A Tribute to Jimi Hendrix (Reprise 45438-2), 1993.
Swallow, Steve. *Home* (ECM 1160), 1980.
Towner, Ralph. *Solstice* (ECM 1095), 1975.
Vaz, Célia. *Mutaçao* (Phillips 6328 300), 1981.
Weather Report. *I Sing the Body Electric* (Columbia KC 31352), 1972.
Weather Report. *Black Market* (Columbia 468210), 1976.
Weather Report. *Heavy Weather* (Columbia PC 34418), 1977.
Weather Report. *Mr. Gone* (Columbia 468208), 1978.
Weber, Eberhard. *The Colours of Chloë* (ECM 1042), 1974.
Weber, Eberhard. *Yellow Fields* (ECM 1066), 1976.
Weber, Eberhard. *The Following Morning* (ECM 1084), 1976.
Weber, Eberhard. *Silent Feet* (ECM 1107), 1978.
Weber, Eberhard. *Little Movements* (ECM 1186), 1980.
Weber, Eberhard. *Later that Evening* (ECM 1231), 1982.
Weber, Eberhard. *Colours* (ECM 2133–35; boxed reissue of 1066, 1107 and 1186), 2009.

VIDEO

Guyer, Peter, and Norbert Wiedmer (dirs). *Sounds and Silence: Travels with Manfred Eicher* (ECM 5050), 2011.
Metheny, Pat. *The Orchestrion Project* (Eagle Vision EREDV 922), 2012.
Pat Metheny Group. Television broadcast of live performance at Montreal Jazz Festival (VHS, author's collection), Channel 4 (UK), 1982.
Pat Metheny Group. *More Travels* (VHS; Geffen GEV-39516), 1992.
Pat Metheny Group. *Imaginary Day Live* (Eagle Vision EREDV 265), 2001.
Pat Metheny Group. *We Live Here: Live in Japan 1995* (Tomorrow fm/Image Entertainment), 2001.
Pat Metheny Group. *Speaking of Now Live* (Eagle Vision EREDV 267), 2003.
Pat Metheny Group. *The Way Up* (Eagle Vision EREDV 596), 2006.
Mitchell, Joni. *Shadow and Light* (Warner Music Vision 5050466-8425-2-7), 1980.
Wertico, Paul. *Paul Wertico: Drum Philosophy* (Alfred DVD 31989), 2009 [1997].

FILM

Apocalypse Now. Dir. Francis Ford Coppola. Zoetrope/United Artists/Paramount, 1979.

Arachnophobia. Dir. Frank Marshall. Hollywood Pictures/Amblin Entertainment, 1990.

Cinema Paradiso. Dir. Giuseppe Tornatore. Cristaldifilm/Miramax, 1988.

Easy Rider. Dir. Dennis Hopper. Columbia Pictures, 1969.

The Falcon and the Snowman. Dir. John Schlesinger. Hemdale Film/MGM, 1985.

Fandango. Dir. Kevin Reynolds. Warner Bros./Amblin Entertainment, 1985.

A Map of the World. Dir. Scott Elliott. Cinerenta/Overseas Film Group, 1999.

Top Gun. Dir. Tony Scott. Paramount, 1986.

Twice in a Lifetime. Dir. Bud Yorkin. Bud Yorkin Productions, 1985.

Under Fire. Dir. Roger Spottiswoode. Lion's Gate, 1983.

INDEX

[*Note:* The principal discussion of an album is indicated by page numbers in bold type.]

University of Arizona, 245
University of Miami, 26, 51

Vandercook, Chris, 23
Vasconcelos, Naná, 156, 163, 164–5, 166,
    178, 180, 183, 185, 189, 190, 197, 200,
    212, 215, 217, 218, 231, 232, 235, 254,
    265, 267 n.69
Vaz, Célia, 166
Violin Phase (Reich), 243
Viva, Luigi, 180, 184, 199, 200, 212, 225, 228
Vu, Cuong, 235

Walcott, Collin, 164
Wang Chung, 268
Warner Bros. Records, 268
Water is Wide, The (Lloyd), 72
Watercolors (Metheny), 2, 14, 27, 32,
    61–91, 93, 97, 122, 124, 156, 165, 168, 271
Waves (Rypdal), 73
Way Up, The (Pat Metheny Group), 3, 163,
    273–5
We Live Here (Pat Metheny Group), 55,
    273
Weather Report, 8, 12, 38, 52 n.43, 64, 98,
    100, 102, 135, 137, 150, 151, 162, 174,
    191, 213
    Black Market, 135, 174
    Heavy Weather, 162
    I Sing the Body Electric, 38
    Mr. Gone, 191

Weber, Eberhard, 32–3, 35, 38, 39, 40, 41,
    49, 54, 62–4, 65, 69, 73, 84, 85, 89, 94,
    108, 135, 267
    Colours of Chloë, The, 32, 39, 63–4, 89
    Later that Evening, 65
    Little Movements, 33, 64
    Silent Feet, 33, 64, 69
    Yellow Fields, 33, 49, 64, 108
Weber, Maja, 63
Wertico, Paul, 15, 34, 67, 231, 232–3,
    234–5, 236, 241, 246, 247, 262,
    265, 275
What's It All About (Metheny), 161
Wichita Jazz Festival, 37, 62
Wieland, Martin, 31
Williams, Buster, 15
Williams, James, 85
Williams, Tony, 70, 233–4
Wilson, Anthony, 22
Winner, Gerd, 196
Wojirsch, Barbara, 96–7, 120, 121, 154, 173,
    174, 175, 226, 245
Wonder, Stevie, 164

Yellow Fields (Weber), 33, 49, 64, 108
Yorkin, Bud, 242
Young, Lester, 14, 20, 24

Zawinul, Josef, 100, 151, 162, 191
Zero Tolerance for Silence (Metheny), 73
Zigmund, Eliot, 62, 84